THE ECONOMY, PRESENT CONTINUOUS

Theory of Economic Time

THE ECONOMY, PRESENT CONTINUOUS

Theory of Economic Time

Elena Popkova

Peoples' Friendship University of Russia (RUDN University),
Moscow, Russia

World Scientific

NEW JERSEY • LONDON • SINGAPORE • BEIJING • SHANGHAI • HONG KONG • TAIPEI • CHENNAI • TOKYO

Published by

World Scientific Publishing Co. Pte. Ltd.
5 Toh Tuck Link, Singapore 596224
USA office: 27 Warren Street, Suite 401-402, Hackensack, NJ 07601
UK office: 57 Shelton Street, Covent Garden, London WC2H 9HE

Library of Congress Cataloging-in-Publication Data
Names: Popkova, Elena G., author.
Title: The economy, present continuous : theory of economic time / Elena Popkova, Peoples' Friendship University of Russia [RUDN University], Moscow, Russia.
Description: New Jersey : World Scientific, [2024] | Includes bibliographical references and index.
Identifiers: LCCN 2023025969 | ISBN 9789811279188 (hardback) | ISBN 9789811279195 (ebook) | ISBN 9789811279201 (ebook other)
Subjects: LCSH: Time and economic reactions. | Economics. | Economic history. | Time--Economic aspects.
Classification: LCC HB147 .P67 2024 | DDC 330--dc23/eng/20230616
LC record available at https://lccn.loc.gov/2023025969

British Library Cataloguing-in-Publication Data
A catalogue record for this book is available from the British Library.

For any available supplementary material, please visit
https://www.worldscientific.com/worldscibooks/10.1142/13495#t=suppl

Desk Editors: Sanjay Varadharajan/Geysilla Jean

Typeset by Stallion Press
Email: enquiries@stallionpress.com

This book is dedicated to the memory of
Oleg V. Inshakov

About the Author

Elena G. Popkova, is a Doctor of Economics, the Founder and President of the Institute of Scientific Communications (Volgograd, Russia), Professor of the Department of Economics, and Chair of International Economic Relations at RUDN University, Moscow, Russia. She is also the author of more than 150 publications in Scopus (h-index: 39), and an editor of more than 50 books and a large number of special issues of international peer-reviewed scientific journals. Member of the editorial board of the *International Journal of Economic Policy in Emerging Economies* and the *International Journal for Quality Research*, she is also the recipient of the Highly Commended Paper Award for the journal *On the Horizon* for 2020 (Emerald). Dr. Elena is also an honoured worker of science and high technologies of the Russian Federation, and an honoured professor of Osh State University (Osh, Kyrgyzstan). She is among Scopus's top 2% of most-cited scholars of the world in 2019–2021.

Contents

Introduction

To this day, His Majesty Time remains a great mystery to man. The impact of physical time on people's daily lives is felt and understood, but the impact of economic time on economic systems is much less pronounced and needs to be independently studied. The economic nature of time as a productive resource is traditionally studied by economic science. Representatives of the classical school of economics (for example, A. Smith, A. Marshall), scientists from the Austrian school (for example, F. von Wieser), and the founder of the Marxist economic school, K. Marx, each held their views on this issue. A generalized microeconomic interpretation of time in the modern economic paradigm is to consider it as a factor of production.

A significant contribution to the formation of the philosophy of time, as an economic category, was made by a Russian (Soviet) philosopher, antiquary, and Soviet cultural figure, Aleksei F. Losev. He built a systematic world outlook, which is characterized by energy symbolism and Orthodox-related Neo-Platonism. In this system, the world is considered a hierarchical and henology-charged whole, shown in the continuous self-development of the one living bodily spirit.

Time has also been studied in sufficient detail from the perspective of macroeconomics. The most famous economic theory that takes into account the influence of the time factor on the development of economic systems is the Theory of Economic Cycles, based on the ideas of N.D. Kondratiev. According to this theory, economic systems develop cyclically (susceptible to fluctuations), which implies a certain sequence of phases in the economic cycle: rise, peak, crisis, and bottom.

Time is a basic (generally accepted) scientific category that objectively affects the functioning and development of micro- and macro-level economic systems, and it is taken into account in economic analysis, predicting changes in economic systems over time. However, managing this process is difficult. In other words, modern economic science recognizes the influence of the time factor on economic systems but does not offer a methodological tool for influencing the time factor to optimize the development of these systems. In economic analysis, the following criteria (factors) are usually used: space (e.g., classification of countries by geographical criteria) and the level of socioeconomic development (e.g., classification of countries by the level of income, level of digital competitiveness, and implementation of the Sustainable Development Goals).

Time is one of the basic characteristics of being, along with matter, from which it is inseparable. In physics, time acts as an axis in the coordinate system. The scientific approach to the study of economics should also be built into the coordinate system of space (which acts as matter) and time. A one-dimensional consideration of the economy leads to its linear perception. Existing attempts to include individual time characteristics (either absolute or relative) in economic research make it difficult to analyze and present a flat economy. This determined the meaning of the work in the book in the interests of creating the Theory of Time in Economics, which allows us to build a scientific and philosophical concept of conducting scientific research in a three-dimensional coordinate system that includes space, absolute time, and relative time and opens the way to a "voluminous" economy.

This is partly hindered by the multiplicity of interpretations of the concept of time in economics and the inconsistency of its study, as well as the significant predominance of theoretical studies over applied research. This book presents a systematic (holistic) view of time as an economic category, presents the results of its balanced study at the theoretical and empirical levels of economic science, and has also developed scientific and methodological support for high-precision forecasting and high-efficiency management of economic time. The study is presented in the form of twenty consecutive chapters, combined into five semantic parts.

The first part deals with the definition of time as an economic category. It identifies the peculiarities of the influence of the time factor on the development of economic systems, as well as the problems of its study and measurement. The first chapter analyzes the problem of the coexistence of economic systems at different stages of development and reveals the phenomenon of the "economic time machine". The second chapter analyzes the temporal dynamics of the development of economic systems, taking into account their cyclicity. On this basis, the phenomenon of economic "vintage" is revealed; its essence and methods of measurement are considered. In the third chapter, time is considered the main category of the modern Theory of Innovation. Innovations are opposed to traditions; the "economic retrospective" and routine economic phenomena and processes are analyzed.

The second part is devoted to the review of scientific theories reflecting the time factor in macroeconomic analysis. It examines F. von Wieser's Theory of Lost Profits (Chapter 4), A. Smith's Theory of Time Savings (Chapter 5), K. Marx's Law of Time Savings (Chapter 6), and A. Marshall's Temporal States (Chapter 7). In the eighth chapter, the author discusses how the time factor determines the source of imbalance in the process of self-organization of economic systems. The ninth chapter reflects on the indicators given in the Modern Theory of Investment. In the tenth chapter, outdated technologies and catch-up development are shown as manifestations of time in the economy. The eleventh chapter compares existing time theories and assesses their applicability to the modern Theory of Innovation.

The third part is devoted to determining the connection between past, present, and future development of economic phenomena and processes in the concept of "underdevelopment whirlpools". The twelfth chapter defines the concept of "underdevelopment whirlpools" as manifestations of temporary imbalances in the development of economic systems. The thirteenth chapter develops a scientific methodology for studying and measuring "underdevelopment whirlpools" in economic systems. The fourteenth chapter presents "underdevelopment whirlpools" as a tool for macroeconomic analysis and provides practical examples of their application.

The fourth part is devoted to the rationale that "underdevelopment whirlpools" are a manifestation of temporary imbalances in the development of the modern world economy. In the fifteenth chapter, "underdevelopment whirlpools" are considered an indicator of the time lag between developing and developed economies, and practical examples are given.

The sixteenth chapter defines "underdevelopment whirlpools" in the system of developed economies and provides practical examples. The seventeenth chapter identifies the "underdevelopment whirlpools" of developing economies by major categories and gives examples.

The fifth part is devoted to determining the prospects for applying the concept of "underdevelopment whirlpools" to fill the methodological gaps in the Modern Theory of Innovation. The eighteenth chapter reflects on the prospects and ways of overcoming the "underdevelopment whirlpools", depending on the degree of time lag, and gives examples from modern economic practice. The nineteenth chapter proposes a concept and develops a methodology for compiling the economic calendar of the economic system as an indicator of its development over time in comparison with the existing technological framework and gives practical examples. In the final study, the Conclusion draws up models for overcoming "underdevelopment whirlpools" in developed and developing economies through the prism of their time lag and an economic calendar, with examples.

In this book, economic time is considered in the format of popular science. In order to systematically represent it in the unity of past, present, and future time, a unit of economic time at the moment of present continuous is chosen as the object of study. An original view of economic time is proposed as a moment that embodies echoes of the past, the essence of the present, and a view of the future, and the author's methodology for studying and understanding economic time using the calculation of "underdevelopment whirlpools" has been developed.

Complex scientific concepts are explained in the book using simple and understandable illustrations, accompanied by practical examples. For example, the competition between countries in the world economy is compared to motor racing, time savings are illustrated through the example of a masquerade ball, and the cyclical effect of time on the economy is reflected through the prism of changing seasons. The book presents amazing phenomena and processes of economic time, including "economic vintage", "the time machine in the economy", "youth" and "old age" of the economy, its "growing up", "the economic calendar", "catching up", and "forward-looking" development (Figure 1). This book will therefore be interesting not only to members of the scientific community but also to a non-academic readership — to everyone who wants to understand the nature of economic time.

Figure 1. A new beginning.

Source: Photo by scholar and photographer Elena Popkova, https://www.saatchiart.com/account/artworks/1599809.

Let's imagine that time is soft, like hot wax. It has neither beginning nor end, and it does not come and go. It's always with us, and it can be in the past, the future, or the present — whichever we want it to be.

Have you ever thought that such a subtle and volatile character as His Majesty Time could be materialized and even used for the benefit of mankind? This book contains my research and ideas and presents a patented theory of using time to stabilize the economic system. How could its development be more comfortable for everyone, overcoming crises or minimizing losses from crises?

This book studies the Theory of Time in Economics. The idea of combining time and the economy and turning this friendship to the advantage of humanity was born in conversations with my friend and teacher, an iconic figure of modern Russian economic science, Oleg Inshakov.

Oleg Inshakov was a man of both his time and the future. In addition, he had a unique gift — he had no boundaries, being above everything and observing the essence of things in general. He is known as the founder of a scientific school and a leader in the evolutionary-genetic approach to the study of economic systems. He published more than 200 works in peer-reviewed Russian and international scientific publications.

Figure 2. Unfading scientific legacy, left by Doctor of Economics, Professor Oleg V. Inshakov.

Source: Photo by scholar and photographer Elena Popkova, https://www.saatchiart.com/account/artworks/1599809.

I dedicate this work to my mentor in all my professional activities. Dear Oleg Vasilievich, you are now in the place into which you tried to look with the help of science — the world of ideas, the world beyond time (Figure 2). Nevertheless, your deeds, thoughts, and ideas live on, here on Earth, in our hearts and our deeds. Thank you for being with us.

Part I

Time as an Economical Category — Features and Problems of Study and Measurement: How Time Helps the Economy Become Stable

This section states that the importance of time in modern economic theory needs to be considered. To ensure the completeness of the picture of the modern world economic system, it is indicated that it is necessary to supplement the spatial (structural) aspect, which has been studied in detail and described in detail in numerous scientific studies and publications, with the temporal (dynamic) aspect of the development of the world economy. This section describes and develops the fundamental provisions of the Theory of Time in Economics: time is considered an economical category, and specific economic phenomena and processes related to time are identified and analyzed, such as the time machine in economics, economic "vintage", and the role and significance of time in the modern Theory of Innovation.

Economic time is an analogue of physical time and its properties. As Anisov (2019) notes in his work, time, like space, is objective. One of its properties is achieving order in the world and overcoming chaos. In economics, the essence of this property of time lies in structuring economic phenomena and processes and determining their logical sequence. Just as in physics, everything has its beginning and end; in the economy, there is a life cycle of products from development to the cessation of production, the life cycle of an enterprise from creation to liquidation, and the development cycle of the national and world economies.

Subjective perception of time and space with the surroundings.

Source: Photo by scholar and photographer Elena Popkova, https://www.saatchiart.com/account/artworks/1599809.

Chapter 1

The Time Machine in the Economy — The Problem of the Coexistence of Economic Systems at Different Stages of Development: The Time Has Come

The measure of time is not in duration, but in the way you used it.

Michel de Montaigne, French philosopher of the 16th century

The chapter explains that the world economy exists beyond physical time.

This chapter deals with the following topics:

- the temporal (dynamic) aspect of the problem of the coexistence of economic systems at different stages of development in the modern world economy;
- the time machine in the economy;
- time density.

The highest value of time is emphasized in all cultures of ancient and modern peoples. According to ancient Greek mythology, the god of thunder and lightning, who owns the whole world, — Zeus — originated from time itself, since his father was the titan Kronos (from ancient Greek: *Κρόνος* — "time"). This shows that, from the philosophical position, time defines the existing order of things. Time is primary, and the environment is secondary. Therefore, time is the primary category, which outlines the limits of the existing reality; this reality in science must be considered and studied through the lens of time. Let us consider the chronology of time formation as a philosophical and scientific category.

In Ancient Greece, ancient Greek thinkers paid much attention to the category of time in their philosophy. In the philosophy of ancient Greece, time was one of the critical categories of the existence of the world and man. The founder of dialectics, Heraclitus of Ephesus (544–483 BC), wrote: "You cannot enter the same river twice because different water flows through it every moment". On the one hand, he identified time with eternity, but on the other hand, he recognized the volatility and variability of time. Another ancient thinker, Aristotle (384–322 BC), defined time as a quantitative characteristic of movement. He wrote that time history means "to be measured by the time", "to be part of the time", and "to be temporary". For example, a person lives at a certain age or can even see several ages. For example, people born in the tsarist empire saw life in the Soviet Union and modern Russia. All these characteristics can be applied to economic systems.

In contrast, representatives of Chinese philosophy believed that a person is primary, and time is secondary. That is, it is not time that determines a person, but a person "gets into time" and adapts to a situation that changes in time, and he can also change it himself, that is, "control time". For example, Red Army soldiers changed the paradigm during the Great October Revolution (1917), facilitating the transition from the Russian Empire to the Soviet Union. Despite specific differences in viewpoints, philosophers of all times and nationalities have recognized the significance of time and somehow delineated past, present, and future times.

Indian mythology considers time cyclical. In one myth, living creatures can reincarnate in new forms and guises. In another myth, time is a dread of the god Visnu-Narayana. Such a philosophy undermines the accounting of time in science since, with the dream of a god, time is unstable, unreliable, and subjective and is susceptible to unpredictable changes.

In Middle Ages, the philosophy of time was further developed. The philosopher of the Enlightenment, Toland (1670–1722), believed that both time and space are inextricably connected with moving matter. That is, humans exist in time and space as coordinates of being.

In modern philosophy and science, the study of the time category entered a new level. Andrey Pravdivtsev is the Scientific Director of the Center for Energy Information and Health Technologies (CEIHT) of the Laboratory of Integrated Bioinformation Technologies (LIBT), the official representative in Russia of the International Center for the Study of the Heritage of Nikola Tesla (Serbia, Belgrade), and a Ph.D. in Technology in the field of artificial intelligence. In his report "The ionosphere, Kozyrev mirrors, and interaction with the information space" at the conference "Unrecognized 2019", which took place on October 12–13, 2019, he examined the properties of physical time. In particular, the scientist noted that time:

- spreads instantly;
- has a current and a direction of travel;
- has *density* (intensity) — time density depends on the distance from its source. For example, in the digital economies, which are leaders in the Fourth Industrial Revolution, the density of present time ("present continuous") is the highest, and in the economies with a slow rate of digitalization and low digital competitiveness, the density of present time is reduced;
- has pressure and torque and is capable of mechanically acting on the matter;
- is capable of being absorbed (accumulated, remembered) by matter;
- can be released by matter;
- can be reflected from surfaces or shielded by matter;
- can change the physical properties of a substance, i.e., affect its structure.

Economic time also has all these properties. It is in a close relationship with matter — the space, the territory in which the economic system is located — and it converts it, by absorbing, accumulating, remembering, or releasing it.

The meta-scientific (philosophical) foundations for the study of time were laid by an academician of the Imperial St. Petersburg Academy of Sciences (1912) and Laureate of the Stalin Prize of the 1st degree (1943), V.A. Vernadsky. In the report "The problem of time in modern science" (Vernadsky, 2019), he notes that "Time — is life if you discard its content". The scientist identifies time with its carrier (person) and notes the subjectivity of the perception of time. Therefore, in economics, each economic system is a time carrier and subjectively interprets it, which causes differences in the economic time of economic systems.

Kozyrev (2019), in his Theory of Time, defines time as "a continuous source of energy into the Universe" and states, "Stars draw energy from the course of time". By analogy with physics, one can imagine a similar abstraction: time is a "source of energy for the growth and development of economic systems". The scientist also notes that "time is not an abstract quantity, but rather a quantity that has direction and energy that does not allow the thermal death of the universe to occur". Agreeing with the scientist, we note that economic time, too, is not abstract but has a direction (from the past to the present and the future) and energy, increasing and realizing the potential for the development of economic systems and scientific and technological progress.

The existing theories of time formed a solid fundamental basis for the understanding of the essence of, and for realizing, modern time. The transition from the past understanding of that time to the present understanding of this time occurred due to the formation of science and the scientific picture of the world.

The present is a snapshot of reality. Looking at this photo, we can assume how things are now in a particular country or the whole world. However, what if this picture is just an illusion? What if it shows only general outlines, leaving out particular scenes, the multiple connections between various events, and their already emerging consequences?

Present Continuous is a time that has already arrived but is still ongoing. This is a moment in the present that has a strong connection with the recent past and future, a moment in which everything can still be changed if one delves into the essence of what is happening in the photo. Nevertheless, how can that be done? One needs to cross the border of time and objective reality and become part of this photo! Let us go together on a fantastic journey through a snapshot of the modern world economy...

The critical meaning of "Present Continuous" time is its continuity. Human thought continuously develops, moving from one item to another and forming increasingly new and complex logical connections and conclusions, as noted in the work of Christakou (2014). Similarly, as the development of a socio-economic system occurs, each moment of its existence is unique but, at the same time, inextricably connected with the previous and future moments, as described by Aydemir (2011).

"Present Continuous" is a snapshot that is unique for each moment. Let us consider such a snapshot of the modern world economy (2023). The first thing we see in the photo is the basketball players. Two players are competing for victory. Nevertheless, they do not see that they are led by someone from above. The course of the game, the behaviour of the players, and the winner will be determined by the hand holding the ball (Figure 1). From a scientific point of view, this picture can be explained as follows: under the influence of intensive and comprehensive globalization, an integrated global economic system has been formed. (In Figure 1, we see only two players, but this is conditional; in fact, whole teams can stand behind them.) However, increased opportunities for global economic cooperation, which ensures the systemic nature of the interaction of the structural elements of the global economic system, have not led to their unification. On the contrary, there has been an increase in competition, as well as an increase in the role of international organizations, symbolized by the hand in Figure 1.

Figure 1. Snapshot of the modern world economy.

One of the characteristics of globalization is the reduction in the time of transactions. Therefore, if *time density* is measured in terms of the time in which an event occurs, globalization accelerates time, including economic time. As the degree of internationalization of economic activities of socio-economic systems increases, their economic time accelerates.

This phenomenon demonstrates the increase in the annual growth rate of GDP as the value of the globalization index increases. The dynamics of these values in Russia from 1992 to 2017 are shown in Table 1.

Table 1. Dynamics of globalization and GDP index values in constant prices in Russia 1992–2017.

Year	Globalization index	GDP at constant prices, billion ₽	Annual GDP growth, %
1992	51.26	43,246.072	—
1993	50.78	39,483.664	−8.70
1994	51.32	34,469.239	−12.70
1995	53.99	33,056.000	−4.10
1996	55.94	31,863.300	−3.61
1997	56.56	32,303.500	1.38
1998	58.79	30,576.800	−5.35
1999	60.73	32,518.900	6.35
2000	67.52	35,785.800	10.05
2001	67.42	37,607.400	5.09
2002	67.95	39,391.500	4.74
2003	69.59	42,286.400	7.35
2004	67.98	45,320.700	7.18
2005	68.56	48,210.400	6.38
2006	69.34	52,141.300	8.15
2007	70.01	56,591.600	8.54
2008	69.90	59,561.400	5.25
2009	70.22	54,903.100	−7.82
2010	69.02	57,375.800	4.50
2011	70.12	59,698.100	4.05
2012	70.55	61,798.300	3.52

Table 1. (*Continued*)

Year	Globalization index	GDP at constant prices, billion ₽	Annual GDP growth, %
2013	70.53	62,588.900	1.28
2014	70.47	63,038.400	0.72
2015	70.98	61,249.400	−2.84
2016	71.01	61,097.500	−0.25
2017	71.03	61,952.886	1.40

Source: Based on materials from KOF (2018) and the International Monetary Fund (2018).

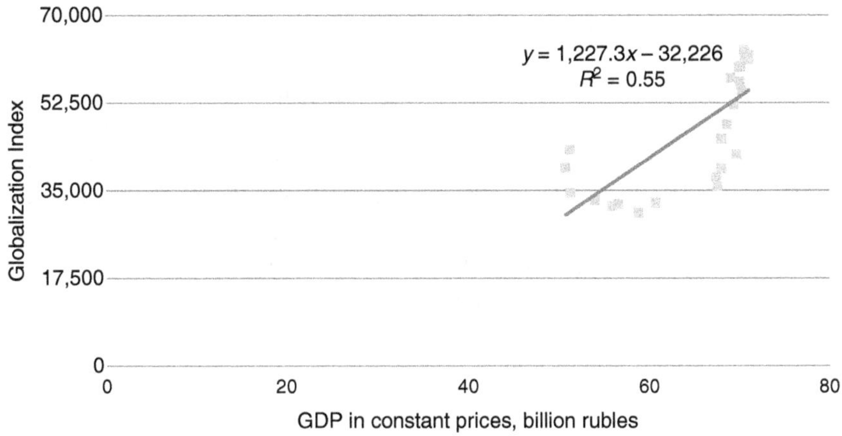

Figure 2. Regression curve reflecting the dependence of Russia's GDP in constant prices on the value of the globalization index.

Based on the data from Table 1, a regression curve is constructed, reflecting the dependence of Russia's GDP in constant prices on the value of the globalization index (Figure 2).

As seen in Figure 2, the 55% acceleration in Russia's GDP growth is due to the growth of the globalization index. This shows the acceleration in the course of economic time in Russia over the past 30 years under the influence of the globalization process.

The specific features of various economic systems not only allow them to maintain competitive advantages[1] on the world stage but also cause structural imbalances in the development[2] of the modern world economy. Its systemic imbalance poses a high risk of global economic crises and necessitates allocating significant resources.

The spatial (structural) aspect of the modern world economic system has been studied in sufficient detail and described in existing scientific papers, while the much-less-studied temporal (dynamic) aspect of the development of the world economy is of no less, and possibly even more, interest to modern science since it can potentially allow us to find answers to questions that remain open due to the limitations of the study of the spatial (structural) aspect of the world economy.

In this book, I propose the scientific hypothesis that the problem of the coexistence of economic systems at different stages of development has deeper roots and has a more substantial influence on the modern world economy than the spatial (structural) aspect of its study reflects. Additional analysis of this problem from the perspective of the temporal (dynamic) aspect will allow a more accurate measurement of the magnitude of differences in the level of socio-economic development of different economic systems, as well as a more reliable prediction (creation of scenarios) of their further development in the future.

Let us turn to modern economic science to help clarify the picture. The aspect of time in the works of modern economists is considered in studies on the following parts of economic science:

- *Theory of economic cycles*: This part studies the cyclical fluctuations of economic systems, as well as socio-ecosystems, in particular, within the framework of the energy economy (Mohammadi *et al.*, 2018).
- *Modelling of socio-economic processes using time series*: This part studies the dynamics of economic development (Shahbaz *et al.*, 2018), transformational processes (transition periods) in economies (Güney *et al.*, 2015), and temporary conditions of stock markets (Sarvan *et al.*, 2014).
- *Forecasting the development of socio-economic systems*: Within the framework of this part, causal relationships are studied, and the future consequences of the implementation of state regulation measures in the economy are predicted (Jalles, 2017).

[1]Competitive advantage is superiority over competitors.

[2]Structural imbalances of the world economy are differences in the level of socio-economic development of economic systems (countries) in the composition of the world economy.

- *Extrapolation*: Within the framework of this part, transport and logistics schemes are developed (Pirker & Lichtenegger, 2018), and the stages of production processes are studied (Mitrouli & Roupa, 2018).
- *The above indicators*: Within the framework of this part, investment design is carried out, and the net present value of investment projects is calculated (Creemers, 2018).
- *Missed opportunities*: This part examines alternative scenarios for the development of socio-economic systems (Stafford *et al.*, 2011).
- *The theory of economy of animated labour*: Within the framework of this part, the labour theory of value was formed, and the modern labour economy is developing (Hecht, 2018).

The above theories shall be considered in the book individually in more detail. These theories affect time in economics, considering it when studying various economic phenomena and processes. For many years, interest in this aspect was minimal but has now been resumed due to the global economic crisis. Therefore, it is through the prism of the crisis that "economic time" is considered in recent scientific publications. This is because *time density* increases during the recovery of the economic cycle and, accordingly, its flow rate in crisis conditions suddenly slows down, which causes resonance. As a result of the systematization of existing scientific and economic research and publications on this topic, we have identified three main approaches to interpreting the phenomenon of the changing *density* and *speed of time* in an economy in a crisis.

The first approach is entrepreneurial. Within the framework of this approach, the decrease in *density* and the slowdown in the *speed of time* flow in the economy during the crisis are explained by a decrease in the level of business activity.

Following this approach, three scientists from Switzerland, Kuntz *et al.* (2017), write that during the crisis, economic conditions worsen and international migration flows increase. This indicates the completion of a certain period of "economic time". The Polish scientists Raźniak *et al.* (2018) note that during a global economic crisis such as that of 2008–2012, the income of the population and the net profit of enterprises do not necessarily decrease, and therefore each country has its own "economic time". By "economic time", scientists mean alternating phases of the economic cycle (rise and crisis).

In Russian economic thought, this approach is presented in the works of scientists such as Ilyin & Kochetkova (2014), Larina (2013), Levchenko & Kuznetsova (2013), Levchenko & Rudychev (2013), and Natsypaeva

(2014). For example, the aggravation of the international sanction crisis in 2022 led to a slowdown of the rate and a decrease in the density of economic time in countries that joined the sanctions.

The second approach is innovative. Within the framework of this approach, the decrease in *density* and the slowdown in the *speed of time* flow in the economy in a crisis are explained by a decrease in innovative activity in the economy.

As part of this approach, Italian economists Castaldo *et al.* (2017) point out that "economic time" is determined by a scientific and technical paradigm. Technological innovation has always been considered the main stimulus for economic growth. The high-speed internet access provided by the spread of broadband infrastructure has been developing rapidly since the late 1990s and has acted as a technological determinant of accelerating the "economic time" of a group of 23 OECD countries over the past 15 years. Overcoming the global crisis of 2008 required the activation of promising technological innovations to launch a new era of "economic time".

The stages of development of economic systems have been studied in sufficient detail within the framework of the Evolutionary Approach and are described in numerous works by various authors. Russian experts Afanasev *et al.* (2015) note that the development of spatially organized systems is cyclic.

Confirming this view, Albanian authors Kupina & Salko (2015) write that the development of the banking system of Albania and Kosovo reflects significant growth with different intensities at different periods. Spanish scientists Gómez & Neves Sequeira (2014) point out that the different industrial experiences of the countries of the world, starting with innovation or education, can be explained not only by different structural parameters or public policies but also by differences in the factors affecting them.

This approach is followed by certain Russian scientists, in particular Barmuta (2009), Komarov (2010), Makarov & Shuval-Sergeeva (2016), and Nekrasov (2012). For example, under the conditions of the COVID-19 pandemic and crisis, due to the lockdowns around the world, the flow of economic time slowed down, and its density decreased — for the rate of the economy's digital development reduced, as well as the rate of implementation of the Sustainable Development Goals (SDGs).

The third approach is structural. Within the framework of this approach, the decrease in *density* and the slowdown in the *speed of time* flow in an economy in a crisis are studied through the lens of differences in these indicators in different economic systems.

Within the framework of this approach, the problem of the coexistence of economic systems at different stages of development is recognized by the modern academic community. It is one of the most critical global problems of our time. It is traditionally formulated as a problem of differentiation of countries in the world economy or imbalances in the development of the world economic system. This problem is the focus of Turkish experts Ari & Sari (2017), who claim that the differentiation between developed and developing countries is one of the essential tasks in implementing the Paris Agreement.

American scientist Syrquin (2015) writes that modern economic growth is characterized by the widespread use of knowledge-intensive technologies for production, which, since the late 18th century, have led to a steady increase in income, population, and productivity, as well as large-scale structural changes. However, most of humanity has yet to realize the potential for economic growth provided by modern technologies, although the per capita GDP of most modern countries is higher than in the 19th and early 20th centuries. The essence of the considered approach is that it allows distinguishing the precise structure of the world economic system, differentiating countries with large density and high rate of economic time flow and countries with small density and low rate of economic time flow.

Regarding the differences in the level of socio-economic development between various regions of Russia, a Doctor of Economics, Professor O.V. Inshakov, found signs of different regions at various stages of economic development. The views of the scientist on this topic are presented in the following works: Inshakov (2003), Inshakov *et al.* (2008a, 2008b, 2009a, 2009b), and Inshakov & Mitrofanova (2007a, 2007b). Based on the differences in economic time, Inshakov introduced in the scientific circulation the notion of the "vicious circle of poverty", which is understood as continuous aggravation of the indicators of socio-economic development (level of income, level of social inequality, global competitiveness, sustainability) of economic systems with a low rate of economic time flow and its small density.

A review of the existing scientific literature on the formulated scientific problem showed that despite the high degree of elaboration of its components, in modern economic theory, there is no precise and uniform (generally accepted) formulation of the problem of the existence of *a "time machine" in economics*, nor methodological tools for measuring and solving it. This necessitates further scientific study of the problem.

The methodology of this study was based on statistical and comparative analysis methods based on the World Monetary Fund, UNDP, and the World Bank versions of official international statistical information on socio-economic development in the years 2012–2022.

Based on the collected and systematized statistical information, we have identified significant differences in the level of socio-economic development of developed and developing countries (Figures 3, 5, 7–10).

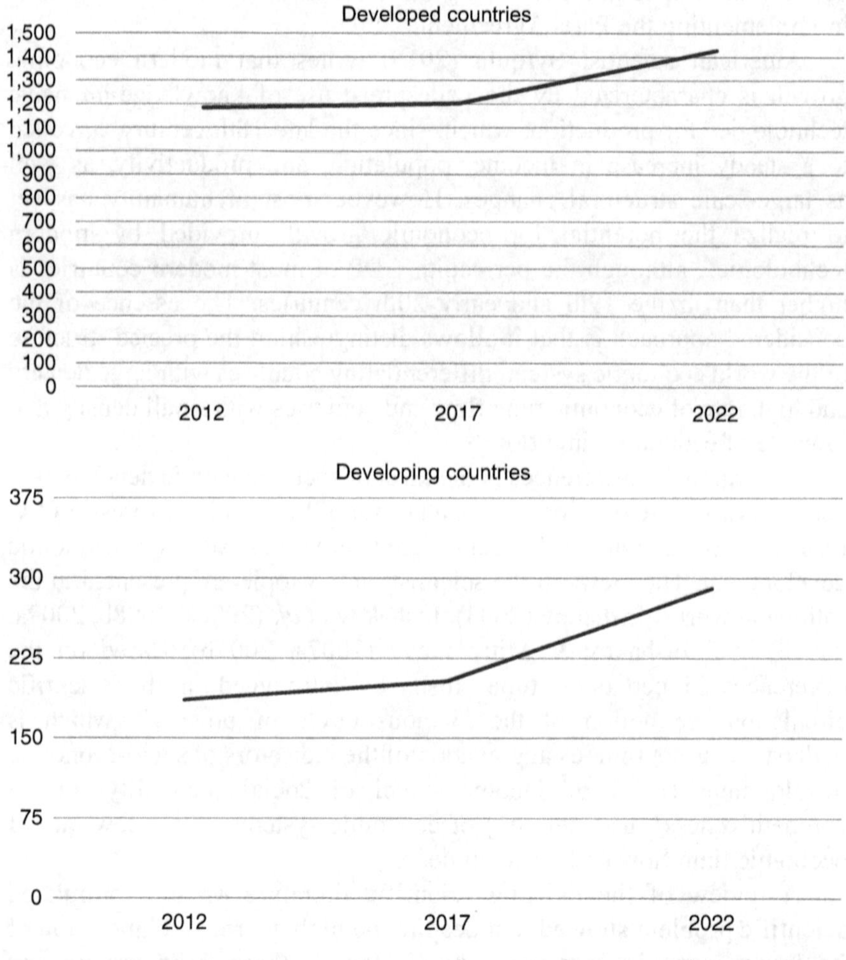

Figure 3. GDP dynamics in current prices in developed and developing countries 2012–2022.

Figure 4. Ageing economies.

Source: Photo by scholar and photographer Elena Popkova, https://www.saatchiart.com/account/artworks/1599809.

As seen in Figure 3, developed countries are far ahead of developing countries in terms of GDP. Moreover, developed countries show a much faster GDP growth rate, leading to a widening gap between the categories of countries under consideration over time.

Behind that is the speed of the flow of economic time and the economic age of the country, which are closely connected (Figure 4). For example, participation in the Fourth Industrial Revolution accelerates the flow of economic time and stimulates the rejuvenation of the economy, making it more modern through technological progress (Figure 6). On the contrary, economies removed from the Fourth Industrial Revolution conditionally age and are behind in technological progress.

As shown in Figure 5, developed countries usually have a high level and growth rate of GDP per capita, which helps them get ahead compared to developing countries.

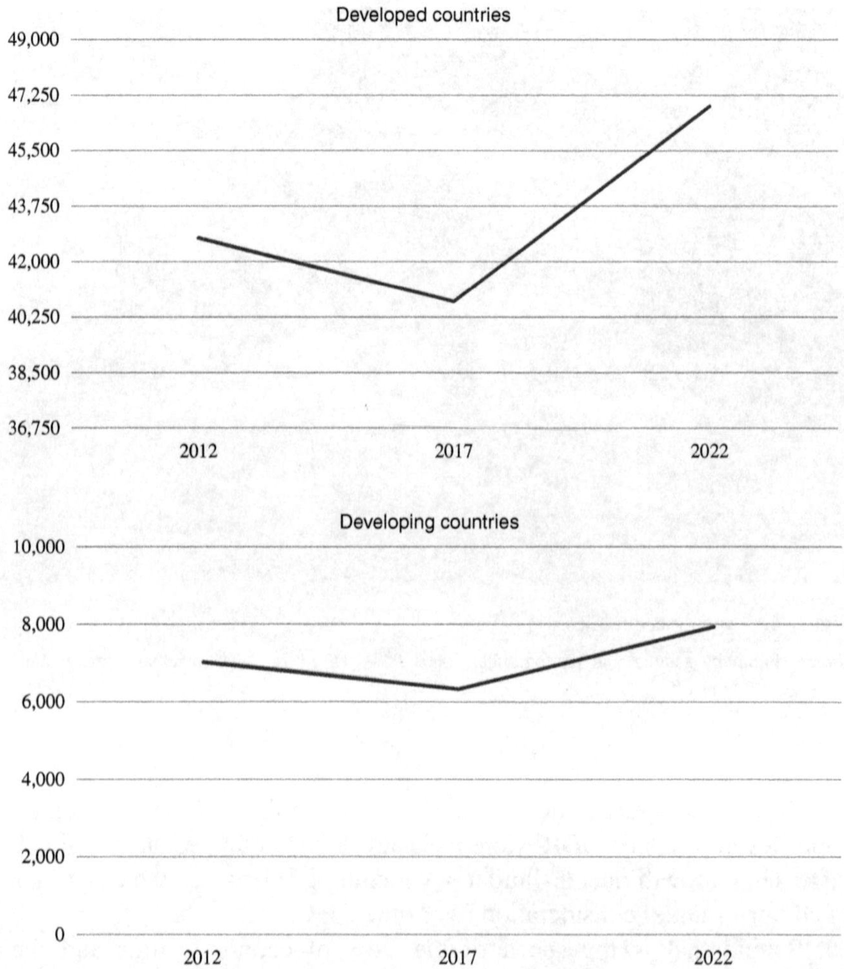

Figure 5. GDP per capita dynamics at current prices in developed and developing countries 2012–2022.

As can be shown from Figure 7, the level of GDP based on purchasing power parity in developed countries is much higher. They are also increasing their exports while developing countries are characterized by declining exports over time.

Figure 6. Result of the ageing of economy.

Source: Photo by scholar and photographer Elena Popkova, https://www.saatchiart.com/account/artworks/1599809.

As shown from Figure 8, while developed countries experience a decline in inflation, developing countries experience a significant increase over time. At the same time, developed countries are increasing their imports, and developing countries are reducing them. Unemployment in developing countries is significantly higher than in developed countries.

As can be shown from Figure 9, developed countries are characterized by lower levels of aggregate public sector borrowing and public debt, as well as declining indicators, while the situation in developing countries is precisely the opposite.

As can be shown from Figure 10, developed countries are far ahead of developing countries in terms of the Human Development Index and the Knowledge Economy Index. This indicates that developing countries need to catch up to developed countries in time; behind these indicators is time that cannot be accumulated and caught up. In modern economic science, the quality of economic growth is determined by the speed of economic time.

The quality of economic growth is a system of stable signs within a particular historical stage (the structure of economic growth factors).

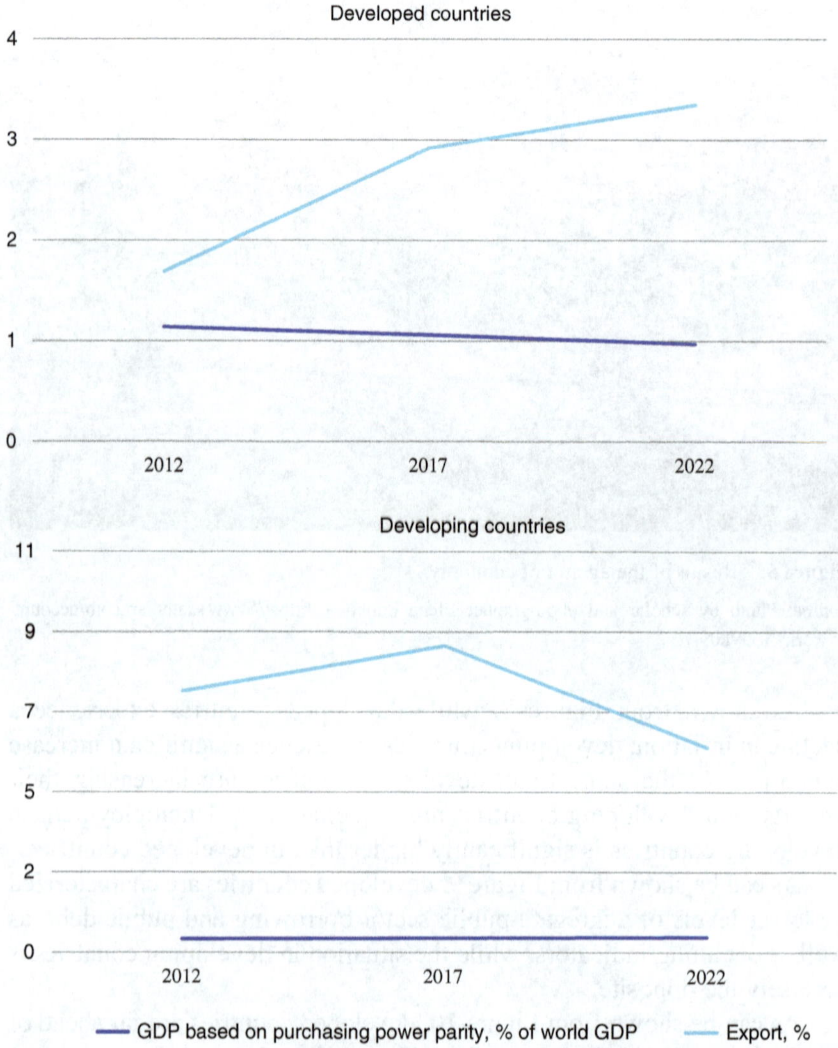

Figure 7. GDP dynamics based on purchasing power parity and exports in developed and developing countries 2012–2022.

It allows us to distinguish the type of economic growth in different space–time coordinates. A new quality of economic growth is present at all stages of the economic development of the world economy, determined by the mode of social production. It is achieved as a result of a system of qualitative transitions, which, during the evolution of the economic system, can

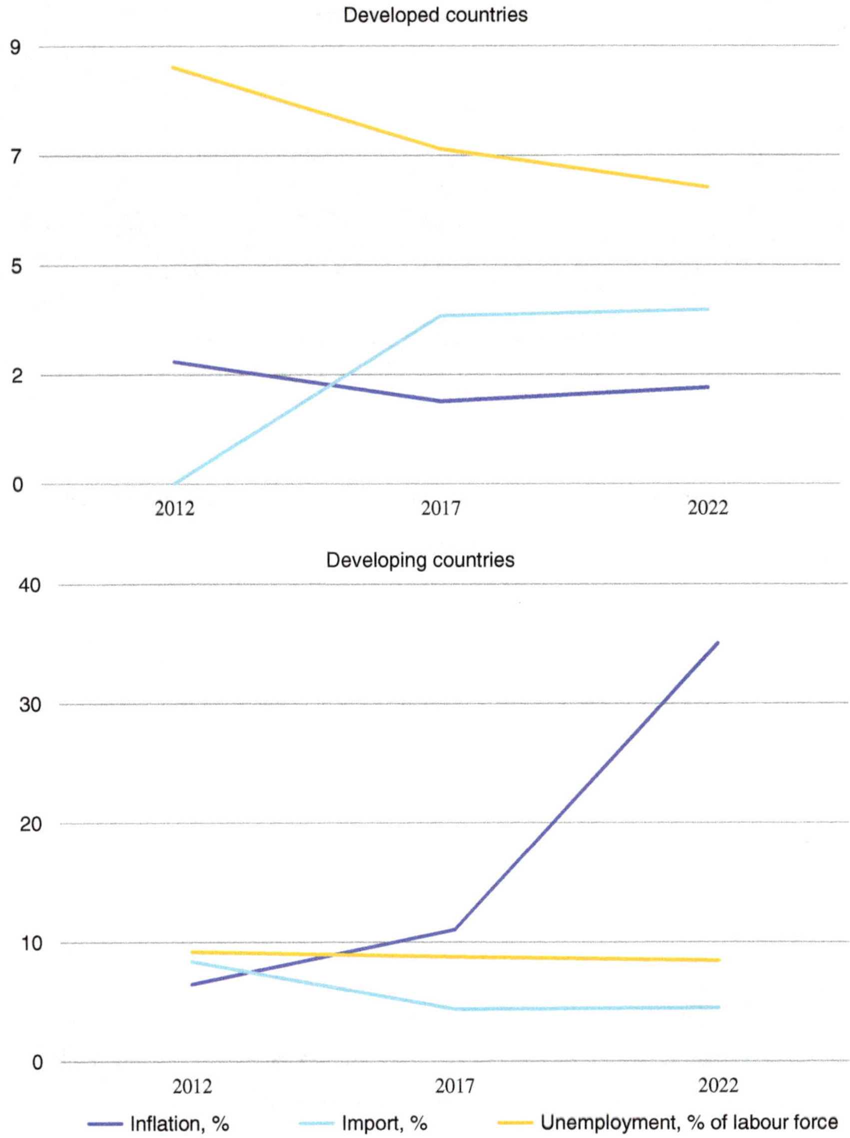

Figure 8. Trends in inflation, imports, and unemployment in developed and developing countries 2012–2022.

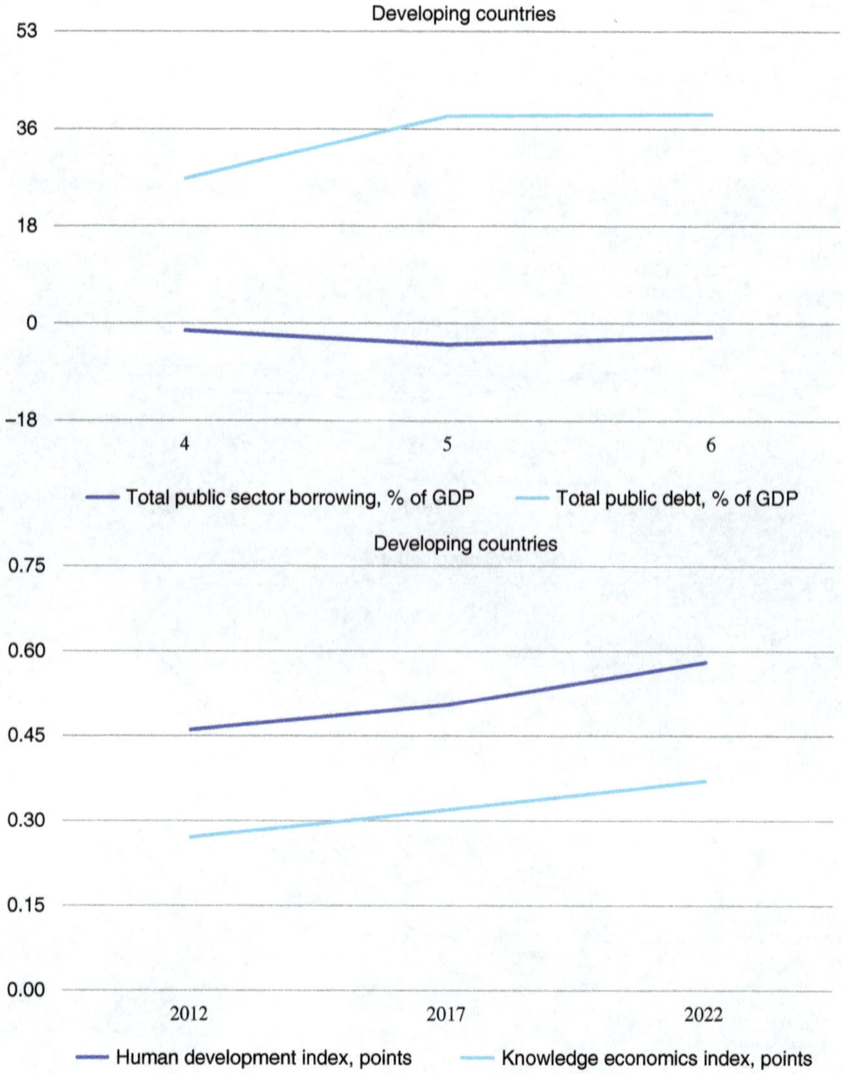

Unemployment in developing countries is significantly higher than in developed countries.

Figure 9. Trends in public sector borrowing and debt in developed and developing countries 2012–2022.

change, disappear, or give rise to new qualitative transitions from the old to the new mode of social production.

The differences in the quality of economic growth between developed and developing countries reflect the differences in their economic times.

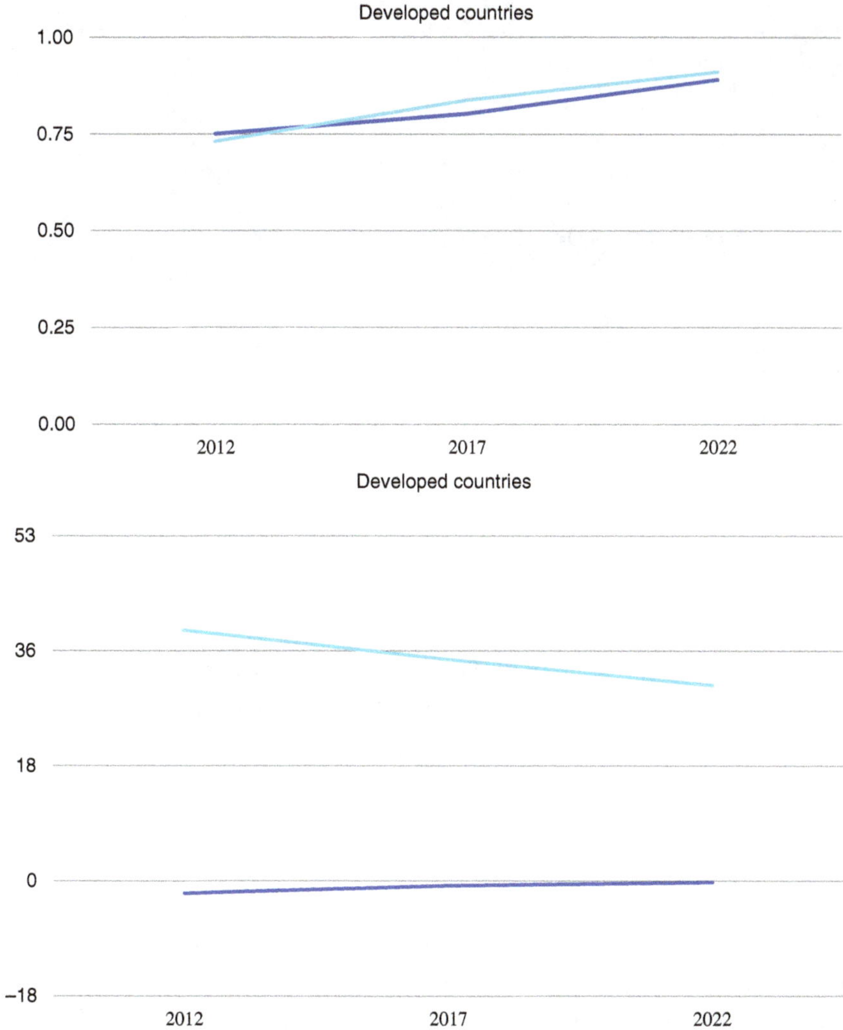

Figure 10. Dynamics of the quality of economic growth of developed and developing countries 2012–2022.

An analysis of the socio-economic development indicators of these countries showed that the differences between them are significant. This indicates the existence of *a time machine in the economy*, the theoretical model of which is presented graphically in Figure 11.

As can be seen from Figure 11, following the current scientific, economic paradigm, four stages of socio-economic development are

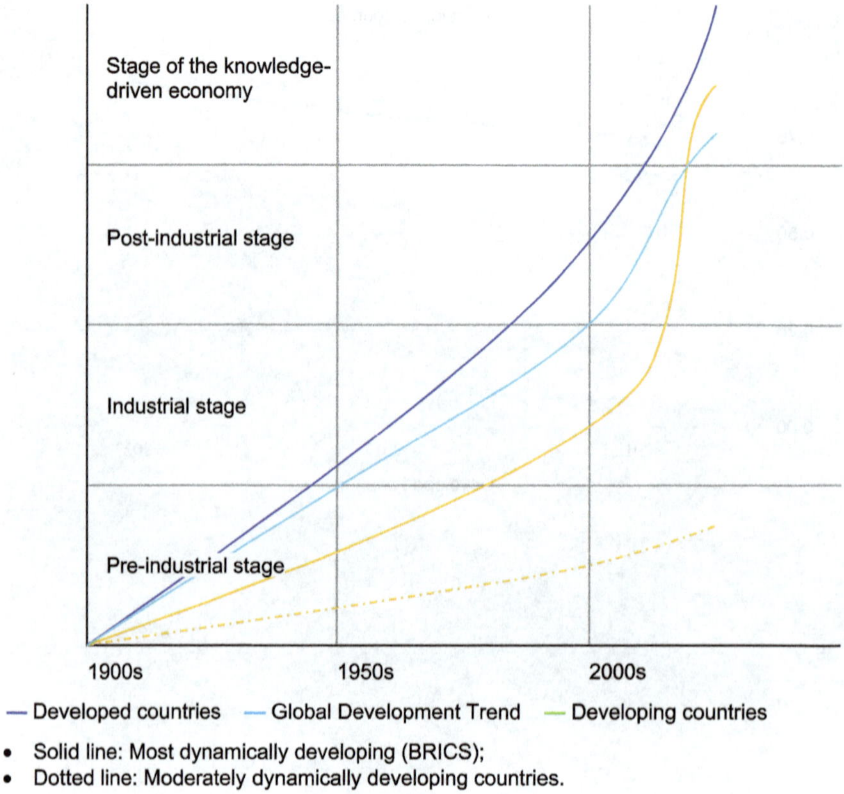

Figure 11. A theoretical model of *the time machine in the economy.*

distinguished: pre-industrial (until the beginning of the 20th century), industrial (until the middle of the 20th century), post-industrial (until the end of the 20th century), and the stage of knowledge economics (from the beginning of the 21st century to the present — 2017). The global trend of economic development implies a consistent transition from one stage to the next.

Developed countries are the engine of the world economic system. They are the first to move to new stages of socio-economic development, even before a global trend has been established. At the same time, many developing countries need to catch up to the global trend, moving more slowly to new stages of development or remaining at the same stage for a long time. However, they can also dramatically overcome the backlog (the phenomenon of the "economic miracle") and almost reach the level of developed countries ahead of the global trend.

The phenomenon in the modern world economy which is associated with the simultaneous existence of economic systems at different stages of development, as well as the possibility of an "elevator" of economic systems that allows them to "travel in time" during one time period, replacing two or more stages of socio-economic development, we call *a time machine in the economy*.

For example, in the age of great geographical discoveries (17th century), travellers from European countries would write in their notes and recollections that, having come to Africa, they would seem to have travelled to the past, facing less technologically developed civilizations. This was vividly shown in the film "Babylon", which simultaneously demonstrates the co-existence of modes. In simple terms, *a time machine in the economy* is the possibility of moving to different technological systems at the same time. For example, we can move to pre-industrial production by flying to underdeveloped countries.

In Africa (Egypt, Congo, Somalia) and Asia (China, India), the income of the average employee is about $100 per month, and this is enough to purchase the entire "commodity bundle" necessary for human life. In other words, the cost of living in these countries is at the level of $100. At the same time, in the advanced countries of Europe (Germany, France, Great Britain) and America (the USA, Canada), the cost of living is about $1,000, and an income of only $100 does not allow a person to purchase even half the goods and services necessary for living.

On the whole, the mode (e.g., the level of development of technologies, communications, finance, and transport) allows identifying young economies (ones that use AI technologies, big data, the Internet of Things, robots, virtual communications, digital finance, crewless vehicles, and electric cars), mature economies (ones that are based on digital technologies: wireless, high-speed and broadband internet, mobile communications, cloud technologies, and fossil fuel cars, with active development of e-commerce and online payments), and old economies (with the domination of personal communications, cash payments, and transport based on human strength).

It should be noted that the phenomenon of "*time machines in the economy*" is not linked to the classification of countries by level and pace of socio-economic development in terms of developed and developing countries. A more accurate gradation of economic systems is needed; the main criterion should be the economic structure. The type of economy should also be taken into account. The matrix for modern Europe (2019) is shown in Table 2.

Table 2. Time matrix (2023).

	Future	Present	Past
Economic structure	Digital economy	Digitalizing economy	Pre-digital economy
Type of economy	Market	Market	Transitional
Structure	Developed countries	Developing countries	Developing countries
Level of income	Countries with a high level of income and income that is higher than the world's average	Countries with income of the world average level	Countries with income that is lower than the world average and with low levels of income

A systemic view of the evolutionary development of economic systems from the position of the theory of economic time, which unifies the provisions of the existing concepts (from Table 1), is presented in Figure 2. The author's view is based terminologically, first, on the notion of the level of development of society's productive forces in economic formations (Marx & Engels, 1959). Second, on the notion of the level of technological development of the economy and the concept of technological revolutions (Kuhn, 1977; Lakatos, 1995). Third, on the notion of economic growth of the eponymous concept (Leontyev, 1966; Kleiner, 1986).

As shown in Figure 12, the economic growth rate is the quantitative characteristic of the evolutionary development of economic systems from the position of the theory of economic time. The quality of economic growth is determined by two parameters: (1) level of the development of productive forces of society: economic formations, determined by the criteria of the value-added type of economic production relations, and (2) level of technological development of the economy: machine level of the development of productive forces of production relations (technological mode).

The first three economic formations (primitive communal, slave-owning, and feudal systems) with a low level of the development of productive forces of society conform to the agrarian economy. The next formations, which differ by the form of ownership for production means — capitalist system (private property) and socialist system (public property) — conform to the industrial economy. Here, the quality of

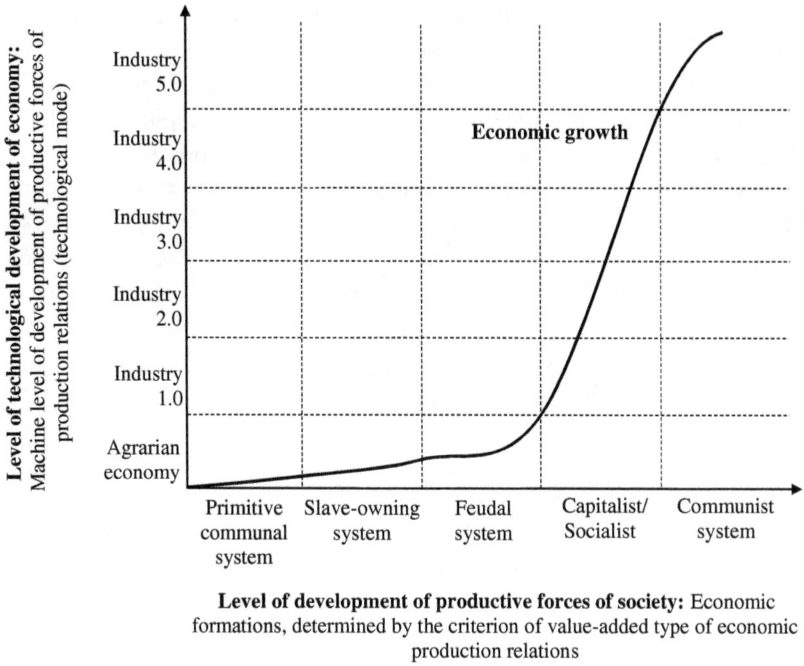

Figure 12. A systemic view of the evolutionary development of economic systems from the positions of the theory of economic time.

economic growth proliferates. The first three industrial revolutions occurred in these formations, and the Fourth Industrial Revolution continued. It is accompanied by the transition to and development of Industry 4.0.

In the definition of K. Marx and F. Engels, the communist system is characterized by "the disappearance of the opposition of mental and physical labour, when labour ceases to be only a means for life, but becomes the initial need of life, when, together with the comprehensive development of individuals there also grow productive forces" (Marx and Engels, 1959). This description conforms to the post-industrial economy, in which the development and unlocking of human potential become the most important need of the "knowledge society" under the conditions of human–machine competition in Industry 5.0. The ongoing Fifth Industrial Revolution may lead to this.

The presented view of the evolutionary development of economic systems from the position of the theory of economic time (Figure 2) determined the order of this development. To specify its causal connections, it is also necessary to discover the conditions of the change in economic formations and technological modes. In this relation, the historical experience of Russia, where formations were changes not in a classical way, is peculiar (Stafford *et al.*, 2011; Vernadsky, 2019). As noted above, Russia skipped the slave-owning system; without realizing the capitalist system, Russia passed to socialism, and now it has returned to capitalism.

In the classic evolutionary development of the economic system by Marx and Engels (1959), socialism is considered the first stage of communism. However, Russia skipped capitalism and formed imperialism after socialism. The signs include, first, foreign political expansion (accession of many socialist republics to the Soviet Union). Second, the foundation of military power is the driving political, social, and economic power. Given the experience of Russia, the classic view of economic formations is corrected in Figure 2, where capitalism (private property) and socialism (public property) are presented at one level as alternatives with different forms of property for production means.

The cause of the violation of the classic logic and smoothness of the flow of economic time in Russia, similarly to other economic systems, is the lack of time for awareness of the process. This means that time is required not only for technological development but, to a more significant extent, for awareness of one's economic time, in which society and economy are at the current moment. Awareness of economic time is a new, previously unknown component of the social factors of the evolutionary development of economic systems (Figure 3).

It is offered to treat awareness of economic time as society's readiness and susceptibility to the current or yet forming level of technological development of the economy (machine degree of development) and the level of development of productive forces of society (economic formation). This readiness is expressed in the achievement of the necessary level of public creation (human development), dissemination, and acceptance (adoption) of certain norms and values, as well as the development of necessary competencies (e.g., digital competencies). The social interpretation of this readiness relates to the fact that public awareness is achieved through forming influential formal and informal institutes.

As shown in Figure 13, the speed and smoothness of the flow of economic time are determined by the social factors — not only technological but also social (awareness of economic time) readiness for the change of the evolutionary form of the economic systems' development. Low social and technological readiness leads to stagnation

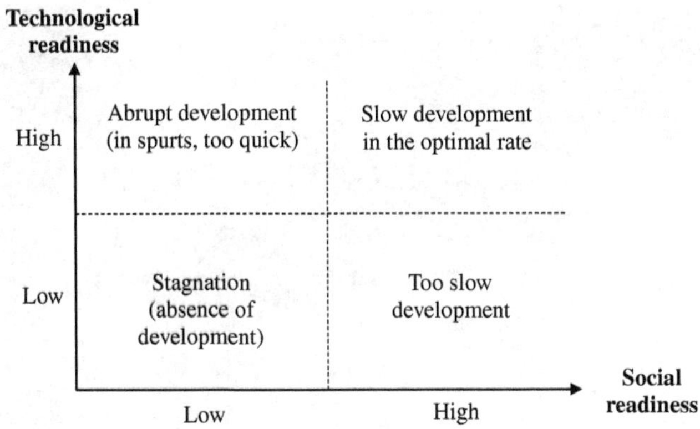

Figure 13. Speed and smoothness of the flow of economic time depending on readiness for the change in the evolutionary form of economic system development.

(absence of development). In the case of high social readiness (progressive society, which supports innovations, strives towards innovations, and realizes its economic time and need for innovations) but low technological readiness (deficit of technologies and dependence on import of technologies and innovations), economic time is too slow, which causes and strengthens the underrun of the economic system from world leaders and reduces its global competitiveness.

In the case of high technological readiness (presence of own leading technologies) but low social readiness (unpreparedness for changes, opposition to innovations), abrupt development (in spurts, too quick) takes place — as in the 1990s in Russia (skipping economic formations and technological modes).

Skipping was facilitated by market (privatization, formation of the institute of private property) and social (formation of capitalist society with the domination of material values and personal motives that prevail over public ones; formation of entrepreneurs as a new social class) reform of the Russian economy. It is only at the high social and technological — at the same time — readiness that smooth development at the optimal rate is achieved. This is precisely what modern Russia should strive towards as an objective (Figure 14).

Modern Western Europe (Germany and Great Britain) represents the future time. Its economic structure is the digital economy. It is characterized by a formed market economy, and it is composed of developed countries. Central Europe (Greece and Poland) represents

Figure 14. The nature of time.
Source: Photo by scholar and photographer Elena Popkova, https://www.saatchiart.com/account/artworks/1599809.

the present. Its economic framework is a digitalizing economy, it is characterized by a formed market economy, and it is composed of developing countries. Eastern Europe (Belarus and Moldova) is in the past. Its economic structure is a pre-digital economy, it is characterized by an emerging (transitional) market economy, and it is composed of developing countries. The time matrix above demonstrates the European "*time machine in the economy*". With it, in less than six hours, an individual can move from one economic structure to another, from the past to the present to the future.

A vivid example of the time machine in the economy is changes in the fuel and energy complexes of countries under the conditions of the 2022–2023 global energy crisis. European countries that were leaders in the sphere of green energy now disassemble wind stations and restore the work of coal mines, returning to the past. Compared to this, the Russian economy develops hydropower and hydrogen energy, moving towards the future.

The results of the research showed that a large dispersion of modern economic systems in terms of the level of socio-economic development leads not only to the formation and consolidation of the roles of leaders and laggards but also to the separation of economic systems in the world economy according to the stages of socio-economic development. Developed countries (Italy, Great Britain, and the USA) are changing over time to the global trend of economic development or running ahead of it.

Developing countries are of the most significant scientific interest in the context of economic time theory, which develops contrary to the natural course of time; that is, they show substantial variations relative to the global trend of economic development. These are countries such as South Africa, Algeria, North Korea, Kazakhstan, Belarus, and Russia. This phenomenon we describe as *a time machine in the economy*. The essence of this phenomenon is contradictory.

On the one hand, it presents a problem for the modern world economy in general and individual (mainly developing) economic systems in particular. The high degree of differentiation among the countries of the world, which are now entrenched in sustainable places in specific categories (developed and developing countries), underestimates global indicators of socio-economic development and slows down the development of the world economy as a whole. On the other hand, the existence of *a time machine in the economy* allows each country to choose its target level and optimal pace of socio-economic development.

Thus, having come to our senses after a dizzying journey through one of the many existing photos, we understand that the time has come. It is time to act to help the new contenders for victory, those we were so desperately rooting for, and the teams watching the game from the side, which caused us sympathy and regret. However, how can we help them?

Moving in time in our imaginary car, we noticed that behind the seeming world harmony lies the fierce struggle for superiority in the game of the world economy. Having travelled in the elevator of *the time machine in the world economy*, we have realized that the "residents of the lower floors" do not want to only watch what is happening from below, and the "residents of the penthouse" are ready to share. However, they have not yet decided what, exactly — they do not want to give up their place in the sun!

In plain scientific language, *the time machine in economics* is a common phenomenon that deserves the close attention of scientists and further research. In this work, the categorical apparatus for studying this phenomenon has been clarified; the scientific term *time machine in economics* has been proposed to denote it. An in-depth study of the nature and causal relations of this phenomenon constitutes the prospects for further scientific research. In this regard, the phenomenon of economic vintage is of great interest.

Thus, the following conclusions can be made:

- *Time machine in the economy* is a possibility of movement to different technological modes simultaneously. That is, as in our photograph, we can move to the pre-industrial type of production, just by flying to underdeveloped countries;
- *The density of economic time* depends on economic activity: the higher the activity, the larger the density of economic time and the higher the level of entropy (chaos) of the economic system.

In the period *Present Continuous* (current period of stationary state) at present, the changes are zero, the density of economic time is minimal, and the entropy of the socio-economic system is also minimal.

References

Afanasev, A. A., Kasyanov, V. F., Lukmanova, I. G., & Silka, D. N. (2015). Synchronization of processes related to economic activity with stages of development of spatially-organized systems. *International Journal of Economics and Financial Issues*, 5(3S): 121–124.

Ari, I. & Sari, R. (2017). Differentiation of developed and developing countries for the Paris agreement. *Energy Strategy Reviews*, 18: 175–182.

Aydemir, I. A. (2011). The present continuous tense in Tuvan [Tuvacada şimdiki zaman]. *Bilig*, 59: 53–66.

Barmuta K. A. (2009). Darwin innovation. Modelling the life cycle of innovation based on the theory of evolution. *Creative Economy*, 1(25): 39–42.

Castaldo, A., Fiorini, A., & Maggi, B. (2017). Measuring (in a time of crisis) the impact of broadband connections on economic growth: An OECD panel analysis. *Applied Economics*, 11, https://doi.org/10.1080/00036846.2017.1343448.

Christakou, A. (2014). Present simple and continuous: Emergence of self-regulation and contextual sophistication in adolescent decision-making. *Neuropsychologia*, 65: 302–312.

Creemers, S. (2018). Moments and distribution of the net present value of a serial project. *European Journal of Operational Research*, 267(3): 835–848.

Gómez, M. A. & Neves Sequeira, T. B. E. (2014). Phases of economic development: Do initial endowments matter? *Journal of Macroeconomics*, 12(1): 21.

Güney, P. Ö., Telatar, E., & Hasanov, M. (2015). Time series behaviour of the real interest rates in transition economies. *Economic Research-Ekonomska Istrazivanja*, 28(1): 104–118.

Hecht, J. (2018). Research and development and labour productivity: do high-tech firms exhibit labour- or capital-saving technical change? *Applied Economics*, 50(16): 1790–1811.

Ilyin, S. Y. & Kochetkova, I. A. (2014). Analysis of business activity and profitability of the enterprise. *Chasopis of Economic Reforms*, 4: 49–55.

Inshakov, O. V. (2003). Social nature and specifics, typology and classification of economic institutions. *Investigations on Sociology* [Sotsiologicheskie Issledovaniya], (9): 42–51.

Inshakov, O. V. & Mitrofanova, I. V. (2007a). The modern appearance of the economic complex of southern Russia. *Regional Economics: Theory and Practice*, 11(1): 3–14.

Inshakov, O. V. & Mitrofanova, I. V. (2007b). Socio-economic indicators of the development of the southern regions of Russia: trends and forecasts. *Regional Economics: Theory and Practice*, 14(1): 14–23.

Inshakov, O. W. *et al.* (2008a). Strategy for the socio-economic development of the Volgograd region (2008–2025). Volgograd: Ministry of Education and Science of the Russian Federation, State Educational Institution of Higher Professional Education "Volgograd State University".

Inshakov, O. W. *et al.* (2008b). Modernization of the economy of southern Russia. Problems, priorities, projects. Moscow: Russian Academy of Sciences, Southern Scientific Center.

Inshakov, O. W. *et al.* (2009a). Strategy for innovative development of the Volgograd region until 2025. Volgograd: Ministry of Education and Science of the Russian Federation, State Educational Institution of Higher Professional Education "Volgograd State University".

Inshakov, O. V., Yakovlev, A. R., Fesyun, A. V., Orlova, A. A., & Moseiko, V. O. (2009b). Mechanisms for implementing the strategy for the formation of the nano-industry in the regions of Russia. Volgograd: Ministry of Education and Science of the Russian Federation, State Educational Institution of Higher Professional Education "Volgograd State University".

International Monetary Fund (2017). World Economic Outlook. http://www.imf.org/en/Publications/WEO/Issues/2017/04/04/world-economic-outlook-april-2017. Accessed: 01 November 2017.

International Monetary Fund (2018). Dynamics of Russian GDP values in constant prices in 1992–2017. http://www.imf.org/external/pubs/ft/weo/2017/01/weodata/weorept.aspx?sy=1992&ey=2017&scsm=1&ssd=1&sort=subject&ds=%2C&br=0&pr1.x=52&pr1.y=2&c=922&s=NGDP_R%2CNGDPD%2CNGDPRPC%2CNGDPDPC&grp=0&a=. Accessed: 07 March 2018.

Jalles, J. T. (2017). Forecasting performance of private sector's unemployment forecasts in advanced economies. *International Review of Applied Economics*, 31(6): 707–733.

Kleiner, G. B. (1986). *Production Functions: Theory, Methods, Application*. Moscow: Finances and Statistics.

KOF (2018). Dynamics of KOF Globalization Index Values in Russia in 1992–2017. https://www.kof.ethz.ch/en/forecasts-and-indicators/indicators/kof-globalisation-index.html. Accessed: 07 March 2018.

Komarov, S. V. (2010). Internal innovations of the company: Their creators and life cycle. Marketing internal innovations of the company. *Russian Entrepreneurship*, 7(2): 73–76.

Kozyrev, N. A. (2019). Time Theory. http://xn----itbbdwiegebisy1c.xn--p1ai/teoriya-vremeni-nikolaya-kozyreva/?ckattempt=1. Accessed: 07 December 2019.

Kuhn, T. (1969). *The Structure of Scientific Revolutions*. Moscow: Progress.

Kuntz, A., Davidov, E., & Semyonov, M. (2017). The dynamic relations between economic conditions and anti-immigrant sentiment: A natural experiment in times of the European economic crisis. *International Journal of Comparative Sociology*, 58(5): 392–415.

Kupina, Q. & Salko, D. (2015). Banking system performance on the actual stage of economic development (A comparison analysis of banking systems of Albania and Kosovo). *Mediterranean Journal of Social Sciences*, 6(2): 345–353.

Lakatos, I. (1995). The methodology of scientific research programmes. *The Issues of Philosophy*, 4: 147.

Larina, E. V. (2013). Indicators of financial and business activity of an automobile enterprise. *News of Moscow State Technical University MAMI*, 5-1(15): 326–328.

Leontyev, V. (1990). *Essays in Economics*. Moscow: Politizdat.

Levchenko, A. S. & Kuznetsova, I. A. (2013). Regulatory and legal aspects of the regulation of business activity of industrial enterprises. *Economics and Entrepreneurship*, 11(40): 875–878.

Levchenko, A. S. & Rudychev, A. A. (2013). Peculiarities of defining the marketing activity of the enterprise as a component of business activity. *Social and Humanitarian Knowledge*, 8: 233–239.

Makarov, V. V. & Shuval-Sergeeva, N. S. (2016). The choice of the funding source for innovation at different stages of its life cycle: The amount of funding and the quality of innovation. *Issues of Radio Electronics*, 1: 78–80.

Marx, K. & Engels F. (1959). *A Contribution to the Critique of Political Economy* (Collected Works, 2nd edn.), Vol. 13. Moscow: Politizdat.

Mitrouli, M. & Roupa, P. (2018). Estimates for the generalized cross-validation function via an extrapolation and statistical approach. *Calcolo*, 55(3): 24.

Mohammadi, A., Ahmadi, M. H., Bidi, M., Ghazvini, M., & Ming, T. (2018). Exergy and economic analyses of replacing feedwater heaters in a Rankine cycle with parabolic trough collectors. *Energy Reports*, 4: 243–251.

Natsypaeva, E. A. (2014). The financial activity of the enterprise and the system of indicators of a quantitative assessment of its business activity. *Science and Society*, 3(18): 122–127.

Nekrasov, D. A. (2012). Development of the theory of innovation. Innovative cycles and socio genetic of innovation. *Bulletin of Samara State Economic University*, 5(91): 68–71.

Pirker, S. & Lichtenegger, T. (2018). Efficient time-extrapolation of single- and multiphase simulations by transport based recurrence CFD (rCFD). *Chemical Engineering Science*, 188: 65–83.

Pravdivtsev, V. L. (2019). The Ionosphere, Kozyrev Mirrors and Interaction with the Information Space. https://www.youtube.com/watch?v=rh2D5jC4eHs&feature=youtu.be. Accessed: 28 December 2019.

Raźniak, P., Dorocki, S., & Winiarczyk-Raźniak, A. (2018). Eastern European cities as command and control centers in a time of economic crisis. [Vzhodnoevropska mesta kot središča Vodenja in upravljanja med gospodarsko krizo]. *Acta Geographica Slovenica*, 58(2): 101–110.

Sarvan, D., Stratimirović, D., Blesić, S., & Miljković, V. (2014). Scaling analysis of time series of daily prices from stock markets of transitional economies in the Western Balkans. *European Physical Journal B*, 87(12): 297, https://doi.org/10.1140/epjb/e2014-50655-5.

Shahbaz, M., Shahzad, S. J. H., Mahalik, M. K., & Sadorsky, P. (2018). How strong is the causal relationship between globalization and energy consumption in developed economies? A country-specific time-series and panel analysis. *Applied Economics*, 50(13): 1479–1494.

Stafford, M. B. R., Reilly, T., Grove, S. J., Carlson, L., Bhandari, R., & Copeland, J. (2011). The evolution of services advertising in a services-driven national economy: An analysis of progress and missed opportunities. *Journal of Advertising Research*, 51(Suppl. 1): 136–152.

Syrquin, M. (2015). Resources, industrial transformation and the structure of the world economy. *Resources, Production and Structural Dynamics*, 323–345. DOI:10.1017/CBO9781139940948.019.

The World Bank Group (2017). KEI and KI Indexes. http://www.worldbank.org/kam. Accessed: 01 November 2017.

United Nations Development Programme (2017). Human Development Index. http://hdr.undp.org/. Accessed: 01 November 2017.

Vernadsky, V. A. (2019). The Problem of Time in Modern Science. http://vernadsky.name/problema-vremeni/. Accessed: 28 December 2019.

[illegible] (20[illegible]). [illegible] analysis of [illegible] leader [illegible] with [illegible] policy [illegible]. [illegible] of the [illegible] and the [illegible] [illegible]. [illegible], 10(2), [illegible].

[illegible] (20[illegible]). [illegible] of the theory of innovation [illegible] and [illegible]. [illegible], [illegible].

[illegible] (2013). [illegible] transport based [illegible]. [illegible], 148, [illegible].

[illegible] (20[illegible]). The [illegible] information [illegible]. Accessed 8 December 2015.

[illegible] (2011). [illegible]. Evaluation [illegible]. [illegible], 2015, [illegible].

[illegible] (20[illegible]). Scaling analysis of [illegible] in the [illegible]. https://doi.org/10.1[illegible].

[illegible] (2013). [illegible] developed [illegible]. [illegible], 11, [illegible].

[illegible] (2018). The evolution of services [illegible] national [illegible]. An analysis of progress and [illegible]. [illegible], 17, 1[illegible].

[illegible] (20[illegible]). [illegible]. https://doi.org/10.1016/[illegible].

[illegible] (2017). [illegible]. Accessed 21 November 2017.

[illegible] Development Programme (2017). Human Development [illegible]. Accessed 21 November 2017.

Vernadsky, V. I. (2019). The Problem of Transition [illegible]. Accessed [illegible] 2019.

Chapter 2

Economic "Vintage" — The Nature of the Phenomenon and Methods of Measurement: Time Stood Still

Choosing time means saving time, and what is done untimely, is done in vain.

F. Bacon, 16th century English philosopher

This chapter is about the world economy developing in a spiral.

It deals with the following:

- a comparison of past and present socio-economic systems;
- classification of approaches to the interpretation of the essence and methods of measuring economic "vintage;"
- highlighting key properties and drawing up a conceptual model of economic "vintage".

In ancient Chinese philosophy, linear-cyclical ideas were dominant. It was believed that space develops in a spiral, and it is divided vertically (time) and horizontally (space) into five levels. The age of a person is etymologically associated with the words "to howl" and "to develop".

The chariot of history moves inexorably forward. Its wheels spin, driving the world economy. It accelerates, then slows down, but it never stops. If you watch the wheels of history for a long time, you'll notice that they make a revolution, returning to the starting point (Figure 1). For example, in the fashion world, styles and shapes that were popular in the past become trendy again over time.

Figure 1. Vintage photograph.

Source: Author's photo by scholar and photographer Elena Popkova, https://www.saatchiart.com/account/artworks/1599809.

The same happens with musical styles. There is a movement aimed at recreating and re-employing old motifs and compositions. Retro cars are also in demand. Outwardly they resemble cars from the past, but they contain updated or new parts, thus combining vintage style with modern capabilities, convenience, and comfort.

This suggests that only by taking a step forward does a person begin to realize all the advantages of his previous position. As a result, interest in subjects and concepts from the past resumes; old things acquire a new interpretation and receive a "second life". I believe that the economy is no exception. In this chapter, we consider examples of a return to the past in the economy and, on that basis, define the concept of economic vintage and discuss methods of measuring it.

The systematization of the existing scientific literature in the field of economic vintage allowed us to classify approaches to its study (Table 1).

Let's consider the approaches highlighted in Table 1 in more detail. As part of the traditional approach, economic vintage refers to traditions laid down in the past and preserved to date. The measurement of

Table 1. Classification of approaches to the interpretation of the essence of economic "vintage" and methods of measuring it.

Conceptual approach	The essence of economic "vintage"	Methods of measuring economic "vintage"	Representatives of the approach
Traditional	Economic vintage is a tradition laid down in the past and preserved to date	Ratio of traditions and innovations in the economy (degree of vintage of the socio-economic system)	Bohner *et al.* (2017) Liao *et al.* (2016) Bolton *et al.* (2016) Takeuchi (2016) Budanov (2010) Muzalevskaya (2007) Khomenko & Vorontsov (2014)
Diversification	Economic vintage is the process of expanding (diversifying) the scope of economic ideas	Degree of diversification (diversity of spheres and uses) of economic ideas	Hwang *et al.* (2018) Thanakijsombat & Kongtoranin (2018) Desmarchelier *et al.* (2018) Garvey *et al.* (2017) Liu *et al.* (2017) Belik (2017) Boltava (2009) Magomedova (2009) Shcherbakov (2011)
Modern	Economic vintage is the process of modernization of economic systems with the preservation of their basic installations	Degree of compliance of basic ideas with current needs and capabilities	Busu & Busu (2017) Andreeva *et al.* (2017) Bulatov (2016) Kyrchaniv (2016) Zheng *et al.* (2016) Inshakov & Yakovlev (2009)

economic vintage is carried out through the ratio of traditions and innovations in the economy; that determines the degree of vintage of the socio-economic system. It is assumed that the more traditions prevail over innovation, the more vintage the socio-economic system.

With this approach, the term "economic vintage" is replaced by the category "tradition" and distinguishes between traditional ("vintage") socio-economic systems, which are least susceptible to change and are characterized by strong public resistance to innovation, and innovative socio-economic systems, which are dynamic and characterized by positive perception and public support for innovation.

Prominent representatives and founders of this approach are Laperche, Galbraith, and Uzunidis, who, in their book *Innovation, Evolution and Economic Change: New Ideas in the Tradition of Galbraith*, released in 2006, studied the phenomenon of economic vintage using the example of the ideas of Galbraith (Figure 2).

Figure 2. Book cover of *Innovation, Evolution and Economic Change: New Ideas in the Tradition of Galbraith* (Laperche *et al.*, 2006).

This French-American team of authors investigated the evolution of capitalism. Given the changes in the general economic climate since Galbraith's ideas were put forward, the scientists describe new ideas that "form fertile ground for new research". The experts concluded that capitalism is a traditional concept that underlies the functioning and development of dynamically developing modern economic systems and defined it as economic "vintage".

This approach is used by Russian researchers such as Budanov (2010), Muzalevskaya (2007), and Khomenko & Vorontsov (2014).

Representatives of the diversification approach define economic vintage as a process of expanding (diversifying[1]) the areas of application of economic ideas. Their focus is on entrepreneurship, which creates and implements various business ideas. This approach emphasizes the creation of patents establishing copyright on original ideas and the subsequent transfer of these rights in various ways, leading to diversification in the use of ideas. As a way of measuring economic vintage, an assessment of the degree of diversification (variety of spheres and methods of use) of economic ideas is used.

According to the diversification approach, economic vintage is the result of multidisciplinary scientific and practical research that adapts ideas and discoveries in one field of knowledge to the current needs of another field of knowledge and economic practice. For example, adapting military developments of the past years for peaceful purposes in our time leads to the creation of an economic vintage. Thus, the Hummer vehicle was launched for mass consumption.

The resumption of production of cars under the Moskvich brand in Moscow in 2022–2023 is also an example of an economic vintage. Another example of economic vintage is the significant popularity of smartwatches. After decades of using mobile phones as the sources of information about time, wristwatches became popular again — though now they have innovative designs and new functions (e.g., measuring pulse and checking messages).

Reference: It was originally termed an HMMWV or Humvee (High Mobility Multipurpose Wheeled Vehicle), an American army all-rounder, mainly in service with the US Armed Forces, as well as the armed forces, police, and other services of some other countries. The car has high

---

[1]Diversification of the scope of the idea is an increase in the variety of areas of application of the idea, leading to a reduction in the risks associated with its implementation and the maximization of economic benefits.

cross-country ability and is suitable for air transportation and parachute landing. It was marketed as the Hummer (HUMMER is the registered trademark of its manufacturer, AM General Corporation), and since 1992 it has been converted to an SUV for civilian use.[2]

Speaking about the proponents of this approach, it is necessary to especially note the contribution of an American scientist who is the representative of the International Monetary Fund, O.E.G. Johnson. In his book *Economic Diversification and Growth in Africa: Critical Policy Making Issues*, he presents evidence that the phenomenon of economic vintage is most characteristic of developing countries (Figure 3).

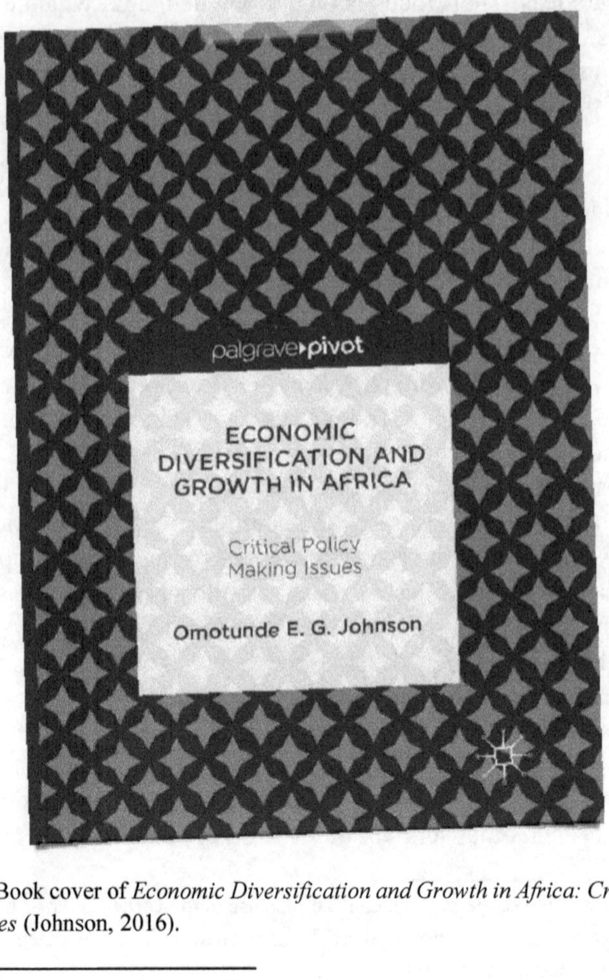

Figure 3. Book cover of *Economic Diversification and Growth in Africa: Critical Policy Making Issues* (Johnson, 2016).

[2]https://ru.wikipedia.org/wiki/HMMWV.

The author focused on exploring policy development in three critical areas for Africa: capacity-building for domestic resource mobilization; regional integration and intraregional trade; and diversification of exports of selected African countries. He showed that African developing countries could improve their policy-making strategies to diversify the economy and accelerate socio-economic development, but the basic concepts of their growth and development remain almost unchanged and represent an economic vintage (Johnson, 2016).

This approach is used in the works of such Russian scientists as Belik (2017), Boltava (2009), Magomedova (2009), and Shcherbakov (2011).

From the point of view of the modernization approach, economic vintage is considered as a process of modernization of economic systems with the preservation of their basic installations. That is, representatives of this approach study macroeconomic objects — entire socio-economic systems — analyzing the process of their modernization. At the same time, vintage includes those socio-economic systems that, in the process of modernization, retain their support for basic concepts, adapting them to new conditions.

Considering the history of developing countries, the logical question arises: how much did external conditions (for example, colonization) affect their economic development? Would these countries achieve a qualitative transition without having been colonies? Would developing countries have grown faster before 1950 if they had been fully independent? Examples of countries that have never been colonized (Ethiopia, Afghanistan, Nepal, and China until 1949) show that independence did not provide additional advantages while ensuring sufficient economic growth.

In this case, a vivid example of the economical vintage is modern Russia, which started the actualization of the Soviet inheritance and its adaptation to new realities in 2022–2023. A precondition to economic vintage was that the model of "pure" capitalism, well established in Western Europe and North American countries, did not meet Russia's expectations. The initiative on the international recognition of higher education diplomas, instead of an influential institute, turned out to be an "institutional trap". To implement this initiative, Russia refused post-Soviet traditions and changed the hierarchy of the higher education system to match European standards. However, the practice of international recognition of diplomas was never developed. That is why, starting in 2022, Russia has been forming a new model of the organization of higher education, which will be based on the unique Soviet inheritance and consider the new experience of Russia. This new reform should ensure unique and sustainable competitive advantages of the system of higher education in Russia and the successful implementation of the program "Priority 2030" in the Decade of Science and Technology in the Russian Federation. It should strengthen the strategic academic leadership of Russia.

The return of most countries of the world — developing (BRICS) and developed (the G7 and the EU) — to the policy of protectionism is yet another specific feature of economic vintage. After World War II, protectionism dominated the global economy. The end of the 20th century marked the age of the development of free trade. Under the guidance of the World Trade Organization, the advantages of the international division of labour as the most effective model of production organization were promoted. Production specialization was considered preferable because it was most effective in terms of economy, with allowance for significant dependence of the national economy on imports. The worsening international sanction crisis in 2022 made further implementation of the free-trading model impossible in principle since it led to significant deficit risks due to the destruction of the global supply and sales chains. Thus, an economic vintage appeared — the restoration of the protectionism model, though with modern features through an allowance for dependence on imports from friendly countries (reliable regional foreign trade partners).

Several positive features characterized the colonial period of various countries. During this period, clear political boundaries were established, the status of statehood increased, the colonial authorities supported and stimulated new exports (coffee, tea, cocoa, sugar, rubber), and invented land management schemes that stimulated the production of traditional cereals. All this was accompanied by a significant increase in infrastructure: the construction of roads, railways, and port facilities and the establishment of river navigation. Domestic order created an enabling environment for economic activity and contributed to population growth.

However, there were just as many negative features of colonialism (unsuccessful economic "breakthroughs"). The colonial authorities did nothing to protect local artisanal producers from competition from imported factory goods. They were usually hostile to domestic industrialization and preferred to continue importing products from overseas. Education, especially secondary and higher education, was not widespread among the population due to the desire to preserve traditions.

According to a study by Lloyd Reynolds, among those countries that were colonies, 17 made material transitions during the colonization period, and eight could not do this (India, Pakistan, Bangladesh, Indonesia, Egypt, Sudan, Mozambique, and Zaire) since colonial rule as an external circumstance created obstacles to qualitative transformations (Reynolds, 1983).

One of the most prominent representatives of this approach is Diego Coletto, who, in his book *The Informal Economy and Employment in Brazil: Latin America, Modernization, and Social Changes*, published in 2010, studied the phenomenon of economic vintage using the example of a shadow economy (Figure 4).

The scientist analyzed some informal (shadow) economic activities in Brazil in this book. Using an ethnographic approach, he investigated social and economic processes that allow the informal economy to be

Figure 4. Book cover of Coletto's *The Informal Economy and Employment in Brazil: Latin America, Modernization, and Social Changes* (2010).

reproduced, revealing the complex and heterogeneous relations between the formal and informal sectors of the economy. The scientist concluded that the shadow economy is an "economic vintage" that remains almost unchanged in modernizing the economy (Coletto, 2010, pp. 44–46).

In his works, Professor Inshakov justified the need to study the evolution of socio-economic systems. The continuity of economic development is emphasized in his works on economic genetics and economic institutionalism. The process of modernization of socio-economic systems described in the works of Inshakov contributed to the development of fundamental provisions of the modernization approach. He described ideas in this regard in the following publications: (Inshakov & Frolov, 2010; Inshakov, 2007a, 2007b; Inshakov *et al.*, 2009; Inshakov & Yakovlev, 2009).

When measuring the economic "vintage" within the framework of this approach, the degree of correspondence of the basic ideas to the actual needs and possibilities of our time is determined. That is, representatives of this approach consider the active use of past concepts and their applicability to current conditions. According to this, they distinguish between successfully developing "vintage" socioeconomic systems (characterized by high efficiency) and systems that are "hostages" of their "vintage"; that is, they do not have the opportunity or are not capable of innovative development when it is needed.

The analysis results showed that, despite the variety of approaches to interpreting the essence of economic vintage and how to measure it, these methods are characterized by low accuracy and reliance on qualitative indicators. These approaches should not be considered an alternative since they reflect various properties of economic vintage. Combining the main ideas of existing approaches, we propose a new integrated approach to studying economic vintage, taking into account all its properties. Let us consider the most striking examples of these properties in modern economic reality.

The first characteristic of economic vintage is a return to the origins — the past economic concept — and its application in the present. For example, when the world was on the verge of the first industrial revolution in the 19th century, there were those advocating that new technologies should be abandoned, fearing their possible harm to humanity. In the 20th century, large-scale scientific discoveries renewed interest in this concept, causing not only individual protests and resistance to the development of new technologies but also an official worldwide ban, for example, on human cloning and the testing of nuclear weapons, due to the risk of a biological crisis.

Another example is vehicles that are an integral part of most people's lives. In the 15th century, Leonardo Da Vinci predicted that in the future people would fly, and he invented a tank and an airplane and made many other discoveries that are actively used today. Despite the exact and detailed drawings of the scientist, his ideas could not be realized due to the imperfection of the technologies of that time. Today's more advanced technologies have made it possible to recreate his ideas, and the similarity between the resulting mechanisms and his designs is striking.

Another example of this characteristic of economic vintage is the rethinking of industrial development through the lens of environmental costs. As a result, modern humanity has chosen as an ideal the model of environmentally sound economic development implemented before the emergence of industry in the 19th century. Just as agrarian (pre-industrial) socio-economic systems of that time existed in harmony with nature, modern high-tech (industrial and post-industrial) systems, on the brink of an environmental crisis, seek to balance the interests of the consumer society and damage to the environment.

Similarly, in the 21st century, under the influence of a global recession, economic systems were forced to move away from the concept of free trade[3] and apply protectionist measures.[4] These measures were not as radical as they were in the 18th and 19th centuries and did not completely exclude foreign competition. However, to a large extent, these measures were restrictive and gave substantial preferences to domestic enterprises.

The second characteristic of economic vintage is a new application or a new interpretation of the past economic concept. For example, the modern shadow economy is rooted in slavery. By depriving a person of labour rights and giving him unlimited duties, the shadow economy turns him into a slave. Without formal employment, the employee has no social guarantees, and the system of "work in debt" plunges him into a state of dependence on the place of work.

The concept of the slave-owning system has received another interpretation today. Just as in slave markets people were perceived as a commodity, in the modern labour market, labour (or human resources) acts as a commodity. Of course, the original concept is now interpreted in

---

[3]Free trade is the concept of free (barrier-free) movement of resources and finished goods across the national borders of states in the world economy.

[4]Protectionism is the concept of restricting the access of foreign competitors to domestic markets and providing domestic enterprises with various preferences aimed at strengthening their market position compared to foreign competitors.

a completely different way, although it retains the basic idea of "man as a product".

Consider another example of this characteristic of economic vintage. Modern technologies for wireless charging of mobile devices (phones, tablet computers, smartwatches, etc.), created as innovations, existed and were successfully used back in the 19th century. In 1894, in New York, Nikola Tesla lit an incandescent phosphorus lamp from a distance due to the inertia of the electromagnetic field.

This technology was not only invented, but also patented, two centuries ago. However, after Tesla's experiments, interest in this technology faded due to a side effect — the negative effect on the human body — as well as the energy intensity of the technology and the short distance at which it could be used. (A mobile device had to be too close to the source of energy for its use to be practical.) Today, this technology has been refined and successfully used.

The third characteristic of economic vintage is the modernization processes' complexity in the new economic conditions. As an example, consider the struggle for energy resources. The discovery of metallurgy caused a massive labour migration to Siberia for iron ore, which was highly valued. Today, oil is called "black gold", and a struggle is underway for the effective use of nuclear energy. Interest in energy sources has accompanied the entire history of human society, and as new technologies arose, the energy concept was gradually modernized.

A similar example is geographical discoveries. In the era of the Great Geographical Discoveries (15–17th centuries), ships were worth their weight in gold, and battles were fought for the seas. Now, space exploration is actively taking place. Spaceships have replaced marine vessels, and the battle for space supremacy continues. Space travel brings discoveries and allows for more detailed maps of the universe. Even though technologies to make other planets habitable for human life have yet to be found, there is an intensive division of alien territories.

These properties formed the basis of our definition of economic vintage.

Reusing economic concepts at different times with the possibility of their new interpretation or new application, as well as modernization in new economic conditions, is an aspect of economic vintage.

In accordance with the proposed definition, we have developed a conceptual model of economic vintage, which is presented graphically in Figure 5.

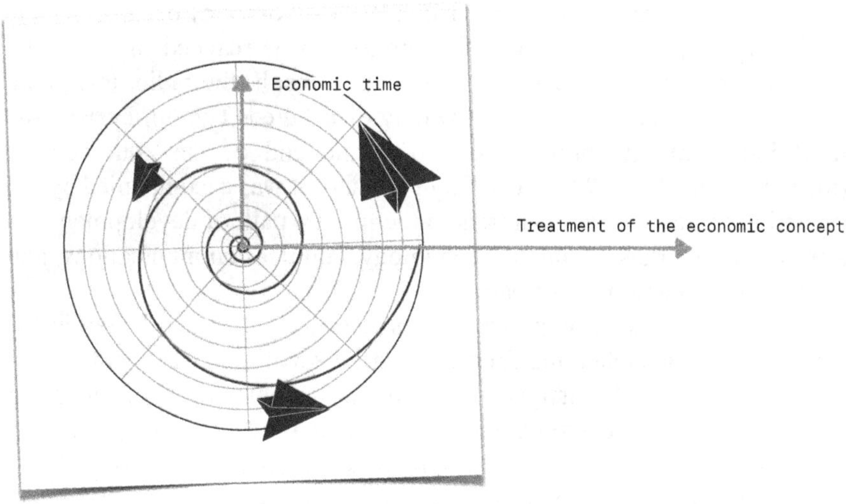

Figure 5. Conceptual model of economic vintage.

As seen in Figure 5, economic vintage can be represented as a spiral ladder, at the bottom of which is the distant past, when the original idea was created. As time passes and the wheel of history moves, this concept is modified and transformed into an economic vintage, becoming a phenomenon of the past in the present.

An essential component of the formation of economic vintage is overcoming the obsolescence of the original concept because otherwise it will lose its relevance and will not receive further application and development. In this regard, economic vintage relies on scientific research and the innovative activity of entrepreneurs. It can be manifested both at the level of micro-structures (enterprises that have introduced vintage ideas into their activities) and at the level of macro-structures (socio-economic systems (countries) that develop vintage).

The proposed term "economic vintage" is comparable to the category of economic crisis, which means an economic recession accompanied by the paralysis of individual industries or the economy as a whole. Throughout modern economic history, crises have coincided with industrial revolutions. The first crisis (the first industrial revolution) occurred in the 18–19th centuries. Its result was the creation of the textile industry and the steam engine.

The second crisis (the second industrial revolution) occurred at the beginning of the 20th century; the "bottom" was reached in 1933 (the Great Depression in the United States). As a result, the radio, telegraph, and telephone were invented and widely distributed. The third crisis (the third industrial revolution) occurred at the end of the 20th century (the market crash of 1991 and 1998 in Russia). It was accompanied by the transition of post-Soviet countries to the market path of development. As a result of the crisis, computer technology, cellular communications, and the internet became widespread.

The fourth crisis (the global depression of 2008, which began in the United States) launched the fourth industrial revolution. Its result should be the transition to Industry 4.0. Already, in the context of the emerging digital economy, the cloud, blockchain, and other progressive digital technologies are becoming widespread. From the perspective of the Theory of Economic Cycles (founded by Kondratyev), a crisis is a downward wave of the economic cycle. Small and large waves of development stand out, which are both logically and visually similar to economic vintage. Kondratiev's theory has many followers around the world. As can be seen, each crisis (cycle wave) combines both recession and subsequent accelerated growth (progress). This emphasizes the contribution of economic vintage to economic growth.

A fifth crisis is expected — it may occur soon, by 2050 or even 2030. The Fifth Industrial Revolution will be accompanied by the socialization of intelligent machines — bright (equipped with artificial intelligence and machine learning) autonomous robots, which will become a part of the machine and human–machine community. The first manifestations of the socialization of intelligent machines exist even now, becoming more prominent each year. For example, intelligent voice assistants (Alisa in Yandex), smart speakers (Marusia), competent consultants (Afina in Sber), and chatbots (Max in public services) communicate with people and help them in many ways, taking the load off employees of organizations that started them. This is economic vintage, for, similarly to the process of socialization (introduction in society: acceptance, recognition, adoption of social statuses and roles) of certain social groups (peasants after the abolition of serfdom and after the Great October Revolution in Russia; black population after the abolition of slavery in the USA; representatives of colonies after the dissolution of the monopolistic system in countries of Western Europe), socialization of intelligent machines takes place now and will take place in the future.

Therefore, following the movement of the wheel of economic history, we see that the famous proverb "New is the well-forgotten old" is also true economically. Through the prism of economics, it can be paraphrased as follows: modern is often the past, demanded in the present, and with a new interpretation. Some economic concepts could not be embodied in the economic practice of the past due to the lack of interest in them or the necessary conditions; others were successfully implemented, but failed; still others were popular, but were forgotten, and so on.

Economic "vintage" allows returning to the past concepts and finding new applications for them or refining or modernizing them in the present to take advantage of already known or hidden advantages. Crises of economic systems create scientific and practical interest in economic "vintage". By making it impossible or impractical to continue the intended course of socio-economic development, crises require a revision of their underlying theoretical concept. Finding a new concept sometimes requires too much time or resources, so resorting to economic "vintage" is an attractive alternative.

The proposed concept of economic vintage allows us to define it as inspired by new life, having received a wider scale and complicated economic ideas than the past, applied in the present. At the same time, original ideas might be created in the past but get used only in the present, or attract new interest and get a new interpretation, or be used continuously, gradually evolving.

Developing this concept, we can conclude that if there is an old one, then there should be a new one. Obviously, not all economic phenomena and processes are vintage. The opposite is innovation. This concept also requires rethinking from the point of view of the economic Theory of Time, since it must be tied to the existing base and compared with it, characterized by a certain proportion and degree of novelty. Therefore, in the next chapter, we need to consider time as a category of the modern Theory of Innovation.

References

Andreeva, E., Myslyakova, Y., Glukhikh, P., & Ratner, A. (2017). Economic and social impact of modernization on cultural values. *Journal of International Studies*, 10(1): 193–208.

Belik, I. A. (2017). Diversification strategy. Concept, essence, and main types of diversification. *Economics and Entrepreneurship*, 12–13(89): 616–620.

Bohner, G., Crutchfield, R. D., Messner, S. F., & Zick, A. (2017). Innovation and tradition (Editorial). *International Journal of Conflict and Violence*, 11: 1–3. DOI:10.4119/UNIBI/ijcv.617.

Boltava, A. L. (2009). Business diversification in the region: Tools opportunities and limitations of various instruments of diversification in the regional economic system. *Russian Entrepreneurship*, 10(1): 150–154.

Bolton, S., Green, L., & Kothari, B. (2016). Optimize the contribution of design to innovation performance in Indian SMEs-What roles for culture, tradition, policy, and skills? *South Asian Popular Culture*, 14(3): 199–217.

Budanov, V. G. (2010). Conservatism — Tradition — Innovation. *Problem Analysis and Public Management Design*, 3(4): 108–109.

Bulatov, A. (2016). Russia's economic model and prospects for modernization. *Mezhdunarodnye Protsessy*, 14(4): 6–27.

Busu, C. & Busu, M. (2017). The role of knowledge-intensive business services on Romania's economic revival and modernization at the regional level. *Sustainability (Switzerland)*, 9(4): 526.

Coletto, D. (2010). *The Informal Economy and Employment in Brazil: Latin America, Modernization, and Social Changes*. UK: Palgrave Macmillan, pp. 1–270.

Desmarchelier, B., Regis, P. J., & Salike, N. (2018). Product space and the development of nations: A model of product diversification. *Journal of Economic Behavior and Organization*, 145: 34–51.

Garvey, G., Kahn, R. N., & Savi, R. (2017). The dangers of diversification: Managing multiple manager portfolios. *Journal of Portfolio Management*, 43(2): 13–23.

Hwang, I., Xu, S., & In, F. (2018). Naive versus optimal diversification: Tail risk and performance. *European Journal of Operational Research*, 265(1): 372–388.

Inshakov, O. V. (2007a). Economic genetics as the theoretical basis of nanoeconomics. *Philosophy of Agriculture*, 5(53): 95–109.

Inshakov, O. V. (2007b). Economic Genetics and Nanoeconomics. Volgograd: Russian Academy of Sciences, Department of Social Sciences, Southern Scientific Center of the Russian Academy of Sciences. Volgograd: Volgograd State University.

Inshakov, O. & Frolov, D. (2010). The evolutionary perspective of economic institutionalism. *Economic Issues*, 9(1): 63–77.

Inshakov, O. V. & Yakovlev, A. R. (2009). Modification is a form of evolution of the company's product. *Bulletin of Volgograd State University. Series 3: Economics. Ecology*, 2(1): 115–123.

Inshakov, O. V., Inshakova, E. I., Mitrofanova, I. V., & Petrova, E. A. (2009). Development of an Evolutionary Approach in the Strategy of Modernization of the Region and Macroregion. Volgograd: Volgograd State University.

Johnson, O. E. G. (2016). *Economic Diversification and Growth in Africa: Critical Policy Making Issues*. Switzerland: Springer International Publishing, pp. 1–129.

Khomenko, V. V. & Vorontsov, D. P. (2014). Interaction of traditions, innovations, and investments in state support mechanisms for foreign economic activity of regions. *Bulletin of TISBI*, 3: 99–116.

Kyrchaniv, M. (2016). Local currencies: Economic anthropology, regional performative and modernization of identity. *Economic Annals-XXI*, 159(5–6): 10–15.

Laperche, B., Galbraith, J. K., & Uzunidis, D. (2006). *Innovation, Evolution, and Economic Change: New Ideas in the Tradition of Galbraith*. UK: Edward Elgar Publishing, pp. 1–333.

Liao, M.-H., Xu, Y.-C., & Sone, H. (2016). Old-established companies' traditions and innovations — Focusing on e-business of Japan and Taiwan. *Proceedings — 2016 10th International Conference on Innovative Mobile and Internet Services in Ubiquitous Computing, IMIS 2016*, 7794525, pp. 531–532.

Liu, M., Fang, Y., Choulos, A. G., Park, D. H., & Hu, X. (2017). Product review summarization through question retrieval and diversification. *Information Retrieval Journal*, 20(6): 575–605.

Magomedova, Z. G. (2009). Export diversification as a condition of economic growth in Russia. *Russian Foreign Economic Gazette*, 3: 35–40.

Muzalevskaya, I. M. (2007). Tradition and innovation in sociocultural practices. Management consulting. *Current Problems of State and Municipal Administration*, 1(25): 149–156.

Reynolds, L. G. (1983). The spread of economic growth to the third world: 1850–1980. *Journal of Economic Literature*, 21(83): 941–980.

Shcherbakov, D. (2011). The impact of the degree of international business diversification on its efficiency: Is there an optimal level of international business diversification? *Corporate Finance*, 5–11(17): 94–102.

Takeuchi, M. (2016). Tradition and innovation in the business of 450 years. *Journal of the Japan Research Association for Textile End-Uses*, 57(6): 4–5.

Thanakijsombat, T. & Kongtoranin, T. (2018). Performance and diversification benefits of foreign-equity ETFs in emerging markets. *Applied Economics Letters*, 25(2): 125–129.

Zheng, J., Wang, L., & Tang, K. (2016). China's road to modernization: Chinese culture and China's model of economic development: A special issue from the 4th world conference on sinology. *Journal of Chinese Economic and Business Studies*, 14(1): 1–8.

Chapter 3

Time as the Main Category of Modern Theory of Innovation — Innovation vs. Tradition: Time Has Changed

Of all things, time is the least ours, and most of all we lack.

Georges-Louis Leclerc, Comte de Buffon,
18th century French scientist and philosopher

This chapter is about the world's economy changing with time.

This chapter considers the following issues:

- classification and description of the existing approaches to studying the time aspect of the modern theory of innovation;
- comparative analysis of traditions and innovations from the position of the time aspect;
- the properties and the model of innovations from the position of the time aspect.

In European culture, time is considered linear and is traditionally compared to a released arrow that flies fast (Figure 1). This emphasizes the uniqueness of the past events, but also their close interconnection and the constant forward movement and development. In European culture, innovations are treated as having the highest value, since it is the novelty that differentiates the current moment from the past and future ones.

Let us close our eyes and imagine that we're standing on a bank of a limitless river of time. We're boarding an imaginary ship and going along the river. The river's flow quickens, then slows down, allowing us to see

Figure 1. Creative process of innovation.

Source: Author's photo by scholar and photographer Elena Popkova, https://www.saatchiart.com/account/artworks/1599809.

the banks. We see that one bank's landscape remains unchanged during our whole trip. The sky above it is clear, and it is possible to see similar unattractive trees on the bank, which are slightly swaying under the weak wind. This flat bank attracts us with its stability and reliability.

On the other bank, the landscape changes all the time. It is shrouded in mist and covered with quicksand. However, sun rays show wondrous plants on this bank. The plants are pressed to the ground by the strong gusts of wind, and mellow fruits are falling to the ground. We hear strange sounds which call to us, but seem daunting at the same time. Perhaps, dangers await us on this bank, but it is also full of riddles and promises of breathtaking adventures.

We're thinking about what we should do — go to the right bank and rest in the shadow of the ordinary trees or take a risk and step on to the left bank and try the delicious fruits of rare plants?

In the same way, in the world economy, some choose the right bank and some choose the left bank. There are traditional economic systems, which prefer not to take a risk and to preserve the usual socio-economic mode, being content with medium, but stable, income. There are also innovative economic systems, which are inclined to meet changes and are ready for risks, hoping for a larger income.

The purpose of this chapter is to show that time is the main category of the modern theory of innovation and that innovations cannot be considered separately but only in comparison with traditions. Traditions and innovations are usually opposed to each other, but we think that they are closely interconnected. Thus, innovations are built on traditions, and traditions are innovations of the past. Let us use the modern scientific treatment of these notions.

The time aspect of the modern theory of innovation has been studied and elaborated on in multiple works of modern authors. We performed their classification; the description is given in Table 1.

Let us consider the approaches to studying the time aspect of the modern theory of innovation described in Table 1 in detail. The relationship approach is called so because its application envisages a strong impact on the subjective, personal attitude of a researcher to

Table 1. Classification and description of the existing approaches to the research of the time aspect of the modern theory of innovation.

Approach	Time criterion used for the classification of innovations	Classification of innovations by the time criterion	Representatives
Relationship	Novelty and timeliness of innovations	• True innovations • False innovations	Coen (1998) Gaynor (2017) Pavlov (2016) Pchelina (2012) Elsner (2018)
Cyclical	Phase of economic cycle at which innovations are created and implemented	• Innovations in the period of stability • Innovations in the period of crisis	Ramella (2017) Ausloos *et al.* (2017) Squire (2017) Breitung *et al.* (2016) Li (2017) Vorontsova (2016) Indrisov (2015) Pevchev (2011) Shchennikova (2011)

(*Continued*)

Table 1. (*Continued*)

Approach	Time criterion used for the classification of innovations	Classification of innovations by the time criterion	Representatives
Consumer-oriented	Demand for innovations at different periods in the economy	• Innovations in countries with developed and developing economies • Innovations in the innovative economy (knowledge economy) • Innovations in the tradition-oriented and innovation-oriented economies, etc.	Asimakou (2017) Rao-Nicholson *et al.* (2017) Crowley & McCann (2017) Neubert *et al.* (2017) Inshakov *et al.* (2015)
Transformational	Form of innovations in time	• Innovations in the form of new ideas • Innovations in the form of utility models and engineering samples • Innovations in the form of innovative products, etc.	Ortiz-Villajos (2017) Kumar *et al.* (2017) Wang & Hu (2017) Velpandian (2017) Hall *et al.* (2016) Nagorny & Kasyanenko (2013) Sitkevich *et al.* (2018) Tkachenko (2013)

innovations. Within this approach, such time criteria as novelty and timeliness are used for the classification of innovations; the following innovations are distinguished:

- true innovations (completely new, modern economic concepts);
- false innovations (economic traditions, obsolete concepts renewed).

Within this approach, research was conducted and the book *Toward true regulatory reform: How to make EU governance innovation fit. Revolutionising EU Innovation Policy: Pioneering the Future* by Bausch was published in 2016 (Figure 2).

The scholar notes that the European Union is a complex adaptive system consisting of various members with often contradictory political tasks and interests; the central goal of managing the EU is to coordinate and interlink these differences and develop compromise solutions, which would serve a common European future. For this, only true, previously non-existent, and unused innovations could be used (Bausch, 2016).

Figure 2. The cover of Bausch's book *Toward true regulatory reform: How to make EU governance innovation fit. Revolutionising EU Innovation Policy: Pioneering the Future.*

This approach is presented in the works of such Russian scholars as Pavlov (2016), Pchelina (2012) and Elsner (2018).

The cyclical approach suggests the classification of innovations depending on the phase of the economic cycle at which they are created and implemented, as well as the differentiation of innovations in the period of stability and innovations in the period of crisis. The essence and logic of this approach are given in detail in the work of Bazhal *The Political Economy of Innovation Development: Breaking the Vicious Cycle of Economic Theory*, published in 2017 (Figure 3).

Figure 3. Cover of the book *The Political Economy of Innovation Development: Breaking the Vicious Cycle of Economic Theory* by Bazhal (2017).

In this book, the author writes that R&D and technological innovations in a country are not the results but the factors of sustainable economic growth. Bazhal develops Schumpeter's theory and states that true economic growth — especially in countries with transitional and developing economies — is possible only due to innovations. They ensure the effective functioning of the market economy and are in special demand during a crisis since they allow for dealing with its consequences and restoring economic growth in a faster way (Bazhal, 2017).

Professor Inshakov (Doctor of Economy) could be considered a representative of the cyclical approach. In his works, he substantiated the necessity for the initiation of innovative activity in modern economic systems for the quick overcoming of the consequences of the global economic crisis. A perspective direction of these systems' innovative development, according to him, is nano-industry. His ideas on this issue are described in a range of works: Inshakov & Inshakova (2015, 2016), Inshakov *et al.* (2014, 2015), Inshakov & Kryukova (2015), and Inshakov & Fesyun (2014a, 2014b).

According to the consumer-oriented approach, the time criterion for the classification of innovations is the demand for them at different times in the economy. Within this approach, there are innovations in countries with developed and developing economies, innovations in the innovative economy (knowledge economy), innovations in the tradition-oriented and innovation-oriented economies, etc. In other words, innovations could perform different roles and have a different value for the economic system's development, depending on its type and socio-economic mode, which is determined by time.

A representative of this approach is Rahman, the author of the chapter "Open innovation in small and medium enterprises: Perspectives of developing and transitional economies" in the book *Human Development and Interaction in the Age of Ubiquitous Technology* (2016) (Figure 4).

This book states that despite the wide recognition of most corporate business entities, there is a need for adaptation of the modern strategies and concepts, created by open and innovative entrepreneurship, to the specifics of countries of the East, West, or South. This is a guarantee of wide public recognition. Innovations could be in larger demand in economies of the same time level, while there could be no need for innovations in economies that are at other levels. This approach is present

Figure 4. Cover of the book *Human Development and Interaction in the Age of Ubiquitous Technology* by Rahman (2016).

in the Russian scientific and economic literature, in particular in the works of Vorontsova (2016), Idrisov (2015), Pevchev (2011), and Shchennikova (2011).

In the transformational approach, the time criterion of the innovations' classification is their form in time; according to this approach, there are innovations in the form of new ideas, innovations in the form of utility models and engineering samples, innovations in the form of innovative products, etc. According to this approach, it is considered that the following transformation of innovations in time takes place: at earlier stages of socio-economic systems' development, the simplest forms of innovations are used, which often are non-formalized and defenceless in the intellectual and legal aspect; in the course of further development of economic systems, innovations take a more complex form and become better protected from the normative and legal position.

This approach is presented in the chapter "Innovation processes in logically constrained time series" Möller *et al.* in the book *Advances in Directional and Linear Statistics: A Festschrift for Sreenivasa Rao Jammalamadaka* (2011) (Figure 5).

The group of authors thinks that when analyzing an innovative process it is necessary to take into account the connection between this

Figure 5. Cover of the book *Advances in Directional and Linear Statistics: A Festschrift for Sreenivasa Rao Jammalamadaka* (2011).

process and its mathematical consequences. The normative and legal foundations of the innovative activities and the social environment, in which these activities take place, play a decisive role in selecting the form of innovations and methods of their practical use. This approach is given in the works of Russian authors, such as Nagorny & Kasyanenko (2013), Sitkevich *et al.* (2018), and Tkachenko (2013).

The performed overview and content analysis of the existing scientific literature in the sphere of the research of the time aspect of the modern theory of innovation have demonstrated a close connection between traditions and innovations and the essential importance of their differentiation. A comparative analysis from the position of the time aspect is given in Table 2.

As is shown in Table 2, traditions belong to the past, and innovations to the present. Traditions are less topical now since they were oriented on the satisfaction of obsolete needs with the use of the possibilities of the past. Compared to them, innovations are more topical at present, since they use the possibilities of the modern time and are oriented toward the satisfaction of current needs.

Table 2. Comparative analysis of traditions and innovations from the position of the time aspect.

	Traditions	**Innovations**
Belonging to time	Past time	Present time
Topicality in present time	Low	High
Accessibility and level of use at present	Multiple mass routine phenomena and processes	Prototypes, test versions in single quantities
Susceptibility to changes with time	Low	High
Opportunities for using in future	Small, there will be a need for substantial modernization	Large, modernization might be unnecessary
Interpretation of successful adaptation to the requirements and possibilities of the present	Economic “vintage”	Modernity

At present, traditions are widespread, are in open access, and have become mass routine processes and phenomena. Contrary to the less available innovations, they are not that widespread and are presented in the form of prototypes and test samples in single quantities. Unlike innovations, traditions are less susceptible to changes in time, since they are already obsolete.

Given the low topicality of tradition at present time, the possibilities of their use in the future could appear only in the case of modernization. A lot of innovations are initially oriented toward the future and are not used at present, so their modernization might not be needed at all or might be of a smaller form. In the case of successful adaptation to the requirements and possibilities of the present, traditions are interpreted as economic "vintage", and innovations as modernity.

For a better description of time as a category of the modern theory of innovation, let us provide examples of applied innovations and the authors of these innovations:

- Wilhelm Röntgen in 1901 was awarded the Nobel Prize for the invention of rays, which were called X-rays or Röntgen rays;
- Pierre Curie and Marie Skłodowska-Curie received the Nobel Prize in 1903 for their study of radiation phenomena;
- Albert Michelson was nominated for the Nobel Prize in 1907 for the creation of precise optical instruments;
- Guglielmo Marconi and Karl Brown invented radiotelegraphy, for which they also received the Nobel Prize in 1909;
- Nils Gustaf Dahlén was awarded the Nobel Prize in 1912 for his invention of automatic regulators for lighthouses and buoys;
- Erwin Schrödinger and Paul Dirac received the Nobel Prize in 1933 for the discovery of new productive forms of atomic theory;
- Isamu Akasaki, Hiroshi Amano, and Shuji Nakamura were awarded the Nobel Prize in 2014 for the invention of efficient blue light-emitting diodes which have enabled bright and energy-saving white light sources.

The above examples show that innovations were changing — qualitatively — society's life over the past centuries. Today, we're using the benefits of inventions, not thinking about their history and creators. Inventions of the past have become routine things and are no longer assigned their previous value, though they continue to be great scientific inventions of humanity.

Based on the above, the following main features of innovations from the position of the time aspect are distinguished.

- *Relativeness in the context of time*: Novelty as compared to traditions and past.
- *Connection to time*: Topicality at present of future time.
- *Foundation on time*: Use of the capabilities of the time.
- *Change in time*: Depreciation of innovations.

Let us consider these features in detail.

The first feature of innovations is relativeness in time. To distinguish innovations, it is necessary to compare them to traditions. The larger the difference between new concepts and traditions, the higher the level of their novelty and the more unambiguous their belonging to innovations. Thus, traditions are the basis for defining innovations, and without the knowledge of traditions, it is impossible to understand whether innovations are true or false or whether they are economic "vintage".

The second feature of innovations is a connection to time. According to the modern theory of innovation, they have to be practice-oriented and have an applied value. Inventions require an analysis from the positions of the human-oriented approach and evaluation as to potential usefulness and danger for humanity. Innovations have to stimulate better satisfaction of the current human needs. If an innovator does not find a prospective direction of the practical application of their innovations or if innovations are potentially dangerous and require special preparation of society for their implementation, they have to be postponed until the proper time in the future. That is, innovations are connected to time — either present or future — at any rate.

The third feature of innovations is the foundation of time. First, innovations do not appear out of thin air — they are always based on traditions. To create something new, an innovator has to possess knowledge of the concepts in a certain sphere. This is only expedient — for the innovator not to make rediscoveries and not to "reinvent the wheel". Ignorance of traditions could lead to vain efforts. Second, this feature is also manifested in the fact that innovations use the possibilities of the present time. Innovators have to know and use the needs and possibilities of the modern times for their further implementation in the created innovations so that they are in demand at the present time and have the current potential of modern times. Incomplete implementation of this potential leads to a slow rate of economy's growth and innovative development, and, therefore, to lost profit.

The fourth feature of innovations is the change with time. Novelty cannot be eternal. Innovations preserve novelty over a short period, after their creation. Innovativeness is a characteristic of economic concepts, phenomena, and processes until they become widespread and become usual things for humanity and available for use by a large number of economic subjects. The duration of the preservation of innovations' novelty in time depends on the normative and legal regulations of patent law protection and the duration of patents. According to Article 1363 of the Civil Code of the Russian Federation (part four) dated 18 December 2006 No. 230-FZ, the direction of a patent for a production piece is five years, for a utility model, 10 years, and an invention, 20 years. This term could be extended by five years at the request of the patent holder, but by no more than 25 years (State Duma of the Russian Federation, 2006). Various countries have different terms, but the general world tendency in the sphere of patenting envisages the patent duration from five to 25 years. To receive a patent for innovations in any country of the world, one should apply to the corresponding body of the executive authorities, e.g., Rospatent in the Russian Federation, and the United States Patent and Trademark Office in the USA. In the world economy, patent law is regulated by international organizations: the World Intellectual Property Organization, the World Trade Organization, etc. Therefore, while the patent is active, the innovation retains its novelty. When the patent duration ends, it becomes available for free use by economic subjects and for mass distribution — not just by the patent holder and those who received official permission. However, there might emerge a unique situation, when an innovation has not been used during the patent duration, and, therefore, has preserved its novelty after the patent duration. In this case, the timeframe of preservation of the innovations' novelty is vaguer and is limited by the period when the innovation receives the practical application and becomes usual for humanity.

Thus, time is a starting point during the definition of innovations. It assigns them with special features and suggests criteria for their definition. We offer the following definition of innovations from the position of the time aspect.

From the position of the time aspect, innovations are economic concepts, phenomena, and processes that are based on the existing economic traditions but have a large share of novelty as compared to them; which are developed and used in view of the needs and capabilities of the modern times; which are topical at present or future times; and which are susceptible to depreciation, turning into traditions or economic "vintage" in the future.

A model of innovations from the position of the time aspect according to the offered definition of innovations and their distinguished properties is presented in Figure 6.

As is shown in Figure 6, the edge between traditions and innovations is unclear. However, we see that the face of the old mechanical watch acquires a modern electronic form over time. The given model demonstrates the described features of innovations from the position of the time aspect and shows that innovations: (a) are based on traditions, (b) are topical at present, and (c) will become traditions or economic "vintage" in the future.

Thus, our journey along the river of time, which we presented at the beginning of this tale, has come to an end. We have seen that both banks of this river are nice and attractive — each in its aspect. Moreover, we have learned that the river along which we moved is just an illusion, a very thin edge between traditions and innovations, between future and present. It is created by our imagination, to differentiate these categories and understand where one bank ends and the other begins.

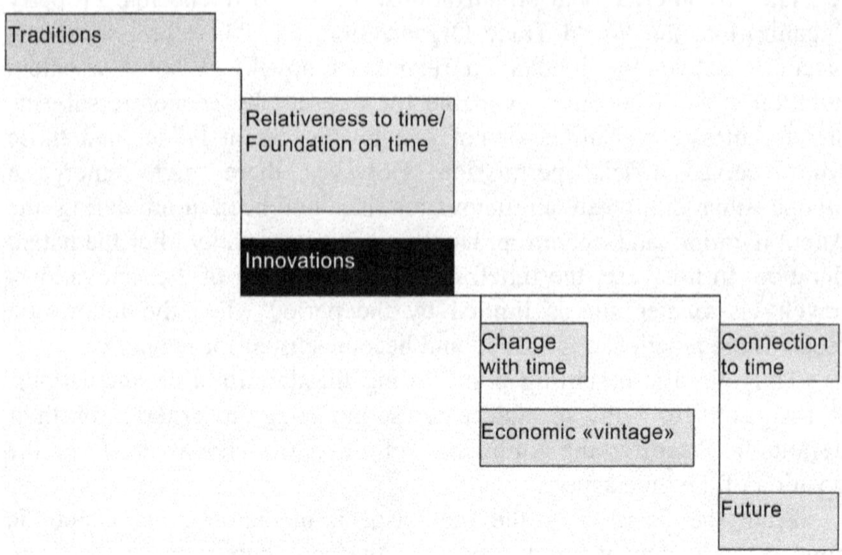

Figure 6. The model of innovations from the position of the time aspect.

In the modern theory of innovation, time is the main category, since from the position of the time aspect it is possible and necessary to differentiate traditions and innovations, which form the basis of the framework of categories and are the key objects of studying this theory. From the position of the time aspect, innovations have the following features: relativeness in time, connection to time, the foundation of time, and changing with time. The substantiated presence and the proven fundamental role of the time aspect in the modern theory of innovation are the basis for an idea of the important role of the factor of time in other economic theories and in the macro-economic analysis which is studied in the next chapter.

References

Asimakou, T. (2017). Time for innovation: Concurrent and conflicting metaphors of time in a knowledge MNC. *Time and Society*, 26(1): 113–134.

Ausloos, M., Bartolacci, F., Castellano, N. G., & Cerqueti, R. (2017). Exploring how innovation strategies at the time of crisis influence performance: A cluster analysis perspective. *Technology Analysis and Strategic Management*, 30(4): 484–497, https://doi.org/10.1080/09537325.2017.1337889.

Bausch, C. J. (2016). Toward true regulatory reform: How to make EU governance innovation fit. In *Revolutionising EU Innovation Policy: Pioneering the Future*. London: Palgrave Macmillan, pp. 215–257.

Bazhal, I. (2017). *The Political Economy of Innovation Development: Breaking the Vicious Cycle of Economic Theory*. Cham, Switzerland: Springer International Publishing.

Breitung, J. & Herwartz, H. (2016). Innovations in multiple time series analysis. *Journal of Econometrics*, 192(2): 329–331.

Coen, D. (1998). Asthma 1997: True and false innovation. [Asma 1997: Vere a false novita]. *Ricerca e Pratica*, 14(81): 125–128.

Crowley, F. & McCann, P. (2017). Firm innovation and productivity in Europe: Evidence from innovation-driven and transition-driven economies. *Applied Economics*, 50(11), 1–19, https://doi.org/10.1080/00036846.2017.1355543.

Elsner, V. (2018). The economy of complexity and innovation: Why innovation's benefits are not guaranteed. *Journal of Institutional Studies*, 10(4): 7–19.

Gaynor, G. (2017). Innovation resources — One more time. *IEEE Engineering Management Review*, 45(2): 6–8.

Hall, C. L., Selby, K., Guo, B., Valentine, A. Z., Walker, G. M., & Hollis, C. (2016). Innovations in practice: An objective measure of attention, impulsivity and activity reduces time to confirm attention-deficit/hyperactivity disorder diagnosis in children — A completed audit cycle. *Child and Adolescent Mental Health*, 21(3): 175–178.

Idrisov, M.-K. M. (2015). Features of financing innovation in developing countries. *Economics and Entrepreneurship*, 11–1(64): 970–973.

Inshakov, O. V. & Fesyun, A. V. (2014a). Impact of Russia's Accession to the WTO on the Development of the National Nano Industry. *Modernization of the Economic System of the Southern Macroregion in the Conditions of the WTO: A Collective Monograph*. Moscow: Volgograd State University, pp. 9–28.

Inshakov, O. V. & Fesyun, A. V. (2014b). The industry as a form of establishment, distribution and domination of the economic structure in the economy. *Bulletin of the Volgograd State University. Series 3: Economics. Ecology*, 2(1): 44–53.

Inshakov, O. V. & Kryukova, E. V. (2015). Special economic zones as an institution for the development of the nano industry: Failures, problems and prospects. *Bulletin of the Volgograd State University. Series 3: Economics. Ecology*, 1(1): 6–17.

Inshakov, O. V. & Inshakova, E. I. (2015). Reconstruction of RF nano industry institutions in an unfavourable global environment. *Bulletin of the Volgograd State University. Series 3: Economics. Ecology*, 4(1): 7–17.

Inshakov, O. V. & Inshakova, E. I. (2016). Development of the world and Russian nano industry: Results and problems. *Economic Science of Modern Russia*, 4(1): 65–78.

Inshakov, O. V., Inshakova, E. I., & Kryukova, E. V. (2014). Special economic zones as an institution for the development of the nano industry: Essence, structure, improvement. *Bulletin of the Volgograd State University. Series 3: Economics. Ecology*, 6(1): 81–95.

Inshakov, O. V., Inshakova, E. I., & Fesyun, A. V. (2015). Nanoindustrialization as a stage in the formation of a new economic order in Russia. Grant research and educational activities: Goals, technologies, results. *A Collective Monograph in 9 Volumes*. Limited Liability Company International Research Center "Scientific Cooperation", Rostov-on-Don. pp. 76–106.

Kumar, R., Sharma, A. K., & Agnihotri, K. (2017). Dynamics of an innovation diffusion model with time delay. *East Asian Journal on Applied Mathematics*, 7(3): 455–481.

Li, C. (2017). Research on economic management innovation model based on market economy environment. *Agro Food Industry Hi-Tech*, 28: 1815–1818.

Möller, C., Rachev, S. T., Kim, Y. S., & Fabozzi, F. J. (2011). Innovation processes in logically constrained time series. *Advances in Directional and Linear Statistics: A Festschrift for Sreenivasa Rao Jammalamadaka*. Germany: Physica-Verlag, pp. 173–188.

Nagorny, E. I. & Kasyanenko, T. V. (2013). Improvement of approaches to marketing testing of ecological innovative products at the stages of the innovation cycle. *Marketing and Management of Innovation*, 4: 291–303.

Neubert, M. J., Bradley, S. W., Ardianti, R., & Simiyu, E. M. (2017). The role of spiritual capital in innovation and performance: Evidence from developing economies. *Entrepreneurship: Theory and Practice*, 41(4): 621–640.

Ortiz-Villajos, J. M. (2017). Forms of innovation throughout time: Insights from the British business elite. *Innovation: Management, Policy and Practice*, 19(4): 428–451.

Pavlov, K. V. (2016). Evaluation of the effectiveness of innovations and investments of intensive and extensive type. *Chasopis of Economic Reforms*, 2(22): 26–32.

Pchelina, Y. S. (2012). Intellectual property as a basis for innovation. *Collection of Scientific Works World*, 23(2): 3–8.

Pevchev, D. A. (2011). Infrastructure support for investment markets in developing countries. *Bulletin of Economic Integration*, 3: 131–139.

Rahman, H. (2016). Open innovation in small and medium enterprises: Perspectives of developing and transitional economies. In *Human Development and Interaction in the Age of Ubiquitous Technology*. Hershey, PA: IGI Global, pp. 250–272.

Ramella, F. (2017). The 'Enterprise of Innovation' in hard times: Corporate culture and performance in Italian high-tech companies. *European Planning Studies*, 25(11): 1954–1975.

Rao-Nicholson, R., Vorley, T., & Khan, Z. (2017). Social innovation in emerging economies: A national system of innovation-based approach. *Technological Forecasting and Social Change*, 121: 228–237.

Shchennikova, Z. V. (2011). Investment activity of countries with emerging markets. *Bulletin of Economic Integration*, 7: 118–124.

Sitkevich, A. M., Sobolevsky, S. B., & Leshko, Y. S. (2018). The volume of shipped innovative products as a result of innovative activities in the region. *Bulletin of the Institute of Entrepreneurial Activity*, 1(18): 91–99.

Squire, K. (2017). Innovation in times of uncertainty. *On the Horizon*, 25(4): 293–308.

State Duma of the Russian Federation (2006). Civil Code of the Russian Federation (part four) of 18.12.2006 No. 230-FZ. http://www.consultant.ru/document/cons_doc_LAW_64629/9e7ee220e4fac9a5158bb4406a5cb4e224e5122e/. Accessed: 21 December 2017.

Tkachenko, D. D. (2013). Modelling cooperation between enterprises in the creation of innovative products and innovative production technologies. *Management of Economic Systems: Electronic Scientific Journal*, 2(50): 11.

Velpandian, T. (2017). Research for innovation: Time for adapting the changes. *Indian Journal of Physiology and Pharmacology*, 61(2): 86–87.

Vorontsova, O. V. (2016). Innovation in emerging markets. *Production Management: Theory, Methodology, Practice*, 7: 19–24.

Wang, R.-K. & Hu, D. (2017). Time-cost substitutability, early cutting threat, and innovation timing. *Economics Letters*, 156: 88–91.

Chapter 4

F. von Wieser's Theory of Lost Profits: Time as a Source of Alternatives

The natural value (utility) of anything is a value due to the utility it has conferred on the final product.

Friedrich von Wieser, 19th century Austrian economist

This chapter is about the world's economy having numerous alternatives.

This chapter considers the following issues:

- definition and the specifics of measuring the true value of time in economics;
- alternative possibilities of using time in economics.

According to the mythological beliefs of the pre-Islamic nomadic Turks, who lived in the territories of Innermost Asia and Southern Siberia in the 6th century A.D. and did farming, time was cyclical and subject to constant recurrence.

We suggest using the skill of imagination again and visualizing metaphors. Now, we are in a magic valley of time (Figure 1). Broken apart by a swift river, it reached far beyond the horizon. The time horizon opens many alternatives for us, and we are at a crossroads. We can go north, following the cold wind, and reach an icy cave, which could be discerned far away. We can go south and join a caravan travelling across a desert. Looking west, we understand that we can overtake a herd of sheep that is pasturing at hand. Setting out east, we can go fishing at a wonderful lake. Each of these alternatives is great and attractive all by itself, but our time is limited — when the last grain of sand falls to the bottom of a sand clock

Figure 1. Time as a source of alternatives.

Source: Author's photo by scholar and photographer Elena Popkova https://www.saatchiart.com/account/artworks/1599809.

in our hands our fantasy journey finishes in a blink of an eye. Thus, we have to choose what exactly we want most.

At first, we decide to follow the caravan in the south, but we understand right away that it is too far from us — we won't be able to reach it and will only lose priceless time. Then we make up our minds to go fishing in the east but realize that we might catch nothing and might spend the time left without any use. Then our choice remains with two options: north or west. What is awaiting us there? We're thinking hard, trying to avoid a mistake. It is as if we are in a labyrinth of time and wish to choose the best option — with the least amount of time and effort required (a path that will lead us from the labyrinth in the fastest and simplest manner possible) and the best result (the most valuable prize has to wait for us at the end of this path).

Economics also lies in the labyrinth of time. von Wieser's Theory of Lost Profits, described by the scholar in his monograph *Theory of Social Economy* ("Theorie der gesellschaftlichen Wirtschaft") in 1914, points out the following properties of economic time (von Wieser, 1927).

- *Value in the future*: It is only after the end of the process of the creation of goods and provision of services (in the future) that we can determine their value precisely.
- *Alternativeness*: During the creation of goods and provision of services, we can use different forms of resources (labour, land, capital), which are the alternatives.
- *Subjectivity*: Costs of the creation of goods and provision of services are subjective and are determined by alternative goods and services, which have not been produced.
- *Lost profit*: True value (cost) of goods and services is a "benefit that was not received" (lost profit) from all other goods and services that we have not produced since we have already used resources for the production of these goods and services — Wieser's law.
- *Alternative costs*: Value (cost) of goods and services is formed of all alternative costs — costs of production of all possible goods and services with the help of the given resources.

Analyses of von Wieser's Theory of Lost Profits and its reconsiderations from the positions of the modern economic reality have been performed in the works of such foreign authors as Arena (2010), Campagnolo & Vivel (2012), Festré & Garrouste (2016), Bebber (2017), Klein *et al.* (2017), Liu *et al.* (2017), Nguyen & Makam (2017), Susilo *et al.* (2017), Tackett *et al.* (2017), Taumoepeau *et al.* (2017), Trinks & Scholtens (2017), van Dijk (2017), Appolloni *et al.* (2018), and Yoon *et al.* (2018), and such Russian scholars as Barkalov *et al.* (2006), Rzhanitsyna (2008), Zhuravlev *et al.* (2008), and Shakirov (2010).

Prof. Oleg V. Inshakov considered these properties of economic time through the lens of institutional economic theory. He introduced the notion of "institutional human", which allows tracking the process of the institutionalization of saving time by a human. This issue is studied in the works of Inshakov (2005), Inshakov & Frolov (2005a, 2005b), and Inshakov *et al.* (2005).

The above properties of economic time are illustrated in Figure 2, with the model of economic time from the positions of von Wieser's Theory of Lost Profits.

As shown in Figure 2, it is only after the slug is turned into gold bullion and the production process ends that its value will be known in the future (shown by the dotted line). The weighing of various options on the scale (double line on the left) reflects their alternativeness, One option

Figure 2. The model of economic time from the positions of von Wieser's Theory of Lost Profits.

has to outweigh. The number of alternatives (gold bullions in the figure) and their weight are difficult to determine by eye, taking into account the fact that some of them go beyond the limits of the considered figure, which is a demonstration of our evaluations' subjectivity.

Lost profit is all the gold bullion that we see and can imagine, finishing the figure in our mind. The true value of the slug, which we have to choose in this figure according to von Wieser's Theory of Lost Profit, includes the weight of its alternative — the gold dust (double line in the right), or the alternative costs.

Economic time itself is the scale at which alternative options of using limited resources for the production of economic goods are weighed. Time in economics is a limited resource, and thus it is necessary to perform weighing for the rationalization of economic activities. This action allows determining the true value of time in economics: the true value of time in economics is the total time spent for the production of other economic goods.

Also, it is necessary to pay attention to the fact that according to von Wieser's Theory of Lost Profit, time in economics is static: economic analysis is performed at a set moment, and dynamics are not taken into account. Each set of alternatives corresponds to its own time, and their comparison is not envisaged. During the determination of the value of economic goods, despite the theory's stating that it happens in the future, time is actually present in the moment of determination of the value. Since the production process is finished, the past time is taken into account — but not the future time.

It should be noted that the described von Wieser theory of alternative costs is popular and is used in many countries in the world (e.g., the USA), but it has not become that widespread in Russian practice. However, many Russian financial managers use the main provisions of this theory in the process of managing the companies' financial flows. The postulates of this theory are most vividly demonstrated in the financial market when the selection of certain financial assets leads to losses for the whole securities portfolio. Such examples in the practice of work of the Russian stock market are numerous. They were manifested most vividly during the financial crises of 2008, 2014, and 2018, when the quick growth of the stock market was followed by its downfall, which led to the mass crisis of companies and the bankruptcy of investors.

Thus, according to von Wieser's Theory of Lost Profits, whatever path in the valley of time we choose, we lose anyway, since we cannot go in all cardinal directions at the same time. Moving only in one direction we bear alternative costs, which are connected to the impossibility to explore and use other directions and lose the connected profit. We can only minimize the alternative costs and lost profit, but it is impossible to eliminate them.

This theory will not help us find the way out of the labyrinth of time, it only says that there is a way or several ways out and suggests criteria for comparing them, but the choice remains with us. However, this theory provides an unambiguous answer to the question of which variant of behaviour is the worst. It is inactivity — the choice at which alternative costs and lost profit are at their maximum, since we have not moved at all and have not taken any of the available directions.

As a result, our question remains open. While we — being impressed by the scientific theory — are thinking about which way to choose, we involuntarily take the worst alternative. The last grains of sand fall to the bottom of the sand clock, our time passes away, and we can just wait for the next opportunity to take a journey in time. We have to continue our search for the "key to time" — a means to choose the best option. Perhaps, Adam Smith's Theory of Saving Time will help us with that.

References

Appolloni, L., Sandulli, R., Vetrano, G., & Russo, G. F. (2018). A new approach to assess marine opportunity costs and monetary values-in-use for spatial planning and conservation; the case study of Gulf of Naples, Mediterranean Sea, Italy. *Ocean and Coastal Management*, 152: 135–144.

Arena, R. (2010). Friedrich von Wieser on institutions and social economics. In *Austrian Economics in Transition: From Carl Menger to Friedrich Hayek*, pp. 109–137.

Barkalov, S. A., Vrublevskaya, S. S., Semenov, P. I., & Serebryakova, E. A. (2006). A method of minimizing lost profits. *Control Systems and Information Technologies*, 3(25): 29–34.

Bebber, M. R. (2017). Tempered strength: A controlled experiment assessing opportunity costs of adding temper to clay. *Journal of Archaeological Science*, 86: 1–13.

Campagnolo, G. & Vivel, C. (2012). Before Schumpeter: Forerunners of the theory of the entrepreneur in 1900s German political economy — Werner Sombart, Friedrich von Wieser. *European Journal of the History of Economic Thought*, 19(6): 908–943.

Festré, A. & Garrouste, P. (2016). Wieser as a theorist of institutional change. *Journal of the History of Economic Thought*, 38(4): 463–483.

Inshakov, O. V. (2005). "Institutional man" is a subject of socially consecrated action. In *Institutional Man*. Russian Academy of Sciences, Department of Social Sciences, Southern Scientific Center of the Russian Academy of Sciences: Volgograd State University, pp. 59–86.

Inshakov, O. V. & Frolo, D. P. (2005a). Man is an institutional system. In *Institutional Man*. Russian Academy of Sciences, Department of Social Sciences, Southern Scientific Center of the Russian Academy of Sciences, Volgograd State University, pp. 195–219.

Inshakov, O. V. & Frolov, D. P. (2005b). Institutional factions in modern society. In *Institutional Man*. Russian Academy of Sciences, Department of Social Sciences, Southern Scientific Center of the Russian Academy of Sciences, Volgograd State University, pp. 37–59.

Inshakov, O. V. *et al.* (2005). *Institutional Man*. Russian Academy of Sciences, Department of Social Sciences, Southern Scientific Center of the Russian Academy of Sciences, Volgograd State University.

Klein, R., Mackert, J., Neugebauer, M., & Steinhardt, C. (2017). A model-based approximation of opportunity cost for dynamic pricing in attended home delivery. *OR Spectrum*, 40(4): 1–28, DOI:10.1007/s00291-017-0501-3.

Liu, J., Fu, B., Wang, Y.-K., Lu, Y.-F., & Xu, P. (2017). Agricultural opportunity costs assessment based on planting suitability: A case study in a mountain county in southwest China. *Journal of Mountain Science*, 14(3): 1–13, DOI:10.1007/s11629-016-4329-0.

Nguyen, O. K. & Makam, A. N. (2017). What are the opportunity costs of self-financing medical education? *Academic Medicine*, 92(12): 1655.

Rzhanitsyna, B. C. (2008). Determination and accounting of compensation for lost profits. *Accounting*, 19: 11–18.

Shakirov, D. F. (2010). Compensation for lost profits in case of violation of obligations in the pre-contractual relationship. *Business in Law*, 3: 130–133.

Susilo, H., Takahashi, Y., & Yabe, M. (2017). The opportunity cost of labour for valuing mangrove restoration in Mahakam Delta, Indonesia. *Sustainability*, 9(12): 2169.

Tackett, B. M., Sheng, W., & Chen, J. G. (2017). Opportunities and challenges in utilizing metal-modified transition metal carbides as low-cost electrocatalysts. *Joule*, 1(2): 253–263.

Taumoepeau, S., Towner, N., & Losekoot, E. (2017). Low-cost carriers in Oceania, Pacific: Challenges and opportunities. *Journal of Air Transport Management*, 65: 40–42.

Trinks, P. J. & Scholtens, B. (2017). Correction to: The opportunity cost of negative screening in socially responsible investing. *Journal of Business Ethics*, 147: 239–240, https://doi.org/10.1007/s10551-017-3726-9.

Van Dijk, M. (2017). Estimating the weight of opportunity costs in housing consumption. *Applied Economics*, 49(57): 5762–5770.

Von Wieser, F. (1927). *Theorie der gesellschaftlichen Wirtschaft, Social Economics*. Translated by A. Ford Hindrichs. https://mises.org/library/social-economics.

Yoon, B., Park, K., & Kang, S.-K. (2018). A design of group recommendation mechanism considering opportunity cost and personal activity using spark framework. *Lecture Notes in Electrical Engineering*, 461: 289–298.

Zhuravlev, Y. V., Prozorovskaya, L. V., & Zhuravleva, T. Y. (2008). Methodology for assessing lost profits in investment design. *Innovation Bulletin Region*, 3: 6–9.

Chapter 5

A. Smith's Time Saving Theory: Time Should Be Saved

> *Every man is rich or poor according to the degree in which he can afford to enjoy the necessaries, conveniences, and amusements of human life.*
>
> Adam Smith, 18th century Scottish economist

This chapter is about saving time in the modern global economy.

This chapter considers the following issues:

- principles of saving time in the economy;
- role and strategies of specialization for saving time in the economy.

In Ancient Egypt, time was considered heterogeneous — it could be bad or good. Stability and consistency were the most important properties of time. It was treated cyclically and followed the set algorithm.

...Time continues its flow again. Now, we're at a masquerade. There are many guests here, and we want to get acquainted with each one. This is similar to the situation when participants in world economic relations gather to discuss an issue that concerns all of them. They put on masks to hide their emotions and intentions and make the results of a general vote unpredictable. We need to look under their masks, to find out whether they are going to support our initiative. Depending on whether the masquerade's guests become our allies or opponents, we shall build our behaviour tactics.

The hands of an old clock move relentlessly, and we have little time left — and much to do...! The time of voting for our initiative comes closer, and we cannot determine the allies before the vote. We want economics to help us. Will it be able to help us to slow the course of time down and do all that we planned? The help is provided by the Theory of Time saving by Adam Smith[1] — the representative of the classical political economy.[2]

This theory is described in Adam Smith's fundamental work *An Inquiry into the Nature and Causes of the Wealth of Nations* (better known under its short title *The Wealth of Nations*), which was published in 1776 (Figure 1).

In his research, Smith defined labour as the source of the "wealth of nations" and built a Theory of Time saving around labour as the central scientific category of his works. It should be noted that A. Smith's theory is devoted to labour, not time. However, it contains important provisions for the Theory of Time. Based on the analysis of Smith's work through the lens of the Theory of Time, we formulated the principles of saving time, offered by the scholar (Smith, 1776).

- *Principle of labour division*: In a commodity society, it is possible and necessary to differentiate business processes and assign certain (fixed) workers to them.
- *Principle of specialization*[3]: Performing the same labour operations every day, the worker improves his skills and performs these operations better than the workers who perform other routine operations or combine various operations in their activities.

---

[1]Adam Smith was an 18th century English economist and recognized as one of the founders of modern economic theory.

[2]Classical political economy is one of the first modern scientific schools of economics, dating back to the end of the 18th century. In the 19th century, the most prominent representatives of this were Smith, Say, Ricardo, Malthus, Mill, who proclaimed economic freedom (liberalism) and formulated the main provisions of the labour theory of value, according to which the value of goods and services is determined by the labour expended on their production.

[3]Specialization is the process of focusing efforts on certain labour processes, provided that other business processes are carried out by other participants in economic relations and there is a free exchange of labour results.

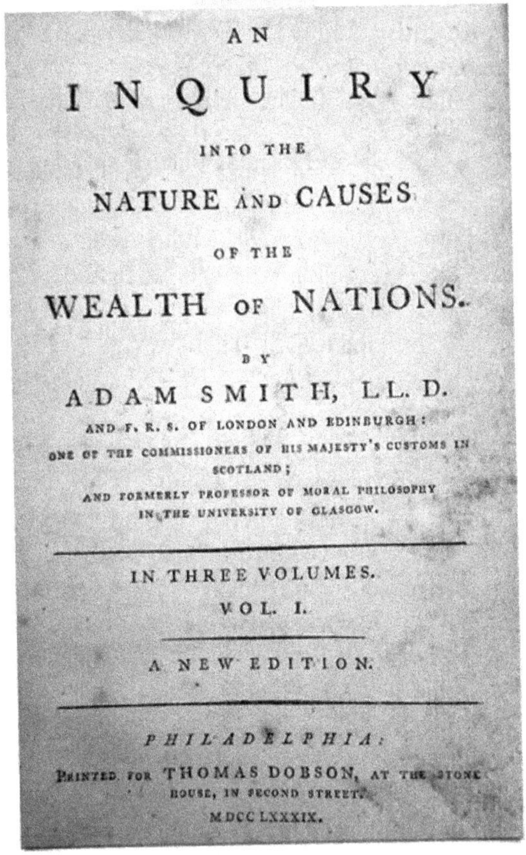

AN
INQUIRY
INTO THE
NATURE AND CAUSES
OF THE
WEALTH OF NATIONS.
BY
ADAM SMITH, LL. D.
AND F. R. S. OF LONDON AND EDINBURGH:
ONE OF THE COMMISSIONERS OF HIS MAJESTY'S CUSTOMS IN SCOTLAND;
AND FORMERLY PROFESSOR OF MORAL PHILOSOPHY IN THE UNIVERSITY OF GLASGOW.

IN THREE VOLUMES.
VOL. I.

A NEW EDITION.

PHILADELPHIA:
PRINTED FOR THOMAS DOBSON, AT THE STONE HOUSE, IN SECOND STREET.
MDCC LXXXIX.

Figure 1. Cover of Smith's book *An Inquiry into the Nature and Causes of the Wealth of Nations* (1776).

- *Principle of automatization of business processes*: Replacement of manual labour by machine labour allows the acceleration of business processes and reduces the number of mistakes caused by the "human factor".
- *Principle of maximization of efficiency*: Focusing on a certain type of activity, a worker does not spend time for the transfer to another workplace and the change of way of thinking, which ensures the maximization of result, i.e., the growth of labour efficiency.

The observation of the above principles ensures the optimization of the worker's efforts and saving of time for the production of a certain set of goods and/or provision of services. These principles are the basis of numerous modern scientific studies in economics that are devoted to the optimization of economic activities, such as Ashby & Gonzalez (2017), Beck *et al.* (2017), Blum (2017), Choi & Han (2017), Folscher & Kruger (2017), Grinstein-Weiss *et al.* (2017), Martens & Di Ciommo (2017), Mitra (2017), Poleacovschi *et al.* (2017), Rolison *et al.* (2017), and Rupprecht & Annuß (2017), Many publications are devoted to the reconsideration of these principles and the adaptation of Smith's works to the modern economic reality, for example, Kolpakov (2006), Erokhin (2007), Fedotova & Kolpakov (2010), Kozyrev (2010), Shchegolevsky (2011), Burnham (2017), Glaze (2017), Hühn (2017), Mahoney (2017), Newbert (2017), Özler & Gabrinetti (2017), Paganelli (2017), Pitts (2017), Ridley (2017), Smith (2017), Viganò (2017), Yamamori (2017), and Thomas (2018).

The idea of time saving is the basis of the works by Inshakov, devoted to the issues of the integration of the theory of economics in the conditions of globalization, reconsideration of the Russian economy's position in the world economic system at the turn of the century, determination of the essence and role of the economic environment, and development of the concept of spatial economics (Inshakov & Frolov, 2005; Inshakov, 2005a, 2005b).

Based on the considered principles, we compiled a model of time saving in economics according to Adam Smith's Time Saving Theory (Figure 2).

As shown in Figure 2, if we're at a masquerade and wish to look under the largest possible number of masks, we have to choose a strategy of specialization. For example, we could specialize only in checking the masks with feathers. This won't allow us to look under all masks, since we do not have enough time, but it will maximize our results. Diversification — the opposite of the strategy of specialization — envisages a chaotic check of masks, and it would only get us perplexed, which could bring the result of our efforts down to zero.

Therefore, the strategy of specialization leads to saving time, allowing one to maximize the result with limited time or minimize the time spent for the receipt of a certain result. In economics, the term "efficiency"[4] is used to describe this phenomenon. Smith's Time Saving Theory, being a

[4]Productivity is the volume of labour results (produced intermediate or final goods and/or services provided) for a fixed period.

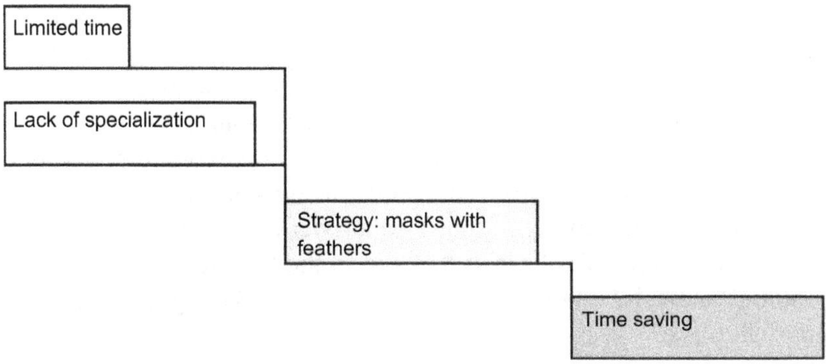

Figure 2. The model of saving time in economics according to Smith's Time Saving Theory.

highly effective tool for the distribution of efforts and allowing for optimal time management, actually provides us with a key to time.

The presented model was created with a condition that labour capabilities are very limited — only one person acts (checks the masks), and this person does not have access to the latest technologies. In more favourable conditions, when we also have other workers, it is possible to divide labour between them and to determine the strategy of specialization for each worker. Thus, one worker will check red masks, the second will check green masks, the third will check blue masks, and so on. We shall coordinate their actions and analyze the result.

By receiving access to the latest technologies, e.g., CCTV in the ballroom, we can spare labour efforts for checking the masks and simply watch the footage from the cameras. With expanded capabilities, Smith's Time Saving Theory allows for the full achievement of the target result (checking all masks) at the minimum cost of labour efforts and time.

Thus, Smith's Time Saving Theory describes economic phenomena and processes that resemble our behaviour at the masquerade. We understand that during the limited time that we have, we won't be able to look under the masks of all guests at the ball. Chaotically checking different masks, we get ourselves perplexed and then forget who we have checked and who is yet to be checked. Smith's Time Saving Theory suggests ordering our actions and checking, for example, only the masks with feathers and thus we will be able to check and remember a larger number of guests.

Elaborating on the scholar's philosophy, it can be observed that Smith's Time Saving Theory allows (conventionally) "putting a mask" on each economic phenomenon and process and systematizing them at the same time. This allows rationalizing the costs of labour and optimizing the efforts, ensuring saving of time. Smith's theory turned out to be useful — but is it perfect? Are there alternative and, perhaps, more modern theories that allow for better saving of time? To answer this question, we have to consider other scientific theories that reflect the time factor in the macroeconomic analysis, among which Marx's Time Saving Law holds an important place.

References

Ashby, N. J. S. & Gonzalez, C. (2017). The influence of time estimation and time saving preferences on learning to make temporally dependent decisions from experience. *Journal of Behavioral Decision Making*, 30(4): 807–818.

Beck, M. J., Hess, S., Cabral, M. O., & Dubernet, I. (2017). Valuing travel time savings: A case of short-term or long term choices? *Transportation Research Part E: Logistics and Transportation Review*, 100: 133–143.

Blum, B. (2017). Saving time and money with remote monitoring: Three ways to improve operations with better data access. *Plant Engineering*, 71(9): 7–9.

Burnham, T. C. (2017). She who understands the fruit fly would do more for economics than Adam Smith: Introduction to the special issue. *Journal of Bioeconomics*, 20: 1–5, https://doi.org/10.1007/s10818-017-9268-5.

Choi, Y. & Han, J. (2017). Time preference and savings behaviour. *Applied Economics Letters*, 25(14): 994–997. DOI:10.1080/13504851.2017.1391989.

Erokhin, A. K. (2007). The political economy of Adam Smith and Nicolas Condorcet as applied to the concept of public education. *Problems of Modern Economics*, 2(22): 371–374.

Fedotova, V. G. & Kolpakov, V. A. (2010). The evolution of economic theory: From A. Smith to neosmitianism. *World of Changes*, 4: 9–25.

Folscher, D. J. & Kruger, K. (2017). Saving time on robot programming: Programming by demonstration using stereoscopic motion capturing. *2016 Pattern Recognition Association of South Africa and Robotics and Mechatronics International Conference*, PRASA-RobMech 2016, 7813133.

Glaze, S. (2017). Adam Smith and William James on the psychological basis of progress. *Cambridge Journal of Economics*, 41(2): bew043, 349–365.

Grinstein-Weiss, M., Russell, B. D., Gale, W. G., Key, C., & Ariely, D. (2017). Behavioural interventions to increase tax-time saving: Evidence from a national randomized trial. *Journal of Consumer Affairs*, 51(1): 3–26.

Hühn, M. P. (2017). Adam Smith's philosophy of science: Economics as moral imagination. *Journal of Business Ethics*, 2(1): 1–15.

Inshakov, O. V. (2005). On the Problems of Integration of Economic Theory in the Context of Globalization. Facets of Integration. Volgograd: Volgograd State University, pp. 7–27.

Inshakov, O. V. (2005b). Russia at the turn of the century. *Economic Issues*, 4(1): 148–151.

Inshakov, O. V. & Frolov, D. P. (2005). Economic space and spatial economics. Reflection on a new economic journal. *Economic Science of Modern Russia*, 4(1): 174–180.

Kolpakov, V. A. (2006). The evolution of economic theory: From A. Smith to neosmitianism. *Questions on Philosophy [Voprosy filosofii]*, 11, 73–84.

Kozyrev, V. M. (2010). Adam Smith and neoclassicism in modern economic theory. *Bulletin of the Moscow State Academy of Business Administration. Series: Economics*, 2(2): 77–87.

Mahoney, P. G. (2017). Adam Smith, the prophet of law and economics. *Journal of Legal Studies*, 46(1): 207–236.

Martens, K. & Di Ciommo, F. (2017). Travel time savings, accessibility gains and equity effects in cost-benefit analysis. *Transport Reviews*, 37(2): 152–169.

Mitra, R. (2017). Domestic saving-investment correlation puzzle revisited: A time series analysis for South Africa. *Economics Bulletin*, 37(2): 1217–1225.

Newbert, S. L. (2017). Achieving social and economic equality by unifying business and ethics: Adam Smith as the cause of and cure for the separation thesis. *Journal of Management Studies*, 2(1): 128–135.

Özler, Ş. & Gabrinetti, P. (2017). *Psychoanalytic Studies of the Work of Adam Smith: Towards a Theory of Moral Development and Social Relations*. New York: Taylor and Francis, pp. 1–207.

Paganelli, M. P. (2017). Adam Smith on the future of experimental evolution and economics. *Journal of Bioeconomics*, 20(2): 1–6.

Pitts, J. (2017). Irony in Adam Smith's critical global history. *Political Theory*, 45(2): 141–163.

Poleacovschi, C., Javernick-Will, A., & Tong, T. (2017). The link between knowledge sharing connections and employee time savings: A social network analysis. *Construction Management and Economics*, 35(8–9): 455–467.

Ridley, M. (2017). Adam smith and the past, present, and future of liberalism. *Journal of Private Enterprise*, 32(3): 1–7.

Rolison, J. J., Hanoch, Y., & Wood, S. (2017). Saving for the future: Dynamic effects of time horizon. *Journal of Behavioral and Experimental Economics*, 70: 47–54.

Rupprecht, M. & Annuß, C. (2017). Savings in times of low interest rates — are German households in need of public support? [Sparen in Zeiten niedriger Zinsen — wirtschaftspolitische Unterstützung nötig?]. *Wirtschaftsdienst*, 97(2): 130–134.

Sen, A. (2011). Adam Smith and modernity. *Economic Issues*, 11: 25–37.

Shchegolevsky, V. A. (2011). From limited economic freedom to economic liberalism in the teachings of F. Quesnay and A. Smith. *Bulletin of the Moscow State Regional University. Series: Economics*, 4: 30–36.

Smith, A. (1776). *An Inquiry into the Nature and Causes of the Wealth of Nations*. London: W. Strahan and T. Cadell.

Smith, V. L. (2017). Adam Smith, scientist and evolutionist: Modelling other-regarding behaviour without social preferences. *Journal of Bioeconomics*, 20: 1–15.

Thomas, A. M. (2018). Adam Smith on the philosophy and provision of education. *Journal of Interdisciplinary Economics*, 30(1): 105–116.

Viganò, E. (2017). Adam Smith's theory of prudence updated with neuroscientific and behavioral evidence. *Neuroethics*, 10(2): C. 215–233.

Yamamori, T. (2017). The concept of need in Adam Smith. *Cambridge Journal of Economics*, 41(2): bew049, 327–347.

Chapter 6

K. Marx's Time Saving Law: Time Is the Basis of Saving

Ultimately, all economy is a matter of economy of time.

Karl Marx, 19th century German economist

This chapter states that time is the source and measure of the development of the modern global economy.

This chapter considers the following topics:

- causal connections that reflect the necessity to save time in the economy;
- role of the time factor as a resource in social reproduction theory.

In the mythological picture of the world of the inhabitants of Ancient Mesopotamia — the Sumerians — time was created and existed only for humans. According to their mindset, there was no time at the very beginning of the creation of the Universe. It appeared together with a man and posed the highest value to him.

...We're turning over the page of our imaginary book of time and are already anticipating the next fantastic journey — but our glance falls, by chance, on the clock, and we realize that we've been travelling for too long. We have other business to attend to, and we cannot travel in time forever. However, our journey is so fascinating that we start thinking about how to save more time for it. Again, economic theory helps us here. It is possible that Karl Marx's Time Saving Law could provide an answer to our question.

This law was derived and described by Karl Marx in his book *A Contribution to the Critique of Political Economy* (*Zur Kritik der Politischen Ökonomie*) in 1859 (Figure 1).

It should be emphasized that this law was not the goal of the scholar's research and was derived by him in the process of studying social reproduction. The title of Marx's book makes it clear that the law is the continuation (or result of critique in Marx's formulation) of the classical political economy, in particular the works of Adam Smith. The foundation of this law is the labour theory of value. We formulated the main provisions of Marx's Time Saving Law, which pose interest in the aspect of reflecting the time factor in macro-economic analysis (Marx, 1859).

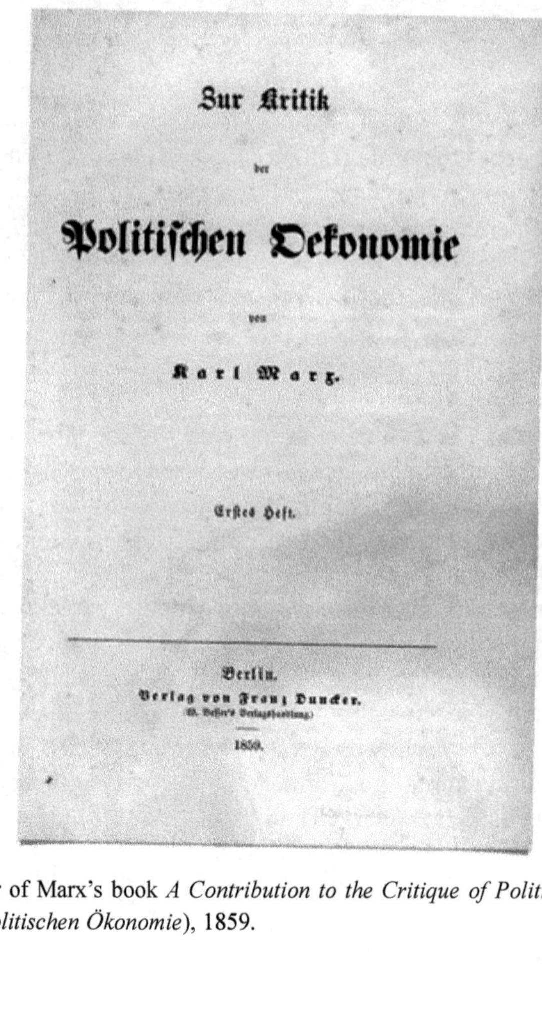

Figure 1. Cover of Marx's book *A Contribution to the Critique of Political Economy* (*Zur Kritik der Politischen Ökonomie*), 1859.

- *There are a lot of alternative means of using time in economics*: This provision was borrowed by Marx from Smith, and after that, it was used in the works of von Wieser, which reflects its high scientific value. Marx's treatment considers the macro-economic aspect of time, and this means that during the set period in a socio-economic system, goods could be produced that are aimed at the satisfaction of the primary needs of a human (according to the scholar, it is "production of grain, cattle, etc.") or goods aimed at satisfying the needs of a higher level, including the spiritual development of society. Marx also provides a treatment of the micro-economic aspect of this provision, according to which humans can perform production activities or consumption of goods, and, as an alternative, develop morally and spiritually.
- *The intensity of society's socio-economic development is determined by the effectiveness of using time*: The effectiveness of using time determines the available combinations of the alternative means of its use. In the micro- and macro-economic aspects, saving time for the production and consumption of goods leaves more time for the spiritual development of a certain human and society on the whole. That's why the intensity (or "comprehensiveness" according to Marx) of society's socio-economic development directly depends on the level of effectiveness of production and consumption of goods and, accordingly, on the time left for spiritual development.
- *Time is the most important economic resource, which is the key object of saving*: Time is defined by Marx as a "form and space for the socio-economic development" of society. Since any socio-economic activities depend on time, it is the most valuable resource. Time is at the basis of all socio-economic phenomena and processes, and so "any saving is eventually brought down to saving of time".

The works of Karl Marx, including his book *A Contribution to the Critique of Political Economy*, are the basis for modern scientific research (O'Hara, 2015; Baizakov *et al.*, 2016; Finelli, 2016; Ince, 2016; Kangal, 2016; Perović, 2016; Shamis, 2016; Simon, 2016; *The Economist*, 2017; Fulk, 2017; Lewis, 2017; Smith, 2017; Warren, 2017). The social reproduction theory and its first law, the law of saving time, is also very popular in scientific economic circles and is the object of close attention of various scholars, as well as the object of discussion and reconsideration in view of the latest experience of economic systems' socio-economic development. Examples of their use are a range of modern authors' publications, for example, Ouellet (2015), Petri (2015), Collins (2016), Cotter (2016), Foley (2016), Roberts (2016), Rotta & Teixeira (2016), Chambers (2017), Furlan (2017), Oittinen & Rauhala (2017), Akhanov (2018), Buzgalin (2018), Gorshkov (2018), Shutova (2018), and Voyeykov (2018).

Prof. Oleg V. Inshakov shared the beliefs of Karl Marx in the aspect of time saving and used them during the creation of his fundamental works on evolutionary economics and economic genetics (Inshakov, 2005a, 2005b). Karl Marx formulated in this works the law of time saving for the past and the present, which predetermined its static character. Scientific studies that were conducted in continuation of Karl Marx's works allowed determining the dynamic aspect of this law, including the future time in it. Based on the considered provisions, the model of time saving in economics, according to Marx's Time Saving Law, should have the following form (Figure 2).

Figure 2 demonstrates the connection between the past, present, and future in Karl Marx's Time Saving Law. This is because this law considers the whole life cycle of a product. As could be seen, the sum of past (previously materialized) labour, which is now expressed in the means of labour, present (in Marx's formulation — "living") labour, and future labour which is spent for consumption (in Marx's formulation — for receipt of useful effect) of a product, determines the total costs of labour.

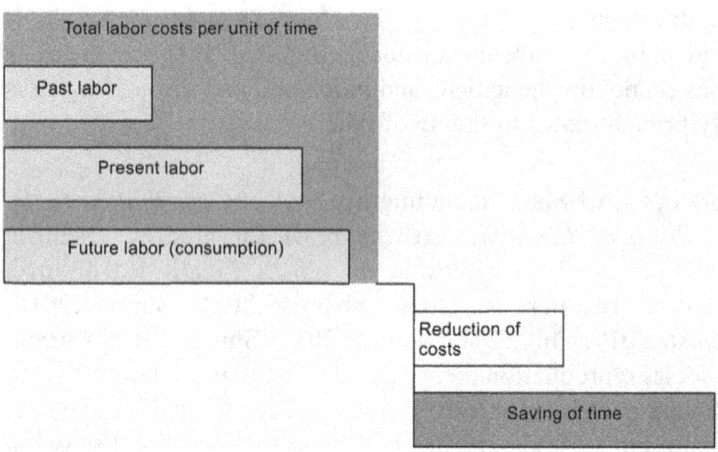

Figure 2. The model of saving time in economics according to Marx's Time Saving Law.

Marx's Time Saving Law states that saving total costs of labour per unit of time leads to the saving of time. In other words, the growth of labour efficiency at present, in the past, and in the future leads to the saving of time. Growth of labour efficiency is accompanied by the reduction of the sum of costs of past, living, and future labour for the production and consumption of goods.

Together with obvious advantages, which are connected to a precise and detailed fundamental description of the essence and specifics of the process of socio-economic systems' development, Marx's Time Saving Law has one drawback: this law is descriptive. It points out the necessity to save time and shows the causal connections of this process, but it does not offer methodological tools for its management. The sole realization of the advantages of time saving does not stimulate the increase of efficiency, for this, as is justly noted in Smith's Time Saving Theory, it is possible to use the mechanism of labour division, specialization, and automatization.

As for our situation, according to Marx's Time Saving Law, we have to finish our usual business as quickly as possible in order to save as much time as possible for the continuation of our journey in time. However, Marx's Time Saving Law has become such an integral part of modern human life that it seems obvious to us now. Critics of this law call this its "scientific nature".

Thus, Marx's Time Saving Law helped us understand that it is necessary to save time, but the question "how exactly?" remains open. Perhaps, an answer to this question will be provided by another economic theory, that of Marshall's time states, which is considered in the next chapter.

References

Akhanov, S. A. (2018). Prometheus: K. Marx and modern political economy (to the 200th anniversary of the birth of K. Marx). *Turan University Bulletin*, 2(78): 261–265.

Baizakov, S., Utembayev, Y., Oinarov, A. R., & Forrest, J. (2016). On mutual coincidence of return on capital measuring principles by Adam Smith and Karl Marx (A critique of "capital in the twenty-first century" by Thomas Piketty). *Advances in Systems Science and Applications*, 16(3): 1–10.

Buzgalin, A. V. (2018). Marx-XXI: Reactualization of the philosophical heritage (to the 200th anniversary of the birth of Karl Marx). *Moscow University Bulletin. Series 7: Philosophy*, 5: 20–34.

Chambers, S. A. (2017). What kind of theory is the labour theory of value? Marx as genealogist in zur kritik. *Political Power and Social Theory*, 32: 63–98.

Collins, J. L. (2016). Expanding the labour theory of value. *Dialectical Anthropology*, 40(2): 103–123.

Cotter, J. (2016). New materialism and the labor theory of value. *Minnesota Review*, 2016(87): 171–181.

Economist Newspaper Ltd. (2017). Bagehot: Labour is right-Karl Marx has a lot to teach today's politicians. *Economist (United Kingdom)*, 413: 9036.

Finelli, R. (2016). The three theories of Karl Marx's work. Replies to my critics. [Le tre teorie del lavoro di Karl Marx. Repliche ai miei critici]. *Etica e Politica*, 18(1): 395–415.

Foley, D. K. (2016). What is the labour theory of value and what is it good for? In *Economic Theory and Its History: Essays in Honour of Neri Salvadori*. London: Taylor and Francis Inc, pp. 370–384.

Fulk, K. (2017). Through the wormhole with Karl Marx: Science fiction, utopia, and the future of Marxism in P.M.'s Weltgeist Superstar. *German Quarterly*, 90(1): 55–70.

Furlan, S. (2017). A reconstruction of Marx's theory of value: An alternative derivation of the concept of abstract labour [Rekonstrukcija Marxove teorije vrednosti: Alternativna izpeljava pojma abstraktnega dela]. *Filozofski Vestnik*, 38(1): 171–187.

Gorshkov, A. V. (2018). The heuristic potential of Karl Marx's "capital" (on the occasion of the 200th anniversary of the birth of K. Marx). *Proceedings of Higher Educational Institutions. Ural Region*, 3: 39–44.

Ince, O. U. (2016). Bringing the economy back in: Hannah Arendt, Karl Marx, and the politics of capitalism. *Journal of Politics*, 78(2): 411–426.

Inshakov, O. V. (2005a). *Evolutionary Economics and Economic Genetics. Socio-economic and Legal Problems of the Development of Territorial-Production Systems: Yearbook*. Volgograd: Ministry of Education and Science of the Russian Federation, Volzhsky Institute of Economics, Pedagogy and Law, pp. 17–25.

Inshakov, O. V. (2005b). Evolutionary economics and economic genetics. Evolutionary theory, innovations and economic changes. *Proceedings of the Third All-Russian Internet Conference on the Problems of Econophysics and Evolutionary Economics*, Yekaterinburg, pp. 45–58.

Kangal, K. (2016). The Karl Marx problem in contemporary new media economy: A critique of Christian Fuchs account. *Television and New Media*, 17(5): 416–428.

Lewis, B. (2017). Marxism after Marx: Karl Kautsky's disputed legacy. *Historical Materialism*, 25(3): 141–147.

Marx, K. (1859). *Zur Kritik der Politischen Ökonomie*. Berlin, Germany: Franz Duncker.

O'Hara, P. A. (2015). *The Contemporary Relevance of Karl Marx's Heterodox Political Economy. Marx, Veblen, and the Foundations of Heterodox Economics: Essays in Honor of John F. Henry*. London, UK: Taylor and Francis Inc, pp. 50–78.

Oittinen, V. & Rauhala, P. (2017). Review of the book "Karl Marx: Economic Manuscripts of K. Marx 1864–1865". *Questions of Political Economy*, 2: 121–128.

Ouellet, M. (2015). Revisiting Marx's value theory: Elements of a critical theory of immaterial labor in informational capitalism. *Information Society*, 31(1): 20–27.

Perović, M. (2016). Labour and division of labour in Karl Marx's work. [Rad i podela rada u delu Karla Marksa]. *Journal of Philosophy ARHE*, 13(26): 259–274.

Petri, F. (2015). On some modern reformulations of the labour theory of value. *Contributions to Political Economy*, 34(1): 77–104.

Roberts, J. M. (2016). Co-creative prosumer labour, financial knowledge capitalism, and Marxist value theory. *Information Society*, 32(1): 28–39.

Rotta, T. N. & Teixeira, R. A. (2016). The autonomisation of abstract wealth: New insights on the labour theory of value. *Cambridge Journal of Economics*, 40(4): 1185–1201.

Shamis, A. (2016). The industrialists of philosophy': Karl Marx, Friedrich Engels, and the discourse network of 1840. *Media History*, 22(1): 67–84.

Shutova, E. A. (2018). Vocation and pay: Public debate and the legacy of Karl Marx. *Bulletin of the Chelyabinsk State University*, 5(415): 83–86.

Simon, J. (2016). A conversation with Karl Marx (1818–1883) on why there is no socialism in the United States. In *The Return of the Theorists: Dialogues with Great Thinkers in International Relations*. London: Palgrave Macmillan, pp. 134–142.

Smith, K. (2017). The discovery of surplus value: Karl Marx and Senior's 'last hour'. *Journal of Classical Sociology*, 17(1): 10–23.

Voyeykov, M. I. (2018). Marx after Marx. *Alternatives*, 2: 182–189.

Warren, P. (2017). Karl Marx and Wilt Chamberlain, or: Luck egalitarianism, exploitation, and the clean path to capitalism argument. *Res Publica*, 23(4): 453–473.

Chapter 7

A. Marshall's Time States: Time Is a Guarantee of Changes

The price of every product increases and decreases from time to time and from place to place, and with each change, the purchasing power of money also changes according to the increase or decrease in the price of a given product.

Alfred Marshall, English economist

This chapter states that time is a criterion of change in the modern global economy.

This chapter considers the following issues:

- treatment of the future time from the positions of forecasting changes in socio-economic systems;
- time states (periods) of socio-economic systems, which reflect their capabilities for changes;
- density as one of the characteristics of time in economics.

In ancient Indian philosophy, time was associated with a cycle of regeneration. Each moment opens new opportunities for the future — lucky, or on the contrary, not so lucky — regeneration. Changeability was considered the most important characteristic of the time (Figure 1).

Turning our glance to time, it seems as if we light a candle. Can it burn down instantly? Of course, it cannot. It needs time to burn down. Looking at the candle after a certain time, we see that some of it has disappeared but the candle continues burning. Later again, we see that there is no wax at all, and the candle has burned down. The periods of time

Figure 1. Pink horse in a winter forest.

Source: Photo by scholar and photographer Elena Popkova, https://www.saatchiart.com/account/artworks/1599809.

between our observations of the candle reflect the opportunities for change. A socio-economic system develops similarly to a burning candle, being connected — same as the candle — to time.

Thinking about the essence and dynamics of the development of socio-economic systems, A. Marshall concluded that, first, they are subject to changes, and, second, the scale of these changes depends on the time given to them. The scholar found out that time opens opportunities for a change of socio-economic systems and showed that changes are impossible in the present time — they are admissible only in the future.

For the economic analysis and forecasting of socio-economic systems, Titenko (2013) suggested treating the future time as a period "with all other conditions being equal", i.e., the period during which these systems will be developing under the influence of the preservation (as compared to the present time) set of factors and along the already set trajectory.

This treatment of the future time allows for compiling forecasts of socio-economic systems' development and, as of now (*in 2018 — author*) is the basis of their modelling and scenario analysis, which is confirmed by the materials of a range of works of modern authors (Poddubny &

Sukhareva, 2006; Naymushin, 2008; Ivanov & Nizhegorodtsev, 2009; Rodina, 2009; Bahloul *et al.*, 2018; Geiger, 2018; Lalwani & Chakraborty, 2018; Lee, 2018; Ma *et al.*, 2018; Ready, 2018).

Prof. Oleg V. Inshakov was also actively studying the dynamics and forecasting the development of socio-economic systems based, in particular, on Marshal's Time States Theory (Inshakov *et al.*, 2005, 2009; Inshakov & Frolov, 2006; Mitrofanova, 2007).

By the criterion of opportunities for socio-economic systems' changes, Alfred Marshall, the English economist, a representative of the neo-classical economic theory, and the head of the Cambridge School of Economics, distinguished three states of time, the descriptions of which, adapted to the specifics of this research, are as follows:

- *Period "Present Continuous"* (*current period or stationary state*). In this period (at the moment of observation), time seems to freeze, and changes are impossible. Socio-economic systems continue functioning, but companies cannot attract additional resources and change the production costs and volumes. That's why the market balance that has been established in this period is unchangeable — the demand price and the offer price are stable.
- *Period "Present Perfect"* (*short-term period*). This period covers two years right after the moment of observation and opens slight opportunities for the changes in the socio-economic systems. Changes in floating capital[1] allow companies to attract additional resources (under the current limitations) and reduce or increase (to a certain extent) the production costs depending on the changes in demand. Fixed capital[2] is stable, but the intensity of its use depends on the volume and price of demand. The market balance could change slightly depending on the fluctuations of demand price and offer price.
- *Period "Future Simple"* (*long-term period*). This period covers a long period (more than two years) after the moment of observation and

[1]Floating capital — objects (which the labour is directed to) of labour involved in production once and influenced by the cost of purchasing raw materials and materials, as well as the cost of paying wages to employees, etc.

[2]Fixed capital — means (tools with which labour is carried out) of labour involved in production many times, while gradually physically and mentally wearing out, gradually transferring their value to the cost of manufactured products (depreciation), and including production buildings, production equipment, etc.

opens large opportunities for changes in the socio-economic systems. During this period, companies can change not only floating capital but also fixed capital and attract the necessary resource (in full volume) depending on the changes in demand. The market balance could change fully, depending on the fluctuations of demand price and offer price. As noted, time is a factor of change in the ratio of production costs and the price for the produced (and sold in the market in the competitive conditions) goods. The considered time states were described by Marshall in his book *Principles of Economics* in 1890 (Figure 2).

Figure 2. Cover of Marshall's book *Principles of Economics*, 1890.

In the context of studying the socio-economic systems' changes, it is also expedient to pay attention to such notions as the density of time. As a physical characteristic, it was offered by a Soviet representative of causal mechanics, Kozyrev, in 1958. The scholar treated the density of time in physics as the level of time's activity (Kozyrev, 1971). The higher the activity, the larger the density of time and the higher the entropy level. The final state of closed physical systems is "black holes" (indefinite period in the future) (Kozyrev, 1982).

Marshall's Theory of Time States allows for a relative measuring of time's density in socio-economic systems. According to this, we compiled the following model of socio-economic systems' changes in various time states (Figure 3).

Figure 3 has two axes — the axis of the dependent variable (y), which is the level of the socio-economic system's entropy, and the axis of the independent variable (x), which is the density of economic time. At the crossing of these axes, the process of the socio-economic system's change in time is shown. At the moment of observation, both variables equal zero.

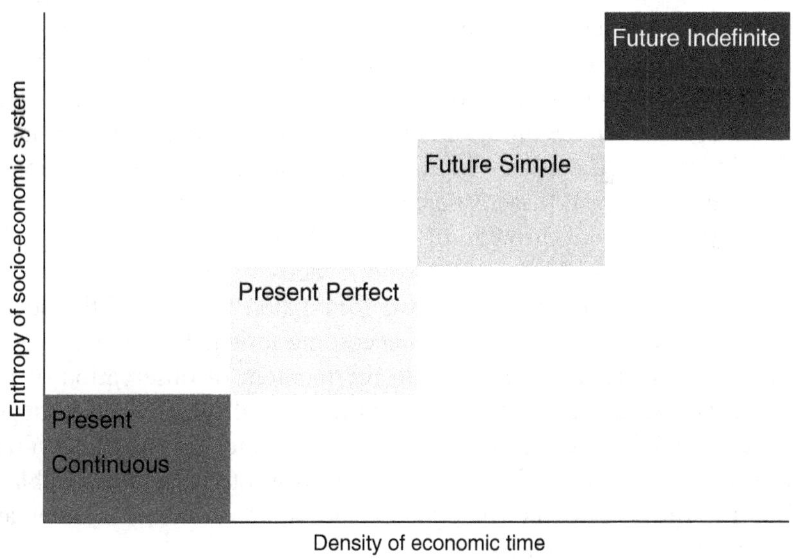

Figure 3. The model of socio-economic systems' changes in various time states according to Marshall's theory and Kozyrev's Theory of Time's density.

In the period "Present Continuous" (current period, or stationary state), at the present time, the changes are zero, the density of economic time is at its minimum, and the entropy of the socio-economic system is also at its lowest. Figuratively speaking, a candle that has just been lit is burning against a light background. As an example, we can consider the existing level of economic systems' socio-economic development.

In the period "Present Perfect" (short-term period), in the future time, the changes are minimal, the density of economic time is small, and the entropy of the socio-economic system is also small. That is, the background has become darker, and the candle has dwindled significantly. As an example, we could consider moving budget planning (short-term plan, forecast).

In the period "Future Simple" (long-term period), in the future time, the changes are substantial, the density of economic time is large, and the entropy of the socio-economic system is also large. The background has become dark, and the candle has burned down. As an example, we could consider the National strategy of development for the period until 2030.

In the period "Future Indefinite" (indefinite period in the future) — "black hole", the changes are at their maximum, and the density of economic time and the entropy of the socio-economic system are also at their highest. As an example, we could consider the strategy of development for 2050, when the limits of the forecast go beyond the modern ideas of the future, which causes a high level of uncertainty. The background has become black, and there is no candle left — only smoke and ash.

The regularity of growth of time's density is explained by the tendency for the increase of economic activity and acceleration of economic growth. Based on this, we formulated the law of the socio-economic systems' changes in time, according to which, in the course of the increase of the time period as to the moment of observation of the socio-economic system, the opportunities for this system's changes increase, which lead to the growth of its entropy and, eventually — if this system is closed — leads it to chaos and turns it into an economic "black hole", in which state the changes of the socio-economic system are unpredictable and unmanageable.

This means that socio-economic systems are subject to changes in time, but these changes could pose danger and lead to the destruction of the systems. Closed development of socio-economic systems, which leads in the uncertain period in the future to the emergence of economic "black holes", should be avoided.

References

Bahloul, W., Balcilar, M., Cunado, J., & Gupta, R. (2018). The role of economic and financial uncertainties in predicting commodity futures returns and volatility: Evidence from a nonparametric causality-in-quantiles test. *Journal of Multinational Financial Management*, 45: 52–71.

Geiger, T. (2018). Continuous national gross domestic product (GDP) time series for 195 countries: Past observations (1850–2005) harmonized with future projections according to the Shared Socioeconomic Pathways (2006–2100). *Earth System Science Data*, 10(2): 847–856.

Inshakov, O. V. & Frolov, D. P. (2006). The Common Man Is a Complex Unit of Measurement of Social Progress. Volgograd (Russia): Russian Academy of Sciences, Department of Social Sciences, Southern Scientific Centre, South Section of the Economy.

Inshakov, O. V. & Mitrofanova, I. V. (2007). Socio-economic indicators of the development of the southern regions of Russia: Trends and forecasts. *Regional Economy: Theory and Practice*, 14(1): 14–23.

Inshakov, O. V., Bogachkova, L. Y., Kuznetsov, M. N., & Nalbandyan, M. O. (2005). On an integrated approach to the analysis of the dynamics of domestic prices for electricity and primary energy carriers. In Davnis, V. V. (ed.) *Economic Forecasting: Models and Methods Materials of the International Scientific and Practical Conference*, pp. 64–77.

Inshakov, O. V. *et al.* (2009). The Program of Anti-crisis Measures for the Volgograd Region for the Year. Volgograd (Russia): Volgograd State University.

Kozyrev, N. A. (1971). On the Possibility of an Experimental Study of the Properties of Time. St. Petersburg: Pulkovo Astronomical Observatory of the USSR Academy of Sciences.

Kozyrev, N. A. (1982). Time as a Physical Phenomenon. St. Petersburg: Pulkovo Astronomical Observatory of the USSR Academy of Sciences.

Ivanov, E. Y. & Nizhegorodtsev, R. M. (2009). Economic coordinate system and Marshall cross. *Bulletin of Economic Integration*, 11(12): 26–30.

Lalwani, V. & Chakraborty, M. (2018). Asset pricing factors and future economic growth. *Economics Letters*, 168: 151–154.

Lee, J. J. (2018). Economic determinants of price informativeness about future earnings. *Journal of Contemporary Accounting and Economics*, 14(1): 83–102.

Ma, F., Wahab, M. I. M., Liu, J., & Liu, L. (2018). Is economic policy uncertainty important to forecast the realized volatility of crude oil futures? *Applied Economics*, 50(18): 2087–2101.

Naymushin, V. G. (2008). The phenomenon of monopoly in the theory of A. Marshall. *Economic Bulletin of Rostov State University*, 6(2): 46–52.

Poddubny, V. V. & Sukhareva, E. A. (2006). Investigation of free and stabilized jerk described by the Walras — Marshall dynamic model with delay. *Bulletin of Tomsk State University*, 290: 190–198.

Ready, R. C. (2018). Oil consumption, economic growth, and oil futures: The impact of long-run oil supply uncertainty on asset prices. *Journal of Monetary Economics*, 94: 1–26.

Rodina, G. A. (2009). Is the Marshall cross relevant in the information economy? *Bulletin of the Ivanovo State University. Series: Economics*, 3: 34–43.

Titenko, E. A. (2013). The time factor as a criterion for the development of production in economic concepts. *Business Education Pravo*, 1(22): 157–160.

Chapter 8

Time Factor as a Source of Imbalance in the Process of Self-Organization of Economic Systems: Time Is Constant Movement

Truly great is the person who managed to master his time!

Hesiod, ancient Greek philosopher

This chapter states that time is the cause of imbalance and a guarantee of development of the modern global economy.

This chapter considers the following issues:

- notion and essence of balance in economics and the time factor's impact on it;
- laws of economic systems' development;
- means of "catching" time in economics for establishing its balance.

In Ancient Greek culture and philosophy, historical time and space time are different. Space time is independent and exists in the space turnover — i.e., in a cyclical manner. It is common for the whole Universe. Historical time is predetermined by social factors, being linear. However, they are closely connected, which leads to the contradiction of time in the unity of space and historical components.

Time is like a floating butterfly, an elusive moth, which is attracted to fire, but dies without reaching its aim. The moth's life is swift, for each day new moths are born and replace others. The development of economic systems could be compared to the flight of a moth. Management of these systems (state governance and market self-management) is aimed at the establishment of balance, which could be compared to catching a moth with the butterfly net. However, similarly to moth's escaping the net, the balance of economic systems is quite brief or even elusive. In modern economic science, there are various factors of imbalance in the process of economic systems' self-organization.

- State regulation, which distorts the effect of the market mechanism — this factor is given in the works of the representatives of the neo-classical economic theory: Langford (2019) and Sum (2019).
- Susceptibility of demand and supply to the constant changes — these factors are noted in the works of the representatives of the neo-Keynesian economic theory, which include Dmitriev *et al.* (2019) and Van Heertum (2013).
- The imperfection of social institutions and the "institutional traps",[1] due to which the connection between production and consumption is weak and unreliable — this factor is specified in the studies of the representatives of the neo-institutional economic theory, which include Hatzis (2018) and Lebel & Lebel (2018).
- Crises of socio-economic systems, the causes of which could be burst economic "bubbles",[2] mistakes (e.g., due to the impact of a "human factor"[3]) — this factor is considered in the publications of the representatives of the theory of economic cycles, which include Jabbour *et al.* (2015) and Wang *et al.* (2019).

The problem of balance and imbalance in economics was considered by such Russian scholars and researchers as Bart *et al.* (2018), Grodsky (2011), Zhukova (2011), Zagulyaev (2009), Moiseev (2013), and Uzyakov (2000).

---

[1]"Institutional trap" is a social institution that has lost its relevance and, instead of the previously provided advantages, began to damage socio-economic systems, but, despite this, continues its full-scale functioning due to the strength of self-sustained institutional ties.

[2]Economic "bubbles" — a sharp deviation of the market value of assets from their actual value, caused by speculative business transactions.

[3]A human factor is a person making irrational decisions due to limited thinking abilities, calculating abilities, incompleteness and inaccuracy of knowledge about the situation in which decisions are made, as well as due to the influence of feelings and emotions.

All the above factors do influence the establishment of balance in the modern economic systems but reflect the essence of this process only in a fragmentary manner. They are unified and manifested by the time factor. According to the empirical data, the balance of socio-economic systems could be achieved in a short period, when the time factor does not influence these systems. In the long term, subject to the impact of the time factor, balance cannot be kept. This is confirmed by the classification of balance, which is accepted in economics — sustainable (preserved during several moments, hard to achieve, and rare in practice) and unsustainable (preserved during one moment, but more frequently met in practice).

The most vivid and typical example, which is usually demonstrated in study guides on economic theory, is balance in commodity markets. This example is illustrated graphically in the two-dimensional geometric space, in which the horizontal axis is the volume (Q) and the vertical axis is the price (P). Each level of market price conforms to a certain volume of demand (D) and offer or supply (S). The curves of demand and offer reflect each other in the inversed manner, for growth of prices leads to an increase of offer with the simultaneous reduction of demand — and vice versa.

The balance of the commodity market is at the crossing of the curve of demand and offer. The equilibrium price is the price at which the whole volume of goods that are sold in the market will be sold. The deficit is below the balance, and profit is above the balance. The advantage of this example is its simplicity and visibility, the drawback — impossibility to consider it based on statistical data. That's why we shall consider a practical example based on government revenues (conventional offer) and expenditures (conventional demand). In this case, we abstract away from price, which is observed only in commodity markets, and focus on the demand/offer ratio — the balance of state budget (Figure 1).

As is shown in Figure 1, under the influence of the time factor, the balance of the consolidated state budget of the Russian Federation in 2000–2022 (the data for 2019–2022 are an estimate) constantly changes. The balance is achieved for short periods — in 2002, 2008, 2011, 2013, and will be achieved — according to the forecast — in 2020; during other periods, either budget deficit or profit is observed.

The scientific explanation of the impact of the time factor on balancing economic systems in the process of their self-organization envisages the determination of the laws of these systems' development. Similarly to

Figure 1. Dynamics of revenues and expenditures of the consolidated state budget of the Russian Federation in 2000–2022.

Source: Based on International Monetary Fund (2018).

technical systems, studied by Altshuller (2018), we formulated the laws of economic systems' development.

- Law of complication of the economic system with time, according to which in the course of the economic system's development, the number of its economic subjects and the structure of their internal and external interconnections grow.
- Law of increase of the level of the economic system's openness for the movement of benefits and production factors with time, according to which the economic system's development envisages its globalization, i.e., increase of its involvement in the global economic processes and the development of its foreign economic activities.
- Law of coordination of the rhythm of the economic system's parts with time, which means that cyclical fluctuations of regional economies — as parts of the national economy — become common, and the integration of structural elements of the system and their movement along the same trajectory of economic growth and development are achieved.

- Law of increase of the level of the economic system's perfection with time, according to which the market mechanism is improved and the need for state regulation reduces, since highly effective self-regulation of the economic system is established.
- Law of inequality of development of the economic system's parts, which is strengthened with time — according to which the disproportions in the level and rate of growth and development of regional economies — as parts of the national economy — increase.
- Law of the economic system's transition to a supra-system with time, which means that globalization leads to erasure of national borders and to the formation of the growing regional and transregional integration unions of countries in the global economy, which become the main participants and basic entities of the international economic connections and relations.
- Law of transition from the level of macro-economics to the level of micro-economics with time, according to which the importance of regional economy grows, since it is at this level that the goals and tasks of the national economy are implemented.
- Law of increase of the level of economic system's manageability with time, according to which the system's development is related to the growth of effectiveness of its regulation.

Scaling the ideas of the Ancient Greek philosopher Hesiod that "Truly great is the person who managed to master his time", it is possible to state that a civilization which was able to master its time is truly great. From the positions of economic theory, this means that forecasting of the time factor's impact on growth and development of the modern economic systems and the management of this factor is one of the top-priority tasks and the key criterion of effectiveness of these systems' regulation.

Modern economic science offers two tools for managing the time factor for balancing economic systems in the process of their self-organization.

First tool — forecasting: Studying the dynamics of the economic system's change in the past allows compiling scenarios of its development in the future. This tool is used within economic statistics (econometrics). The larger the period and, accordingly, the more representative the sample of statistical data, based on which the forecasting is performed, the more correct the forecasts. This tool is actively used in the stock market.

Second tool — marketing: Collection of individual orders from consumers, which has become possible due to the development of online commerce in the conditions of the digital economy, allows producing goods in the volume that conforms to the demand in the market. This envisages the management of stock based on the "just-in-time" principle. This tool is actively used by trading companies, which collect orders and prepayment from consumers and then pass them to manufacturers, who, in their turn, collect a lot of orders and start a conveyor production, gaining advantages from the "scale effect".

Based on the above, the traditional static two-dimensional model of market balance in economies is supplemented because of the time factor, which allows compiling a three-dimensional model of the socio-economic system's development because of the time factor's impact (Figure 2).

As shown in Figure 2, each moment (T) conforms to its combination of demand and offer, depending on the quantity (Q) and price (P). At the moment of time t_1, there is deficit (demand exceeds offer) — the net passes nearby, and the moth can escape; in the moment of time t_2, there is balance (demand equals offer) — the moth is in the net; in the moment of time t_3, there is profit (offer exceeds demand, overproduction) — the moth escapes from the net and flies away.

The above allows the formulation of the notion of balance in economics because of the time factor: balance in economics is the moment in

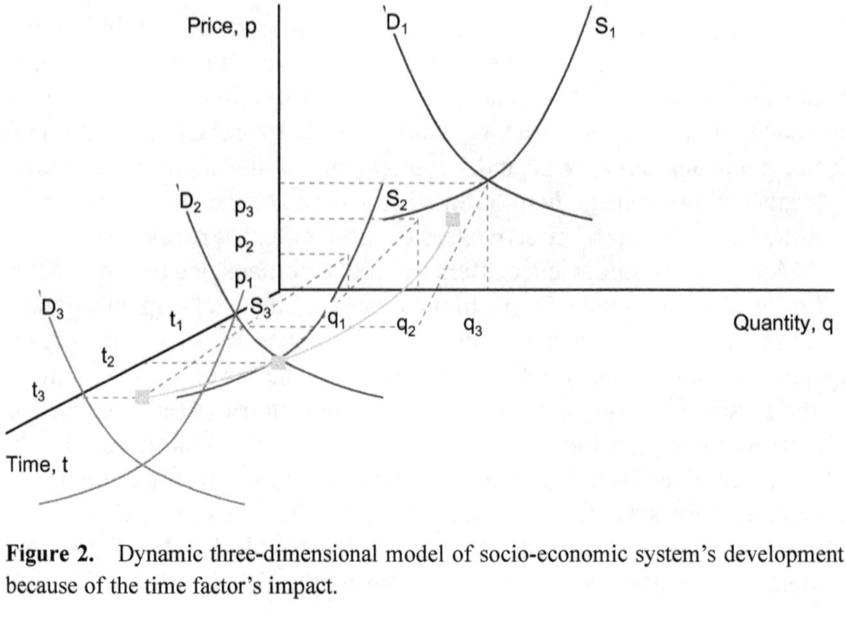

Figure 2. Dynamic three-dimensional model of socio-economic system's development because of the time factor's impact.

which demand equals offer; its sustainability directly depends on its duration; a change of the moment of time, as a rule, leads to the violation of balance in the economy due to the change of conditions in the market environment.

In the system of factors, which influence the market development, the time factor is one of the most significant factors. As an example, let us consider Marshall's "cross" from the positions of economic time (Figure 3).

As shown in Figure 3, at the moment of time t_1, at the crossing of demand and offer, the balance is established at one level of price and quantity, and at the moment t_2 — at another. In other words, the time factor influences the establishment of the market balance and its parameters.

Thus, time puts socio-economic systems in motion, violating their balance — which is treated as the balance of demand and offer. The two-dimensional model of the market, which includes also the price factor and volume factor, shows only the consequence — violation of balance — but does not reflect the reason, since it does not take into account the impact of the time factor. That's why, from the scientific point of view, the three-dimensional model of the socio-economic system's development because of the impact of the time factor is more preferable, since it reflects — in the most complete, precise, and correct manner — the causal connections of the change of the market's state.

In other words, in the two-dimensional space, we see only three fragments: (1) the moth is being caught by the net, (2) the moth is already

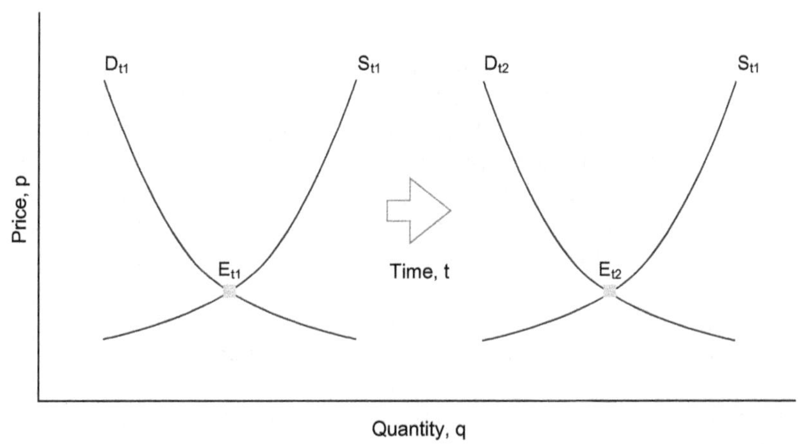

Figure 3. Marshall's "cross" from the positions of economic time.

caught and is in the net, and (3) the moth escapes the net. The connections between these fragments are unclear — we could see them only in the three-dimensional space because of the time factor.

Time is the universal characteristic of socio-economic systems since it has the whole set of their characteristics, including state regulation, change of demand and offer, functioning of social institutions, and crises — and, therefore, must be taken into account during the study of balance in economics.

References

Altshuller, G. S. (2018). Development Laws of Technical Systems. https://www.altshuller.ru/triz/zrts1.asp. Accessed: 30 December 2018.

Bart, T. V., Glasnova, V. P., & Fedyukova, G. K. (2018). Preservation and transformation of investments in the "dynamic equilibrium system" of the economy. *Transport Business of Russia*, 6: 59–61.

Dmitriev, A., Silchev, V., & Dmitriev, V. (2019). A simple econophysics model of the stock market as a nonequilibrium open system. *Lecture Notes in Electrical Engineering*, 489: 237–243.

Grodsky, V. S. (2011). Mathematical modelling of the reproductive equilibrium of the economy. *Samara State University Bulletin. Series: Economics and Management*, 6(87): 26–38.

Hatzis, A. N. (2018). Greece's institutional trap. *Managerial and Decision Economics*, 39(8): 838–845.

International Monetary Fund (2018). Dynamics of revenues and expenditures of the consolidated state budget of the Russian Federation in 2000–2022. https://www.imf.org. Accessed: 30 December 2018.

Jabbour, C. J. C., Neto, A. S., Gobbo, J. A., Ribeiro, M. D. S., & De Sousa Jabbour, A. B. L. (2015). Eco-innovations in more sustainable supply chains for a low-carbon economy: A multiple case study of human critical success factors in Brazilian leading companies. *International Journal of Production Economics*, 164: 245–257.

Langford, N. J. (2019). The governance of social standards in emerging markets: An exploration of actors and interests shaping Trustea as a southern multi-stakeholder initiative. *Geoforum*, 104: 81–91.

Lebel, L. & Lebel, P. (2018). Policy narratives help maintain institutional traps in the governance of floods in Thailand. *International Journal of Water Resources Development*, 34(4): 616–631.

Moiseev, N. A. (2013). Model of spatial dynamic equilibrium of the economy. *Audit and Financial Analysis*, 5: 134–137.

Sum, N.-L. (2019). Ordoliberal authoritarian governance in China since 1978: World market, performance legitimacy, and biosovereign ordering. *South Atlantic Quarterly*, 18(2): 382–400.

Uzyakov, M. N. (2000). Problems of constructing an intersectoral equilibrium model for the Russian economy. *Problems of Forecasting*, 2: 18–33.

Van Heertum, R. (2013). The case for Neo-Keynesianism: In defence of the welfare state. *International Studies in Sociology of Education*, 23(3): 224–250.

Wang, S., Chen, L., & Xiong, X. (2019). Asset bubbles, banking stability and economic growth. *Economic Modelling*, 78: 108–117.

Zagulyaev, D. G. (2009). On the paradoxes of the theory of economic equilibrium in labour economics. *Bulletin of Izhevsk State Technical University*, 1: 58–60.

Zhukova, E. B. (2011). Institutional interests as a factor in ensuring the institutional equilibrium of the economy. *Bulletin of the Saratov State Agrarian University named after N.I. Vavilov*, 7: 73–75.

Chapter 9

Present Indicators in the Modern Theory of Investment: Time Is a Source of Uncertainty

The future is filled with uncertainty, but this deceitfulness of the future is the greatest blessing.

Thucidides, ancient Greek philosopher and historian, founder of historical science

This chapter states that time is a factor of risk and that the global economy's susceptibility to changes in time leads to uncertainty and requires the compilation of scientific forecasts for its reduction.

This chapter considers the following topics:

- classification of the types of economic forecasts of the future;
- present indicators as the tools for reducing uncertainty and risk in economics (Figure 1);
- model of forecasting with the use of present indicators in the modern theory of investment.

The future and attempts at guessing or predicting it have always been the object of human interest. In Ancient Egypt, the future was predicted by stars, based on knowledge of astronomy. It was believed that the month of a person's birth determines his fate, and based on this, astrological forecasts were compiled. In Ancient Greece, when people had to make fateful decisions, they consulted oracles — priests who, according to ancient

Figure 1. Time is a source of uncertainty.

Source: Photo by scholar and photographer Elena Popkova, https://www.saatchiart.com/account/artworks/1599809.

beliefs, could communicate with gods. For example, before declaring war, an army commander would ask an oracle whether the battle would bring victory and whether it was worth entering the battle.

In the Russian heather, pre-Christian (i.e., existing until the end of the 10th century) culture, divination was popular. This practice has survived in our days. Under the influence of technological progress, a new form of divination — digital — has emerged, though the questions remain the same — health, love, power, and material well-being.

In economics, the prediction of the future is defined by the term "forecasting". In the most general dichotomic classification, two types of forecasts are distinguished. The first type involves "other conditions being equal" (Latin *ceteris paribus*). In this case, the future values of economic indicators are determined based on their past values. Here, forecasting is based on the provisions of Aristotle's common logic and envisages the continuation of a semantic row. For example, in the simplest IQ test, any person who can think logically can continue the semantic row "2, 5, 8, 11,

14, …". It is obvious that this is a time row with the initial value "2" and lag "3". To determine the next value of the row's element, it is necessary to add the lag to the previous value. We have the following: 14 + 3 = 17. In economic practice, of course, time rows are more complex, but the principle of forecasting is similar. For example, when planning the budget for the next year, a household takes into account that two years ago prices grew by 4% on average, and in the previous year by 5%; hence, this year prices will grow by (4 + 5)/2 = 4.5%. Also, the confidence interval of 4–6% could be used. However, in reality, prices could grow by 10% if, for example, a crisis takes place, as in 2008. Therefore, forecasting is very conventional and its precision is low.

The foundations of forecasting with the principle "other conditions being equal" in economics were set by Alfred Marshall. In his famous work *Principles of Economics*, the scholar wrote the following:

> "The element of time is the main reason for those difficulties in economic research, which makes it necessary for a person with his limited abilities to go step by step, breaking down a complex issue, studying it in parts, and, finally, combining its partial solutions into a more or less complete solution to the whole riddle. Thus, the more this question is narrowed down, the more accurately it can be resolved, but also less closely related to real life. That is, the more we apply the *ceteris paribus* rule, the further we distance ourselves from reality, for example, if the hydrocarbon fuel is infinite, then the society is stable" (Marshall, 1890).

Thus, the scholar acknowledged the limitations of forecasting "other conditions being equal", which is connected to the applicability of its results in theory but separation from practice.

The second type of forecasting involves "present indicators", which are actively used in investment analysis, which is one of the directions of economic science. In this case, not past experience but the totality of factors that influence the expected profitability of the project is taken into account. As a rule, the factors are as follows:

- change of cost of money in the future under the impact of inflation and macro-economic policy (e.g., key rate, which is set by the Central Bank);

- alternative costs — expected profitability from other projects (advantages of other variants of placement of investments, including deposits in banks and purchase of stock in the stock market);
- macro-economic risk (e.g., expert evaluation of the probability of a crisis).

One of the creators of present indicators in economics is Irving Fisher, an American economist, representative of the neo-classical direction in economic science. In his works *The Nature of Capital and Income* (Fisher, 1906) and *The Rate of Interest* (Fisher, 1907), he substantiated the necessity of taking into account the forecasts for the future to reduce uncertainty during investing.

Before Fisher's works, the experience of investing in project n was assessed according to the classical formula of efficiency calculation: $P_n = PR_n/I_n$, where P_n = profitability of project n, which reflects the efficiency of investing in it; PR_n = profit from the implementation of project n, which reflects its results; I_n = investments in implementation of project n, which reflect expenditures.

Formula (1) could be applied to the already realized (past) projects, but not the future ones, since the total volume of investments in their realization and profit cannot be precisely determined before investing. If $P_n > 1$, project n is deemed attractive (though its profitability could be compared to other projects), and in the opposite case, if $P_n \leq 0$, it is deemed unprofitable or with zero return from investments. In formula (1), the time factor is not considered, so the results of the preliminary assessment of the investment projects are not very precise.

In the modern theory of investment, which is based on the works of I. Fisher, an improved formula, which takes into account the time factor, is used:

$NPV_n = \sum_{t=1}^{T}(c_{tn}/(1 + r)^t)\text{-}C_{on}$, where NPV_n = Net Present Value (NPV = expected future profitability of the project at present) of project n, which reflects the efficiency of investing in it;

t — time (calendar year), $t = 1, \ldots T$; c_{tn} — free financial flow (expected profit from implementing project n);

r — discount rate;

C_{on} — investments in the implementation of project n: initial and annual.

The main difference between formula (1) from formula (2), which allows taking into account the time factor, is the discount rate — the interest rate that is used for recalculating the future flows of revenues in the unified value of the current cost of money. This is a flexible indicator, during the determination of which value different experts may use different methods in different projects. This could be the level of inflation, the interest rate for bank deposits, the expected profitability of alternative investment projects, or a combined indicator, e.g., the weighted average cost of capital (WACC).

Though formula (2) is logically correct, its practical implementation is difficult due to the absence of a methodology of correct assessment of the discount rate (r), which is a subjective indicator. Fisher's scientific works were developed further in the works of Hanke & Wentworth (1981) and Dimand (1994). In recent years, economists have been making multiple attempts to improve present indicators, overcome their subjectivity, and raise the precision of assessing investment projects with their help. Examples are the publications by Bertini Junior *et al.* (2019), Elariane & Dubé (2019), Gaspars-Wieloch (2019), Wicaksono *et al.* (2019), Woo *et al.* (2019), and Zativita & Chumaidiyah (2019), in which present indicators are used to evaluate the perspectives of creation of "smart" homes, technological development of the oil and gas industry of the economy, and implementation of other investment projects.

In Russian scientific thought, one of the first researchers of present indicators was Azgaldov (1970). In the work of Vorobyeva (2014), the author suggests using net present value as an alternative to the indicator of the internal rate of return during the evaluation of investment projects. In the work of Demakov *et al.* (2014), the authors provide methodological recommendations for improving the indicator of present expenditures for the economic evaluation of an investment project. In the work of Bobkova (2014), the author also deems it necessary to evaluate investment projects based on the indicator of net present value. Dorosheva (2012) considers the main features of net present value. Kuvaldina & Lapin (2013) point out the necessity to calculate the discount (present) value during the evaluation of assets and liabilities.

Ivanova (2013) provides applied recommendations for evaluating the present value in financial accounting. Yastrebinsky (2014) provides the economic substantiation of the market criteria of present expenditures and results. Masalov (2012) deems it necessary to use the method of net present revenues during the evaluation of the efficiency of an investment project. Brovkin & Medvedeva (2018) recommend assessing the cost of business with the help of the method of adjusted present value. Ivanovskaya & Biktagirova (2019) reflect on the problematic aspects of using the present value in the assessment of an organization's accounts payable for financial accounting.

Prof. Oleg V. Inshakov substantiates the necessity to take into account the time factor during the implementation of investment and innovative projects. Examples of this are the works of Inshakov *et al.* (2008) on the modernization of the South of Russia and Inshakov *et al.* (2009) on the strategy for Volgograd Region's innovative development until 2025. The author of this book, Prof. Elena G. Popkova, also notes in her work the mandatory consideration of the time factor during evaluation of the perspectives of investment and innovative projects and forecasting the economy's future, in particular, the global financial system and development of human capital. This is reflected in the works of Popkova *et al.* (2017, 2019), Popkova & Parakhina (2019), and Popkova & Alferova (2019).

Based on the modern theory of investment, a model of forecasting with the use of present indicators is compiled (Figure 2).

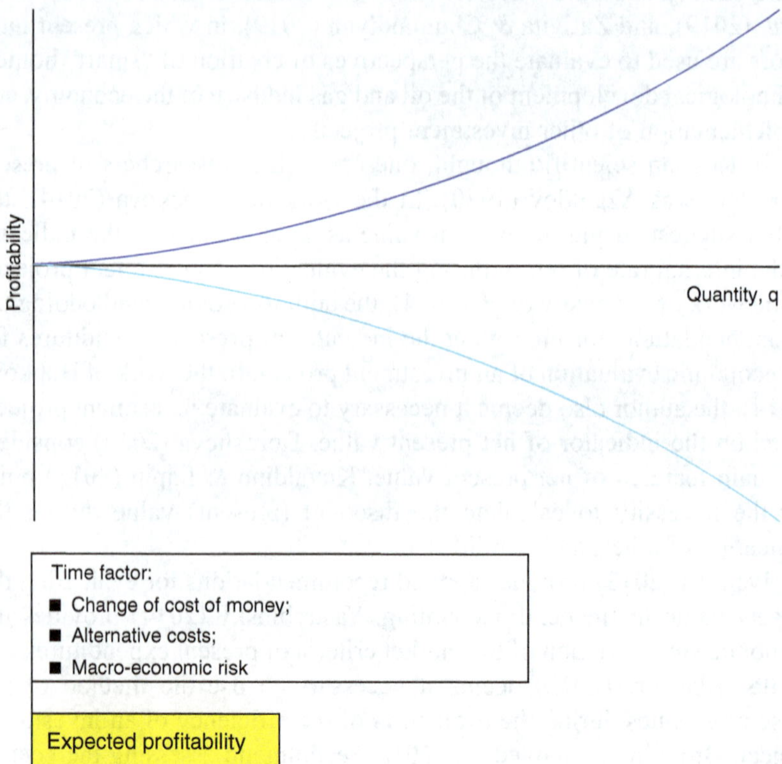

Figure 2. The model of forecasting with the use of present indicators in the modern theory of investment.

Evaluation of an investment project is conducted at the initial moment, the moment of its start (decision on the start), when investments and profits equal zero. Figure 2 shows that under the impact of the time factor, investments in the future might bring profits or losses. It should be noted that physics also acknowledges the different directions of development of matter under the impact of the time factor. BBC (2019) notes that "The Universe has a double of anti-matter, where time flows in the opposite direction; our Universe could only be a "plane reflection" of a parallel world, which is created of anti-matter and moves in the opposite direction from the Big Bang along the scale of time".

In economics (Figure 2), this phenomenon is shown by the straight line and the dark blue line, which is inverse to it. Present indicators have a very contradictory scientific basis and thus could be compared to divination. They allow making a decision but provide a very ambiguous response to the question in which the investment is interested and whose treatment is subjective. This allows the formulation of the notion of present indicators in the modern theory of investment given the time factor: present indicators are indicators that reflect the future (forecasted and subjective) profitability of investments at present, thus allowing making decisions on investing taking into account the time factor. They allow for reducing the uncertainty during investing, but do not allow for its full overcoming.

Thus, despite a rather high level of elaboration, the future time in economics does not have a methodology for high-precision research. This diminishes the value of economics substantially since its primary task is the reduction of uncertainty for rational decision-making. The theoretical approach to studying the future time in economics has been created, but the scientific methodology for implementing this approach has not been formed. Due to this, during the calculation of present indicators in the modern theory of investment, we usually use the method of expert evaluations (expert's subjective opinion) or the methods of random numbers analysis (e.g., Monte Carlo method).

Therefore, time is the source of uncertainty in the economy and the factor of risk of investing. The modern theory of investment urgently requires a scientific methodology for forecasting the future of economic phenomena and processes, and analysis of their change under the impact of the time factor. This will allow avoiding mass bankruptcies during crises as was the case during the Great Depression (1929) and the Great Recession (2008). However, the issue of the transition from the actual divination to forecasting about the economy remains open, while uncertainty and risk are inseparable components of investing.

References

Azgaldov, G. G. (1970). About qualimetry, effective meters and present value. *Construction Economics*, 9: 45–48.

BBC (2019). Scientists: The Universe Has an Antimatter Twin, Where Time Flows in the Opposite Direction. https://www.bbc.com/russian/features-46784520?ocid=wsrussian.8ms.social.sponsored-post.facebook.keywee.RussianLaunch-Universe-Russia.nneed2.ParallelUniverse.mktg&kwp_0=1170115&kw9549_4=3781581989. Accessed: 10 November 2019.

Bertini, Junior, J. R., Funcia, M. A., Santos, A. A. S., & Schiozer, D. J. (2019). A comparison of machine learning algorithms as a surrogate model for net present value prediction from wells arrangement data. In *Proceedings of the International Joint Conference on Neural Networks*, July 2019: 8851708.

Bobkova, A. S. (2014). Evaluation of investment projects based on the net present value. *Scientific Bulletin of MGIIT*, 6(32): 38–43.

Brovkin, A. V. & Medvedeva, N. I. (2018). Business valuation using the adjusted present value method. *Economics: Yesterday, Today, Tomorrow*, 8(10A): 27–39.

Demakov, I. V., Novikov, M. V., & Pavlova, I. A. (2014). Improvement of the reduced cost indicator for the economic assessment of an investment project. *Modern Problems of Science and Education*, 6: 472.

Dimand, R. W. (1994). Irving Fisher's debt-deflation theory of great depressions. *Review of Social Economy*, 52: 92–107.

Dorosheva E. I. (2012). Analysis of the main properties of net present value. *Modern Aspects of Economics*, 11(183): 122–124.

Elariane, S. A. & Dubé, J. (2019). Is smart housing a good deal? An answer based on Monte Carlo net present value analysis. *Sustainability* (*Switzerland*), 11(15): 4193.

Fisher, I. (1906). The nature of capital and income. *Bulletin* of the *American Mathematical Society*, 15(4): 169–186.

Fisher, I. (1907). The rate of interest. *Bulletin* of the *American Mathematical Society*, 15(4): 169–186.

Gaspars-Wieloch, H. (2019). Project net present value estimation under uncertainty. *Central European Journal of Operations Research*, 27(1): 179–197.

Hanke, S. H. & Wentworth, R. W. (1981). Hanke, Steve H. Project evaluation during inflation, revisited: A solution to Turvey's relative price change problem. *Water Resources Research*, 17: 1737–1738.

Inshakov, O. B. *et al.* (2008). Modernization of the Economy of the South of Russia. Problems, Priorities, Projects. Moscow: Russian Academy of Sciences, Southern Scientific Center.

Inshakov, O. B. *et al.* (2009). Strategy for Innovative Development of the Volgograd Region until 2025. Volgograd: Ministry of Education and Science of the Russian Federation, State Educational Institution of Higher Professional Education.

Ivanova, O. V. (2013). Estimation of the present value in accounting. *Accounting and Statistics*, 3(31): 78–92.

Ivanovskaya, A. V. & Biktagirova, E. T. (2019). Problematic aspects of the use of the present value in the assessment of an organization's accounts payable for accounting purposes. *Horizons of Economics*, 3(49): 86–89.

Kuvaldina, T. B. & Lapin, D. R. (2013). The discounted (present) value in the assessment of assets and liabilities. *Auditing Statements*, 11: 63–71.

Masalov, E. I. (2012). Using the method of net present value in assessing the effectiveness of an innovative project. *Intelligence. Innovation. Investments*, 3: 93–97.

Popkova, E. G. & Alferova, T. V. (2019). The concept of restoration of the leading role of the global financial system in the activation of growth and development of the global economy. *Lecture Notes in Networks and Systems*, 57: 407–413.

Popkova, E. G. & Parakhina, V. N. (2019). Managing the global financial system based on artificial intelligence: Possibilities and limitations. *Lecture Notes in Networks and Systems*, 57: 939–946.

Popkova, E. G., Morozova, I. A., & Litvinova, T. N. (2017). New challenges for human capital from the positions of its infrastructural role in the system of entrepreneurship. In *Human Capital: Perspectives, Challenges and Future Directions*. New York: Nova Science Publishers, Inc, pp. 257–275.

Popkova, E. G., Fetisova, O. V., Zabaznova, T. A., & Alferova, T. V. (2019). The modern global financial system: Social risks vs. technological risks. *Lecture Notes in Networks and Systems*, 57: 1013–1019.

Vorobyeva, A. V. (2014). Evaluation of investment projects: Net present value versus internal rate of return. *Russian Economic Internet Journal*, 2: 3.

Wicaksono, F. D., Bin Arshad, Y., & Sihombing, H. (2019). Monte Carlo net present value for techno-economic analysis of oil and gas production sharing contract. *International Journal of Technology*, 10(4): 829–840.

Woo, J., Kim, E., Sung, T.-E., Lee, J., Shin, K., & Lee, J. (2019). Developing an improved risk-adjusted net present value technology valuation model for the biopharmaceutical industry. *Journal of Open Innovation: Technology, Market, and Complexity*, 5(3): 45.

Yastrebinsky, M. A. (2014). Economic justification of the market criterion of the reduced costs and benefits. *Mining Information and Analytical Bulletin (Scientific and Technical Journal*), 6: 327–330.

Zativita, F. I. & Chumaidiyah, E. (2019). Feasibility analysis of Rumah Tempe Zanada establishment in Bandung using net present value, internal rate of return, and payback period. *IOP Conference Series: Materials Science and Engineering*, 505(1): 012007.

[illegible] of the company.

[illegible] (20[illegible]) [illegible]

[illegible] (20[illegible]) [illegible]

[illegible] (20[illegible]) [illegible] Journal of [illegible] Science [illegible]

Chapter 10

"Outdated Technologies" and "Catch-Up Development" as Manifestations of Time in the Economy: Time Is Opportunity

Our old age is a disease that needs to be treated like any other.

Ilya I. Mechnikov, Russian biologist,
Nobel Prize Laureate

This chapter states that time is an opportunity to change the status quo (state of affairs, balance of powers) in the global economy with the help of innovative technologies.

This chapter considers the following issues:

- the life cycle of technology through the lens of its influence on the development rate of the economy;
- the development of the classification of models of economy from the positions of the Time Theory concepts: "catch-up development" and "economic miracle";
- definition of "youth" in economics as a characteristic of technologies and economic systems;
- classification of technologies and economic systems by the criteria of "youth", with examples (Figure 1).

Over whole centuries, the influence of time on humans has been a subject of debate. On the one hand, a human's appearance becomes less attractive with time. Through all times, women have been eager to use any means available to look more beautiful and younger — from natural cosmetics and cosmetics based on poisons (in Ancient Egypt: powder blusher

Figure 1. Land of milk and honey.

Source: Photo by scholar and photographer Elena Popkova, https://www.saatchiart.com/account/artworks/1599809.

of arsenic or drops with death cherries) in Medieval Europe to radioactive cosmetics in the 20th century and plastic surgeries in the 21st century. On the other hand, people become wiser with age. It is no wonder that the Ancient Greeks preferred the wisest elite to govern the state, the mention of which is seen in the works of Aristotle.

The influence of time on the economy is also contradictory. On the one hand, under the influence of time, technologies become outdated and innovations lose their topicality and novelty. On the other hand, it is only in the mid-term and long-term that an economic system receives an opportunity to change its position in the global economy, which is impossible in the short-term period and in the set time when the status quo is already established. The idea of "youthification" is very important in economics. Economic systems are interested in keeping their "youth", but the essence of this notion is unclear.

In the research literature, the classification of technologies by the criterion of their novelty has been adopted. The works of Dreyer *et al.*

(2016), Schmitz *et al.* (2019), Arrona & Zabala-Iturriagagoitia (2019), and Christoforakos *et al.* (2019) emphasize the necessity of refusing outdated technologies, which is explained by the depletion of their potential to stimulate the economy's innovative development. The works of Russian authors focus on the inexpedience of using the model of "catch-up development". They prove, by the example of the Russian economy, the low effectiveness of using outdated technologies, which is caused by slightly reduced (compared to the leading technologies) expenditures for their implementation with almost zero contribution to the increase of entrepreneurship's competitiveness and acceleration of economic growth.

The work of Matveev (2012) notes the mutual dependence of the growth of energy-saving measures and the saving of financial resources in the mechanism of ousting outdated technologies. Makarov (2015) determines the reasons for managers' refusal of innovations and the possible ways of solving this problem by the example of using outdated technologies in logistics. Burenok *et al.* (2017) classify the samples of equipment, distinguishing as outdated, modern, and prospective equipment. Novikova (2019) outlines the perspectives on the development of state management in the context of information technologies. Tikhonov *et al.* (2019) develop and evaluate the effectiveness of the project of implementing IT in management on the example of CRM technologies.

The works of Prof. Oleg V. Inshakov pay special attention to substantiating the necessity for a refusal of outdated technologies and the "catch-up development" model in Russia. Many works of Prof. Inshakov are devoted to determining the innovative potential of nanotechnologies as the leading technical solutions, in particular, Inshakov (2007a, 2007b), Inshakov *et al.* (2009, 2014, 2015), Inshakov & Fesyun (2014), Inshakov & Inshakova (2015, 2016), and Inshakov & Kryukova (2015).

The author of this book, Prof. Elena G. Popkova, also notes in her works the importance of technologies' novelty for their application in the interest of accelerating the economy's innovative development. This is stated in the works of Popkova *et al.* (2015, 2017, 2018).

The notion of life cycle is actively used in economics. It is often used in relation to a product, but not so often in relation to a company. It is like an evolutionary life cycle in biology, which is called "ontogenesis". In economics, the life cycle is treated as the process of development of the studied object from the beginning (e.g., development and issues of products, creation of company) to the end of its existence (e.g., termination of production, liquidation of company). In this work, we shall consider the life cycle of technology through the lens of its impact on the economy's rate of development (Figure 2).

As shown in Figure 2, the influence of technology on the level of the economic system's development decreases in the course of its "ageing" (growing-up, depreciation), which is shown by the blue line. In the moment of development, technology has the highest innovative potential — it is essentially new and, perhaps, a breakthrough. Implementation of essentially new technology ensures the acceleration of the economic system's innovative development and economic growth.

Under the influence of technological progress, during the transition to the next technological mode, the technology becomes outdated, and its innovative potential decreases. The period of "old age" of the technology in Figure 2 could be compared to an image of an elderly woman. Implementation of outdated technology has a small influence

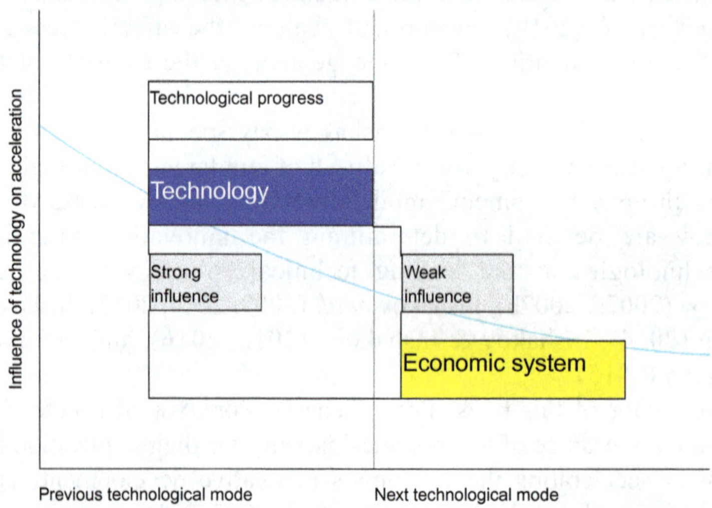

Figure 2. Life cycle of technology through the lens of its influence on the economy's rate of development.

on the acceleration of the economic system's development. Based on this, let us consider the compiled classification of the models of the economy's development from the positions of the Time Theory, which distinguishes between "catch-up development" and "economic miracle" (Figure 3).

As shown in Figure 3, during the classification of the models of economy's development from the positions of the Time Theory, it is necessary to consider the economic system in comparison with the sample system. At the moment of time t_0, the difference in the level of development of the sample economic system and considered economic system equals β. During the implementation of the "economic miracle" model, which envisages the use of breakthrough technologies, the considered economic system exceeds the sample economic system — during the period t_1 — by the level of development (e.g., by the criterion of GDP per capita) and reaches the level d_1.

This allows for "youthification" of the considered economic system: increase of the innovative activity of entrepreneurship, society's inclination toward and susceptibility to innovations, improvement of the demographic

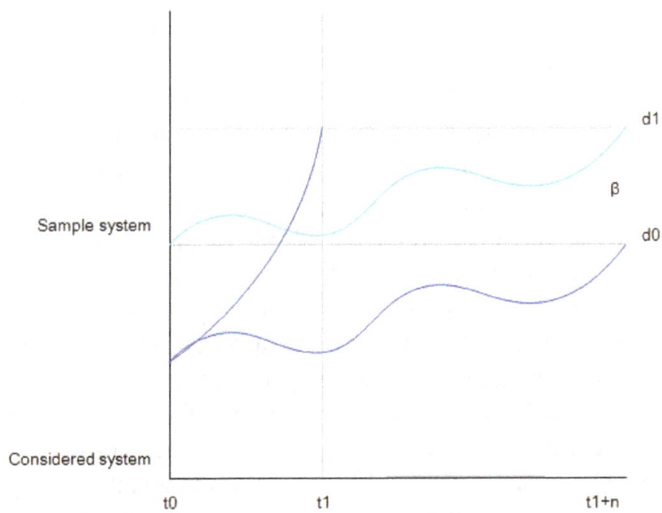

Figure 3. Classification of the models of economy's development from the positions of the Time Theory: "catch-up development" and "economic miracle".

situation (due to the increase of living standards and quality of life), reduction of the average age of the population, reduction of the speed of "ageing of personnel", and increase of economic growth rate.

The sample economic system reaches level d_1 over a large period $(t_1 + n)$. Its cyclical character is more vivid. During the implementation of the "catch-up development" model, the considered economic system "copies" the path of development of the sample system. In Figure 3, this is shown by the identical function of development (dark blue line). However, as a result of the period $t_1 + n$, the difference in the level of development of the sample and considered economic systems does not change compared to the initial period t_0, still equalling β. Though the considered economic system reaches a higher level of development (d_0), compared to the initial period t_0, its underrun from the sample economic system has not been overcome and remains at the same level.

Therefore, the development of the considered economic system during the period $t_1 + n$ was not innovative but was connected to economic growth without using the opportunities of technological progress. This symbolizes the deceitfulness of the "catch-up development" model, at which "youthification" of the economic system is not achieved and expectations do not come true, but economic indicators are purposefully increased to justify them.

Based on the above, the notion "youth" is defined in economics as a feature of technology that reflects its innovativeness (novelty and potential of influence on the acceleration of the economic system's development) and a feature of the economic system that reflects the level of its innovativeness, the average age of the population, speed of "ageing of personnel", and the rate of the system's development.

Let us consider the examples of economic systems that are classified by the criterion of their "youth". The data on society's inclination and susceptibility to innovations and on the speed of "ageing of personnel" are absent in the official statistics and are actually difficult to measure (since they are subjective). So, let us focus on the indicators of the official statistics: GDP per capita, the Global Innovation Index, the average age of the population, and economic growth rate. Let us compare these indicators in countries of BRICS in 2010–2022 (Table 1).

Table 1. Examples of economic systems that are classified by the criterion of their "youth" and the models of development used.

Period	Indicators of the level of development	Sample: USA	"Catch-up development"		"Economic miracle"		
			Brazil	Russia	India	China	South Africa
t0 2000	GDP per capita*, $	50,145.354	11,669.346	14,529.964	2,360.633	3,430.959	11,050.498
	Compared to sample	—	0.23	0.29	0.05	0.07	0.22
	Global Innovation Index, points 1–100 (2013)	60.3	36.3	37.2	36.2	44.7	—
	Compared to sample	—	0.60	0.62	0.60	0.74	—
	Average age of population, years	35.2	25.1	36.5	22.7	30.1	20.9
	Compared to sample	—	0.71	1.04	0.64	0.86	0.59
	Economic growth rate, %	4.077	4.388	10.046	3.975	8.472	4.200
	Compared to sample	—					
t1 2019	GDP per capita*, $	62,417.549	14,799.450	27,341.101	6,689.367	15,893.004	13,690.072
	Compared to sample	—	1.08	2.46	0.97	2.08	1.03
	Global Innovation Index, points 1–100	61.7	33.8	37.6	36.6	54.8	34.04
	Compared to sample	—	0.55	0.61	0.59	0.89	0.55

(Continued)

Table 1. *(Continued)*

Period	Indicators of the level of development	Sample: USA	“Catch-up development”		“Economic miracle”		
			Brazil	Russia	India	China	South Africa
	Average age of population, years	38.3	33.5	39.6	28.2	38.7	26.6
	Compared to sample	—	0.87	1.03	0.74	1.01	0.69
	Economic growth rate, %	2.289	1.221	2.198	3.738	5.951	0.303
	Compared to sample	—	0.53	0.96	1.63	2.60	0.13
t2	GDP per capita*, $	638,920.193	15,028.332	27,167	7,047.8	18,094	13,220
2022	Compared to sample		0.02	0.04	0.01	0.03	0.02
	Global Innovation Index, points 1–100	61.8	32.5	34.3	36.6	55.3	29.8
	Compared to sample		0.53	0.56	0.59	0.89	0.48
	Average age of population, years	37.9	33.2	39	27.9	38.5	27.4
	Compared to sample		0.88	1.03	0.74	1.02	0.72
	Economic growth rate, %	1.641	2.788	−3.408	6.844	3.205	2.098
	Compared to sample		1.70	−2.08	4.17	1.95	1.28

Note: *Constant prices.

Source: Based on International Monetary Fund (2022), Our World in Data (2022), and WIPO (2022).

As shown in Table 1, the models of development of Brazil and Russia could be conventionally assigned to "catch-up development", since although they have the features of "economic miracle", the features of "catch-up development" dominate. Thus, the GDP per capita of Brazil and Russia grew compared to the sample (USA), from 0.23 and 0.29 in 2000 to 0.24 and 0.44, respectively, in 2019; however, in 2022, the values reduced to 0.02 and 0.04, respectively. The value of the Global Innovation Index in Brazil and Russia reduced compared to the sample, from 0.60 and 0.962 in 2013 to 0.55 and 0.61, respectively, in 2019 but grew in 2022 to 0.53 and 0.56, respectively. The average age of the population in Brazil and Russia changed compared to the sample, from 0.71 and 1.04 in 2000 to 0.87 and 1.03, respectively, in 2019, and to 0.88 and 1.03, respectively, in 2022. The economic growth rate in Brazil and Russia reduced compared to the sample, from 1.08 and 2.46 in 2000 to 0.53 and 0.96, respectively, in 2019, and to 1.70 and −2.08 in 2022, respectively.

The models of development of India and China could be conventionally assigned to "economic miracle" since although they have features of "catch-up development", the features of "economic miracle" dominate. Thus, the GDP per capita of India, China, and South Africa grew compared to the sample (USA), from 0.05, 0.07, and 0.22, respectively, in 2000, to 0.11, 0.25, and 0.22, respectively, in 2019 but reduced to 0.01, 0.03, and 0.02, respectively, in 2022. The value of the Global Innovation Index in India, China, and South Africa changed compared to the sample, from 0.60 and 0.74 (no data for South Africa) in 2013 to 0.59, 0.89, and 0.55, respectively, in 2019, and to 0.59, 0.89, and 0.48, respectively, in 2022.

The average age of the population in India, China, and South Africa changed compared to the sample, from 0.64, 0.856, and 0.59 in 2000 to 0.74, 1.01, and 0.69, respectively, in 2019, and to 0.74, 1.02, and 0.72, respectively, in 2022. The economic growth rate in India, China, and South Africa changed compared to the sample, from 0.97, 2.08, and 1.03 in 2000 to 1.63, 2.60, and 0.13, respectively, in 2019, and to 4.17, 1.95, and 1.28, respectively, in 2022. Let us consider the examples of technologies, classified by the criterion of their "youth", through the lens of their life cycle. The corresponding matrix is compiled in Table 2.

Table 2. Examples of technologies, classified by the criteria of their "youth", through the lens of the life cycle.

	Technology and its "age" (stage of life cycle)					
Technological mode	**Calculating frame**	**Calculator**	**Desktop**	**Laptop**	**AI**	**Machine learning**
Pre-industrial economy	Adult	—	—	—	—	—
Industrial economy (Industry 1.0)	Outdated	Young	—	—	—	—
Post-industrial economy (Industry 2.0)	Outdated	Adult	Young	—	—	—
Digital economy (Industry 3.0)	Outdated	Outdated	Adult	Young	—	—
Industry 4.0	Outdated	Outdated	Outdated	Adult	Young	—
Industry 5.0	Outdated	Outdated	Outdated	Outdated	Adult	Young

Thus, it is proved by the example of the technology of numerical data processing that the calculating frame was an adult technology in the pre-industrial (agrarian) economy, and it made a limited contribution to the acceleration of the development of economic systems that used it. When the technological mode was changed under the influence of technological progress, the calculating frame became an outdated technology. The calculator appeared in the industrial economy — a young technology, which grew up in the post-industrial economy with the appearance of a computer, and now — in the digital economy — it is outdated. In the modern digital economy, the laptop (tablet, smartphone) is a young technology. In Industry 4.0, it will be replaced by AI, and in Industry 5.0, by machine learning.

Thus, the economy, similarly to a human, is subject to ageing. Similarly, each technology has its life cycle — from invention to depreciation. Ageing of a population decreases its susceptibility to changes, which, together with the decrease of the innovative activity of entrepreneurship, leads to "ageing" of the economy. Its youthification during the implementation of the "catch-up development" model is impossible with the use of outdated technologies; this requires young (preferably breakthrough) technologies and implementation of the "economic miracle" model.

Therefore, time provides the economy with opportunities for innovative development, whose results depend on the selected model and implemented technologies.

References

Arrona, A. & Zabala-Iturriagagoitia, J. M. (2019). On the study and practice of regional innovation policy: The potential of interpretive policy analysis. *Innovation*, 32(1): 148–163.

Burenok, V. M., Durnev, R. A., & Kryukov, K. Y. (2017). A sample of technology: outdated, modern or promising? *Armament and Economics*, 5(42): 5–14.

Christoforakos, L., Tretter, S., Diefenbach, S., Bibi, S. A., Fröhner, M., Kohler, K., Madden, D., Marx, T., Pfeiffer-Leßmann, N., & Valkanova, N. (2019). Potential and challenges of prototyping in product development and innovation: Insights from an expert discussion among researchers and practitioners. *I-com*, 18(2): 179–187.

Dreyer, A., Fischer, S., Gräwe, A., Keilholz, L., Kokotek, D. & Lüders, J. (2016). International Genetically Engineered Machine (iGEM). Cell-free protein synthesis: Outdated technology or modern methods? [Zellfreie Protein-synthese: veraltete Technik oder moderne Methode? International Genetically Engineered Machine (iGEM)]. *BioSpektrum*, 22(5): 546–547.

Inshakov, O. V. (2007a). Economic genetics as a theoretical basis for nanoeconomics. *Philosophy of Economy*, 5(53): 95–109.

Inshakov, O. V. (2007b). Economic Genetics and Nanoeconomics. Volgograd: Russian Academy of Sciences, Department of Social Sciences, Southern Scientific Center of the Russian Academy of Sciences, Volgograd State University.

Inshakov, O. V. & Fesyun, A. V. (2014). Impact of Russia's accession to the WTO on the development of the national nano industry. In *Modernization of the Economic System of the Southern Macroregion in the Conditions of the WTO: A Collective Monograph*. Moscow: Volgograd State University, pp. 9–28.

Inshakov, O. V. & Inshakova, E. I. (2015). Reconstruction of RF nano industry institutions in an unfavourable global environment. *Bulletin of the Volgograd State University. Series 3: Economics. Ecology*, 4(1): 7–17.

Inshakov, O. V. & Inshakova, E. I. (2016). Development of the world and Russian nano industry: Results and problems. *Economic Science of Modern Russia*, 4(1): 65–78.

Inshakov, O. V. & Kryukova, E. V. (2015). Special economic zones as an institution for the development of the nano industry: Failures, problems and prospects. *Bulletin of the Volgograd State University. Series 3: Economics. Ecology*, 1(1): 6–17.

Inshakov, O. V., Inshakova, E. I., & Fesyun, A. V. (2015). Nanoindustrialization as a stage in the formation of a new economic order in Russia. Grant research and educational activities. In *Goals, Technologies, Results: Collective Monograph in 9 Volumes*. Limited Liability Company International Research Center "Scientific Cooperation", Rostov-on-Don. pp. 76–106.

Inshakov, O. V., Inshakova, E. I., & Kryukova, E. V. (2014). Special economic zones as an institution for the development of the nano industry: Essence, structure, improvement. *Bulletin of the Volgograd State University. Series 3: Economics. Ecology*, 6(1): 81–95.

Inshakov, O. V., Yakovlev, A. R., Fesyun, A. V., Orlova, A. A., & Moseiko, V. O. (2009). Mechanisms for Implementing the Strategy for the Formation of the Nano Industry in the Regions of Russia. Volgograd: Ministry of Education and Science of the Russian Federation, State Educational Institution of Higher Professional Education, Volgograd State University.

International Monetary Fund (2022). World Economic Outlook Database, October 2022: Report for Selected Countries and Subjects. https://www.imf.org/en/Publications/WEO/weo-database/2022/October. Accessed: 05 January 2023.

Makarov, A. N. (2015). The use of outdated technologies in logistics, the reasons for leaders' refusal to innovate and possible solutions to this problem. *Young Scientist*, 10(90): 720–722.

Matveev, V. V. (2012). The interdependence of the growth of energy-saving and the saving of financial resources in the mechanism of replacing outdated technologies. *Issues of Economics and Law*, 45: 153–156.

Novikova, V. S. (2019). Prospects for the development of public administration in the context of information technology. *Diary of Science*, 3(27): 73.

Our World in Data (2022). Age Structure. https://ourworldindata.org/age-structure. Accessed: 05 January 2023.

Popkova, E. G., Grechenkova, O. Y., Boris, O. A., Przhedetskaya, N. V., & Gornostaeva, Z. V. (2017). The prospects of using social marketing in economic criminology in the conditions of an emerging innovative economy. *Russian Journal of Criminology*, 11(2): 280–288.

Popkova, E. G., Khmeleva, G. A., & Ostrovskiy, V. I. (2015). The innovative approach to providing economic security. *Actual Problems of Economics*, 169(7): A002, 99–105.

Popkova, E. G., Poluyufta, L., Beshanova, Y., Popova, L. V., & Kolesnikova, E. (2017). Innovations as a basis for marketing strategies of Russian oil companies in the conditions of oil prices reduction. *Contributions to Economics*, (9783319606958): 449–455.

Popkova, E. G., Sozinova, A. A., Grechenkova, O. Y., & Menshchikova, V. I. (2018). Deficiencies in the legislative support of innovative activities in contemporary Russia and ways of addressing them. *Russian Journal of Criminology*, 12(4): 515–524.

Schmitz, T., Bukowski, M., Koschmieder, S., Schmitz-Rode, T., & Farkas, R. (2019). Potential technologies review: A hybrid information retrieval framework to accelerate demand-pull innovation in biomedical engineering. *Research Synthesis Methods*, 10(3): 420–439.

Tikhonov, S. V., Khachko, O. I., & Biyatov, N. V. (2019). Development and evaluation of the effectiveness of the project for the implementation of information technologies in management on the example of CRM technologies. *Scientific Notes of the Russian Academy of Entrepreneurship*, 18(1): 97–108.

WIPO (2022). Global Innovation Index 2022 Rankings. https://www.wipo.int/edocs/pubdocs/en/wipo-pub-2000-2022-section1-en-gii-2022-at-a-glance-global-innovation-index-2022-15th-edition.pdf. Accessed: 05 January 2023.

Chapter 11

Comparative Analysis of the Existing Time Theories and the Assessment of Their Applicability to the Modern Theory of Innovation: Time Is the Key to Innovations

In a world of locked rooms, the man with the key is the king.

Arthur Conan Doyle, English writer and philosopher

This chapter states that time is the key to understanding and managing innovations in the world economy.

This chapter considers the following topics:

- scientific theories (schools), which reflect the time factor in the macroeconomic analysis, and the assessment of their applicability to the modern theory of innovation;
- postulates of the modern theory of innovation on economic time;
- concept of economic time according to the modern theory of innovation (Figure 1).

In Babylon and Ancient Greece, the night was divided into three guards — three periods in which the guard of camps and cities was replaced. At beginning of our era, the night was divided into four periods, which were also connected to the change of guard. The period of one shift of guard was a measure of time. The Gospel tells about four night guards. Christianity led to the philosophical reconsideration of time in human life;

Figure 1. Time is the key to innovations.

Source: Photo by scholar and photographer Elena Popkova, https://www.saatchiart.com/account/artworks/1599809.

time was associated with the guard and time was treated in the form of a guard. In philosophical works and fiction, there are a lot of abstract notions of time, and the guard is one of its most vivid images. This abstraction harmoniously describes time, which shades humans through the events of the past and opens a door to the future.

The ideas of time as a socio-economic phenomenon and process are reflected in the works of philosophers and theologists: Plato, Augustine, Thomas Aquinas, George Berkeley, Georg Wilhelm Friedrich Hegel, David Hume, and Kant; in the works of scholars: Newton, Descartes, Leibniz, von Holbach, and Diderot; and in the considerations of Russian thinkers: Lomonosov, Chernyshevsky, and Tolstoy.

In economics, time is studied by various theories, but it is an ordinary indicator. This leads to the fragmentary and inconsistent character of the research of time in economics. In the theory of innovation, time is the central category. However, the theory of innovation is not studied by any independent school of economics and is thus formed spontaneously based on a whole range of theories. The aggregate information on the existing scientific theories, which reflect the time factor in the macro-economic analysis, is given in Table 1.

As shown in Table 1, the existing scientific theories study economic time in a very limited way, considering only certain aspects. In the classical political economy, in particular in the works of its representative,

Table 1. Scientific theories that reflect the time factor in the macro-economic analysis.

Economic theory	Approach to studying the time factor	Possibility of use in the theory of innovation
Classical theory of political economy (Smith, 1723)	Assessment of profit from saving time through specialization (labour division)	Only the present is considered (saving time at present), without consideration of the past and future
Marx's theory (1857)	Studying the perspectives of saving time through the increase of labour efficiency to reduce the production cost and increase the capital turnover	The factual and normative time at present is compared, without consideration of the past (though the norm is sent based on past experience) and the future
Neoclassical economic theory (marginalism) — Marshall (1890)	Classification of time periods by the criterion of opportunities for changing the market situation with distinguishing between the short-term, mid-term, and long-term periods, forecasting "all other conditions being equal" based on the past experience and information on the present Planning of the production cycle	Time periods are studied separately, there is no systemic idea of time
Theory of the Austrian school of economics — von Wieser (1914)	Analysis of lost profit — alternative costs	Alternative variants of the present are taken into account; the past and the future are not considered

(*Continued*)

Table 1. (*Continued*)

Economic theory	Approach to studying the time factor	Possibility of use in the theory of innovation
Theory of investment — Fisher (1906)	Calculation of present indicators for determining the comparative economic effectiveness from capital investment and the selection of the best option of investing	Emphasis is on the future, calculations are performed at present, the past is not considered
Scientific Theory of management — Abalkin (1978), Korotkov (2004)	Taking into account the time factor during decision-making: determining and accounting the precise deadlines for projects, stimulation of saving of time Evaluation of the duration of the process of management through the lens of the used resources	Time is considered as a factor, but not an object of management

A. Smith, the assessment of profit from saving time through specialization was performed. However, only the present was considered (saving time at present) without consideration of the past and the future.

Marx's theory was based on the scientific methodology of dialectical materialism and envisaged the study of the perspectives of saving time through increasing labour efficiency to reduce production costs and increase capital turnover. In this case, the factual and normative time at present was compared, without consideration of the past (though the norm is set based on past experience) and the future. This is stated in the work of Makhamatov & Makhamatova (2018), which considers the concepts of Marx on economic space and time and the development of modern dialectical materialism.

The neoclassical economic theory (marginalism), presented in the works of Marshall, envisaged the classification of time periods by the criterion of possibilities for changing the market situation by distinguishing the short-term, mid-term, and long-term periods and forecasting "all other conditions being equal" based on the experience and information on the present. In the works of another representative of this economic school — Galbraith — the planning of the production cycle was performed. In marginalism, time periods are studied separately, and there is no systemic idea of time.

The theory of the Austrian school of economics, presented in the works of Von Wieser, envisaged analysis of lost profit — alternative costs. It takes into account the alternative variants of the present, but the past and the future are not considered.

The theory of investment as reflected in the works of Fisher is a modern theory, which envisages the calculation of present indicators to determine the comparative economic effectiveness of capital investments and the best option for investing. The emphasis is made on the future and calculations are performed at present, while the past is not considered.

The modern scientific theory of management, presented in the works of Abalkin, takes into account the time factor during decision-making: precise deadlines for projects are determined and taken into account and saving of time is stimulated; the works of Korotkov assess the duration of the process of management through the lens of the used resources. In both cases, time is considered a factor, but not an object of management. This is stated (presenting a corresponding table) by a modern Russian scholar in the work Titenko (2013); the author considers time as a factor and criterion of development of production in economic concepts.

Thus, the works of the representatives of economic schools are devoted to the research of only one of the time aspects: as a rule, this is the present or the future. The past — as an economic phenomenon — remains poorly studied. The existing views of economic time are contradictory and inconsistent. This does not allow for forming a comprehensive concept of economic time. Economic time is an independent object of research in the modern theory of innovation. In their work, the modern researchers of the theory of innovation emphasize the duration of the innovative process, from the appearance of an idea to the commercialization of innovations, as well as the significant applied value of innovations. Examples are the works Cipollone & Giordani (2019), Clohessy & Acton (2019), Costanzo & Sánchez (2019), da Silva Lopes *et al.* (2019), Mercure *et al.* (2019), Min *et al.* (2019), and Sony & Naik (2019).

Russian scholars, who research the theory of innovation, in particular, Fedorov *et al.* (2012), describe the possibilities of interpreting the main provisions of the theory of innovation and the methodology of cognition of the theory of innovation based on the classical laws of thermodynamics. Nekrasov (2012) considers the perspectives of development of the theory of innovation through the lens of innovative cycles and sociogenetics of innovations. Kovalev (2013) focuses attention on the future time and studies foresight as a forecast of innovations.

Dadaev (2012) emphasizes the necessity for the applied direction of innovations and the unacceptability of its absence (so-called innovations for innovations' sake), noting this tendency in the commercialization of intellectual property. Bdaytsieva (2013) defines the notion, classification, and problems of consideration of innovations and innovative activities in the Russian Federation. Egorova *et al.* (2015) point out the significance of consumers' attitudes to innovations and innovations' opposition to their commercialization and derive the notion of clever innovativeness.

Khorshikyan (2015) studies the market of innovations and the problems of innovations' transfer. Titov *et al.* (2015) study strategic innovations and offer a complex approach to creating competitive advantages through innovations in a company's business model. Shegelman *et al.* (2015) note the perspectives of the development of the methodology of innovations' classification by building a matrix of innovations. Dydrov (2015) provides the discourses of philosophy of the 20th century on innovations.

Professor Oleg V. Inshakov notes the mutual influence of time and innovations — time determines the opportunities for implementing innovations, which, in their turn, determine the technological mode. This has been written about in the works of Inshakov *et al.* (2009, 2015). Prof. Elena G. Popkova also notes the key role of economic time in the modern theory of innovation in the following works: Popkova *et al.* (2015, 2017, 2018), and Popkova & Sergi (2018).

The modern theory of innovation is based on other economic theories, in particular, on the theory of economic growth, the systems theory, and the theory of economic cycles, and suggests the following postulates on economic time.

- Innovations are created and implemented at a certain (favourable) moment at present: Present continuous.
- During the creation of innovations, traditions are always used as the basis: Experience, accumulated knowledge, and existing technologies.
- Innovations create the delayed effect, which is achieved in the future — Change of technological mode during the accumulation of innovations

(according to the law of dialectics on the transition from quantity to quality).

- Innovations are cyclical: They are subject to the influence of time and they change, becoming traditions in the course of growing outdated.
- Innovations should have a practical application: Being a factor of production, joining with other production factors of innovations to ensure advantages for a company and the economy, which are connected to the acceleration of their development and increase of quality of economic growth.

The above postulates are formulated according to the works of Schumpeter and Kondratyev and allow an illustration of the concept of economic time according to the modern Theory of Innovation (Figure 2).

As shown in Figure 2, economic time is systemic: traditions of the past in a favourable macro-economic environment (with a stimulating impact of external conditions, the sufficiency of resources, and under the influence of technological progress) and organizational environment (with sufficient internal resources and favourable conditions) stimulate the creation of innovations. In their turn, they, with a systemic use with other production factors at present, create a synergetic effect at the

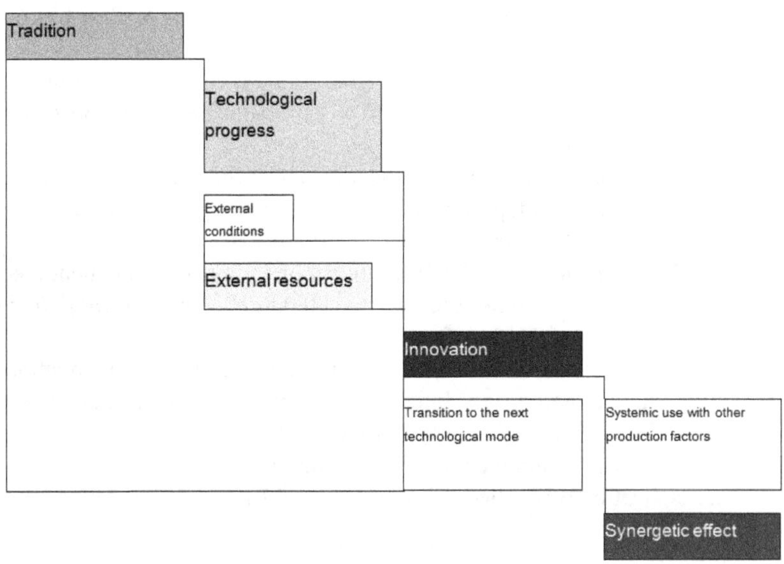

Figure 2. The concept of economic time according to the modern Theory of Innovation.

moment, Present continuous. The synergetic effect is connected to an increase in efficiency, effectiveness, and competitiveness of economic subjects and economic systems. In the future, the time effect from innovations accumulates, and a transition to the next technological mode takes place, due to which innovations become traditions; after this, the cycle is repeated from the very beginning.

Thus, economic time pierces the modern Theory of Innovation. The year 2009 saw a unique invention in physics: Moscow scholars were able to turn time in the opposite way. Researchers from the Moscow Institute of Physics and Technology, together with scientists from the USA and Switzerland, made a quantum computer go back to the past — for one second — thus violating the second law of thermodynamics. In economics, there is a demand for an accelerated transition from the present to the future. The natural course of physical time in the Theory of Innovation is opposed to the differentiated course of economic time. Time is the key to innovations in an economy, but the scientific search for this key is not yet finished.

References

Bdaytsieva, L. Z. (2013). Innovation: Concept, classification, problems of accounting for innovations and innovative activities in the Russian Federation. *Bulletin of the Leningrad State University Named After A.S. Pushkin*, 6(4): 109–115.

Cipollone, A. & Giordani, P. E. (2019). Market frictions in entrepreneurial innovation: Theory and evidence. *Journal of Economic Behavior and Organization*, 163: 297–331.

Clohessy, T. & Acton, T. (2019). Investigating the influence of organizational factors on blockchain adoption: An innovation theory perspective. *Industrial Management and Data Systems*, 119(7): 1457–1491.

Costanzo, B. P. & Sánchez, L. E. (2019). Innovation in impact assessment theory and practice: How is it captured in the literature? *Environmental Impact Assessment Review*, 79: 106289.

da Silva Lopes, T., Casson, M., & Jones, G. (2019). Organizational innovation in the multinational enterprise: Internalization theory and business history. *Journal of International Business Studies*, 50(8): 1338–1358.

Dadaev, A. A. (2013). Innovation for innovation: Emerging trends in the commercialization of intellectual property. *Federalism*, 4(72): 165–172.

Dydrov, A. A. (2015). Discourses of philosophy of the 20th century. On innovation and innovation. *Bulletin of the Moscow State Regional University. Series: Philosophical Sciences*, 4: 8–14.

Egorova, M. S., Kalinkina, E., & Mayer, S. (2015). Determination of consumer attitudes towards innovation, resistance to innovation, reasonable innovation. *Young Scientist*, 7(87): 396–398.

Fedorov, V. K., Marin, V. P., & Beklemishev, N. N. (2012). Possibilities of interpreting the main provisions of the theory of innovation and the methodology of cognition of the theory of innovation based on the classical laws of thermodynamics. *Science-Intensive Technologies*, 13(4): 74–78.

Institute of Scientific Communications (2019). Scientists: You Can Return from the Present to the Past. http://archilab.online/tekhnologii/314-uchenye-iz-nastoyashchego-mozhno-vernutsya-v-proshloe. Accessed: 12 November 2019.

Inshakov, O. V. *et al.* (2009). Strategy for Innovative Development of the Volgograd Region until 2025. Volgograd: Ministry of Education and Science of the Russian Federation, State Educational Institution of Higher Professional Education, Volgograd State University.

Inshakov, O. V., Inshakova, E. I., & Fesyun, A. V. (2015). Nanoindustrialization as a stage in the formation of a new economic order in Russia. In *Grant Research and Educational Activities: Goals, Technologies, Results. A Collective Monograph in 9 Volumes*. Limited Liability Company International Research Center "Scientific Cooperation", Rostov-on-Don. pp. 76–106.

Khorshikyan, S. V. (2015). The market of innovations and problems of transfer of innovations. *Age of Quality*, 2: 46–47.

Kovalev, V. I. (2013). Foresight: Forecasting innovation or innovation in forecasts? *Bulletin of Omsk University*, 2(68): 169–172.

Makhamatov, T. M. & Makhamatova, S. T. (2018). Karl Marx's concept of economic space and time and the development of modern dialectical materialism. *Theoretical Economics*, 6(48): 27–32.

Mercure, J.-F., Knobloch, F., Pollitt, H., Paroussos, L., Scrieciu, S. S., & Lewney, R. (2019). Modelling innovation and the macroeconomics of low-carbon transitions: Theory, perspectives and practical use. *Climate Policy*, 19(8): 1019–1037.

Min, S., So, K. K. F., & Jeong, M. (2019). Consumer adoption of the Uber mobile application: Insights from the diffusion of innovation theory and technology acceptance model. *Journal of Travel and Tourism Marketing*, 36(7): 770–783.

Nekrasov, D. A. (2012). Development of the theory of innovation. Innovation cycles and socio genetic of innovation. *Bulletin of the Samara State University of Economics*, 5(91): 68–71.

Popkova, E. G. & Sergi, B. S. (2018). Will Industry 4.0 and other innovations impact Russia's Development? In Sergi, B. S. (ed.) *Exploring the Future of Russia's Economy and Markets: Towards Sustainable Economic Development*. Bingley, UK: Emerald Publishing Limited, pp. 51–68.

Popkova, E. G., Popova, E. V., & Sergi, B. S. (2018). Clusters and innovational networks toward sustainable growth. In Sergi, B. S. (ed.) *Exploring the Future of Russia's Economy and Markets: Towards Sustainable Economic Development*. Bingley, UK: Emerald Publishing Limited, pp. 107–124.

Shegelman, I. R., Pakermanov, E. M., & Odlis, D. B. (2015). Towards the development of a methodology for classifying innovations by constructing an innovation matrix. *Education and Science in Modern Conditions*, 2(3): 281–282.

Sony, M. & Naik, S. (2019). Six Sigma with C-K theory for innovations in operational excellence: A case study. *Benchmarking*, 26(7): 2105–2121.

Titenko, E. A. (2013). The time factor as a criterion for the development of production in economic concepts. Business. Education. Right. *Bulletin of the Volgograd Institute of Business*, 1(22): 157–160.

Titov, S. A., Titova, N. V., Chernyshev, V. P., & Titarenko, R. B. (2015). Strategic innovation: An integrated approach to creating competitive advantage through innovation in a company's business model. *Fundamental Research*, 10(1): 193–197.

Part II

Connection of Past, Present, and Future Development of Economic Phenomena and Processes in the Concept of "Underdevelopment Whirlpools": How to Measure Economic Time

This part states that economic time flows differently from physical time. It is more difficult to measure, but it is important for studying and forecasting the dynamics of economic systems' development. An overview of the existing scientific and methodological approaches to measuring economic time is presented: innovative (based on the theory of innovations) and cyclical (based on the theory of economic cycles). Also, their limitations are shown, which are connected to the low precision of determining the current time in economics and the speed of its flow, as well as to the impossibility of comparison of various economic systems from the positions of their economic time.

As a preferable alternative, a cone-shaped ("whirlpool") approach based on the theory of economic growth is offered. Within this approach, a methodology of calculating "underdevelopment whirlpools" is offered, and another methodology of calculating "underdevelopment whirlpools" is developed, with recommendations for using this methodology for macro-economic analysis from the positions of the theory of economic time. The approbation of the methodology of "underdevelopment whirlpools" calculation by the example of modern Russia's economy is performed, a chronogram is created, the time asymmetry of economic development is determined, the process of the economic system's sucking into the "underdevelopment whirlpool" from the positions of the theory of economic time is analyzed, and a 3D graph of the economy's development from the positions of the time, GDP per capita, and the "whirlpool's" depth is built (economic chronotope).

Similarly to physical time, whose properties were determined and systematized in Anisov (2019), flow is also peculiar to economic time. It changes constantly, but there is always a strong connection between the past, the present, and the future.

Chapter 12

The Concept of "Underdevelopment Whirlpools" as a Manifestation of Temporary Imbalances in the Development of Economic Systems: Time is a Whirlpool

The future depends on what you do in the present.

Mahatma Gandhi, Indian philosopher

This chapter states that time is a measure of the development of the global economy.

This chapter considers the following topics:

- notion and essence of "underdevelopment whirlpool" as a process of the change of economy in time in relation to other economies;
- the process of sucking into an "underdevelopment whirlpool" through the slowdown of economic time in an economic system;
- means of accelerating economic time in the economic system to overcome the "underdevelopment whirlpool" (Figure 1).

In myths and legends of Ancient Greece, time is one of the central factors of the story but is, however, described in the allegorical form, which is traditional for Ancient Greek literature. Thus, in Homer's "Odyssey", the protagonist Odysseus meets a lot of obstacles on his way home, to Ithaca, which slows him down. First, he gets in a whirlpool when

Figure 1. Time is a whirlpool.

Source: Photo by scholar and photographer Elena Popkova, https://www.saatchiart.com/account/artworks/1599809.

sailing between the monsters Scylla and Charybdis, and then remains on the island of Calypso, and, as a result, returns home only after 20 years. Reconsidering Odysseus's wandering from the position of modern philosophy, it is possible to say that Odysseus gets trapped in a whirlpool of time and goes to the very bottom — but he can get out.

The literary and philosophical treatment of time as a whirlpool or eddy is universal. In economics, the course of time can also accelerate or slow down the development of economic systems. Differences in the rate of economic systems' development or the speed of their economic time became the basis of development and were reflected in the two following concepts of economic science.

The first concept is the concept of developed and developing countries. According to this concept, national economic systems are divided into two main types:

- developed countries, which were the first to start the processes of capitalistic (market) transformations and which demonstrate the highest level of socio-economic development;
- developing countries, which implemented — in the "second wave" — the processes of market reformation of their economy and are characterized by a lower level of socio-economic development.

At the same time, this concept acknowledges that developing countries develop at a higher rate. This concept is presented in the works of Schuh (2003), Grassetti *et al.* (2018), Ahmad *et al.* (2019), Luo *et al.* (2019), and Younsi & Nafla (2019).

Second is the concept of rapid and catch-up development. Representatives of this concept, which include Nassif *et al.* (2015), Khavari *et al.* (2016), Bacon (2017), Hare (2019), and Li *et al.* (2019), consider regional (meso-economic) economic systems and compare them, distinguishing two types:

- regions that demonstrate rapid development: progressive regions which are the first to test new models of socio-economic development, implement breakthrough innovations in their economy, and choose the course of its development;
- regions characterized by catch-up development: regions that are guided in their development by the example of more successful regions and implement the models of socio-economic development that have already been tested by the sample regions.

Though the purpose of developing countries and regions that are characterized by catch-up development is the achievement of the level of the sample, in practice they acquire the role of outsiders, participants of the global (or regional) competitive struggle. They underrun growth with time, i.e., they are sucked into an "underdevelopment whirlpool".

The term "underdevelopment whirlpool" could be met in the existing scientific and economic literature in various contexts. For example, Ashenfelter *et al.* (2013) compare the process of change of prices during large mergers and acquisitions of companies with a whirlpool — prices grow in the course of the whirlpool's becoming deeper. Elida (2018) determines the negative dynamics of the development of local cities in the "whirlpool" of the global economy, which is connected to an increase in their underrun from the capital (shown by the example of Medan-Siantar-Sibolga).

Berta *et al.* (2017) describe deals in the European carbon market as a "whirlpool of speculations", which leads to the formation of a financial "bubble". Borup (2017) notes the cyclicity of the increase of disproportions between different regions of the world and describes it as a whirlpool (shown by the example of East and West). Karkoulian *et al.* (2013) note the increase in complexity of employment in the course of the increase in unemployment's duration, calling this the "whirlpool of chronic weakness". Laptev & Sozinova (2018) describe the process of increase of the differences between companies in the process of their innovative development through "underdevelopment whirlpool" (shown in the example of companies' reorganization).

Certain issues of disproportions in the development of the global economy through the lens of the underrun of certain countries from other countries by the level of socio-economic development are studied in the works of Bulatov (2014), Zabrodotsky (2006), Gurova (2009), Safronov (2009), Kindzersky (2010), and Semenov & Derunov (2016). "Underdevelopment whirlpool", as a phenomenon of economic time, is presented in the works of Shakhovskaya & Popkova (2004), Popkova (2004a, 2004b, 2004c, 2005, 2014, 2017a, 2017b), and Popkova *et al.* (2018), the systematization of which allows defining the considered phenomenon in the following way: "underdevelopment whirlpool" is a process of the change of an economic system in time and the increase of its underrun in the level of socio-economic development as compared to another, sample, economy. An increase of the underrun at a slow rate of socio-economic development (i.e., slowdown of economic time) leads to the economic system's sucking into a "whirlpool", and a decrease of the underrun at a quick rate of socio-economic development (acceleration of economic time) leads to overcoming of the "underdevelopment whirlpool".

The economic essence of "underdevelopment whirlpool" is explained by Bolotin (2001) through economic systems' passing the "vicious circles of poverty", during the attempts to occupy their niche in the international division of labour. "Poverty" is understood as a lower level of income and lower living standards as compared to the sample. "Vicious circle of poverty" is an increase of the underrun from the sample by the level of income and living standards.

Inshakov & Frolov (2002) describe the process of the economic system's sucking into an "underdevelopment whirlpool" as an "institutional trap". Striving to reach the level of the samples' development, economic systems implement obsolete models of development and technologies. The practices of repeating after samples, instead of the search for their unique opportunities for growth and development, are established (institutionalized) and are self-supporting ineffective institutions ("institutional traps").

From the positions of the theory of economic time, "underdevelopment whirlpools" are a process of an increase of the underrun of the economic system in time from the sample. Its scientific concept is shown in Figure 2.

As shown in Figure 2, both economic systems (the considered system and the sample system) are initially at the same level of development — at present. Then, the sample system "develops in tune with the times", using the capabilities of technological progress — i.e., it remains at present. The considered economic system lags behind it more and more, ignoring or trying — unsuccessfully — to use technological progress. It is in the past time and goes deeper into the past.

Economic time in the "underdevelopment whirlpool" passes differently as compared to the surface (Figure 3). Development of the economic system stimulates the overcoming of the "underdevelopment whirlpool", but the system does not get into the future or the present. It remains in the past, orienting at obsolete technologies and opportunities that already lost their topicality. As the economic system is getting sucked into an "underdevelopment whirlpool", the level of its dependence on the model system grows (its investments, technologies, goods, and services). The considered economic system becomes a supplier of resources for the sample system.

Getting to the very bottom of the "underdevelopment whirlpool", the economic system forms a conventional economic "black hole" — it remains in the geographical space, but its underrun from the sample and other participants of the international competitive fight in the set market is so large that it cannot implement economic relations and connections to the required extent. The economic system finds itself in forced economic isolation, being limited to internal processes. To go up from the bottom of the "underdevelopment whirlpool", it is necessary to change the model of the economic system's development.

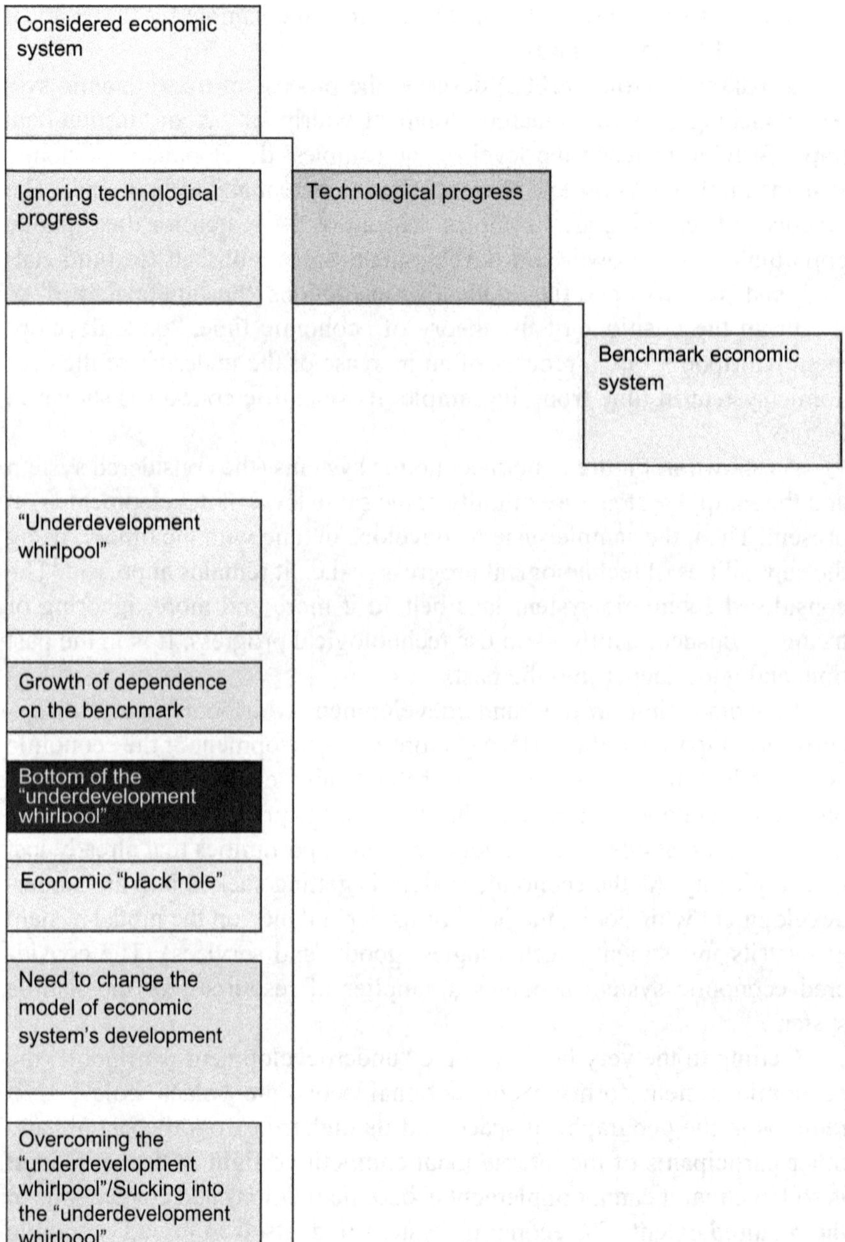

Figure 2. Scientific concept of "underdevelopment whirlpool" from the positions of the theory of economic time.

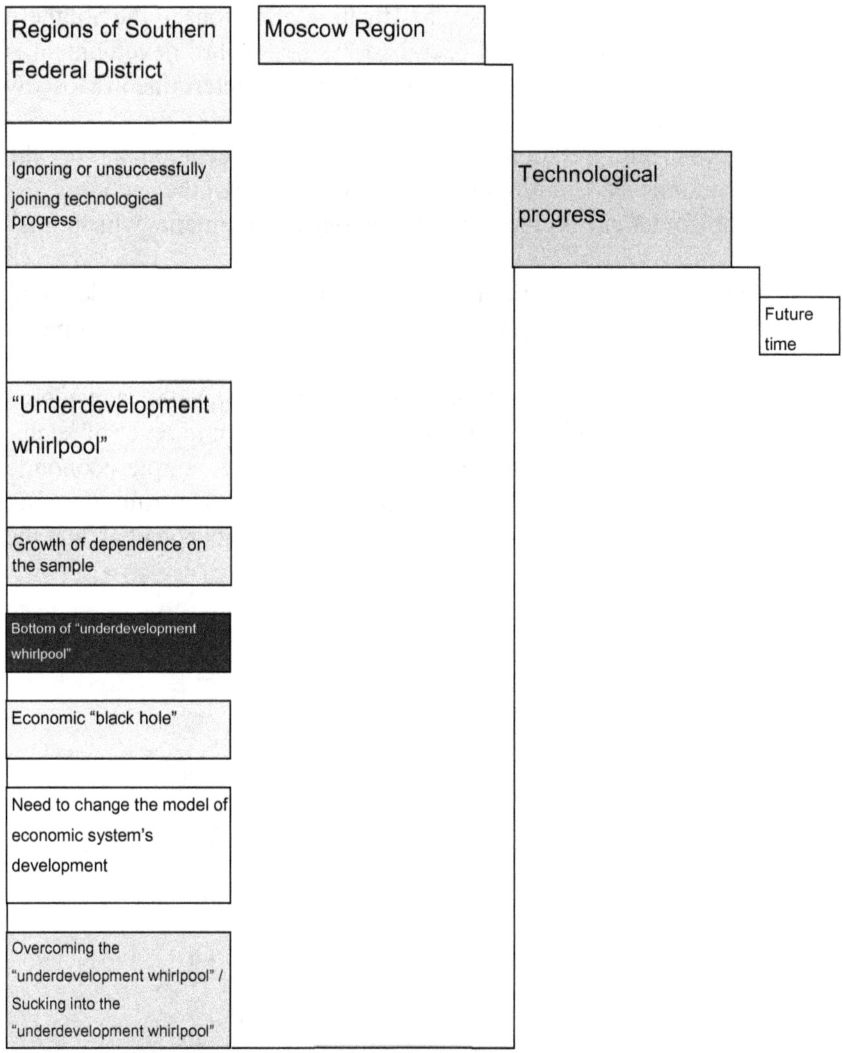

Figure 3. The scientific concept of "underdevelopment whirlpool" from the positions of the theory of economic time.

According to this concept, the classification of regions of the Southern Federal District of the Russian Federation by the level of development is performed, and their positions in the whirlpool are determined (Moscow Region is the sample).

The given interpretation of socio-economic development of the national economic system provides a complex picture of the economy and reflects the practical value of the "underdevelopment whirlpools" concept.

The process of economic system's sucking into an "underdevelopment whirlpool" from the positions of the theory of economic time is shown in Figure 4.

As shown in Figure 4, at the initial moment (t_1), the considered and the sample economic systems demonstrate the same level of socio-economic development. At the next moment (t_2), the sample economic system implements — to the fullest extent — external opportunities (first of all, the opportunities of technological progress) and its potential, and the

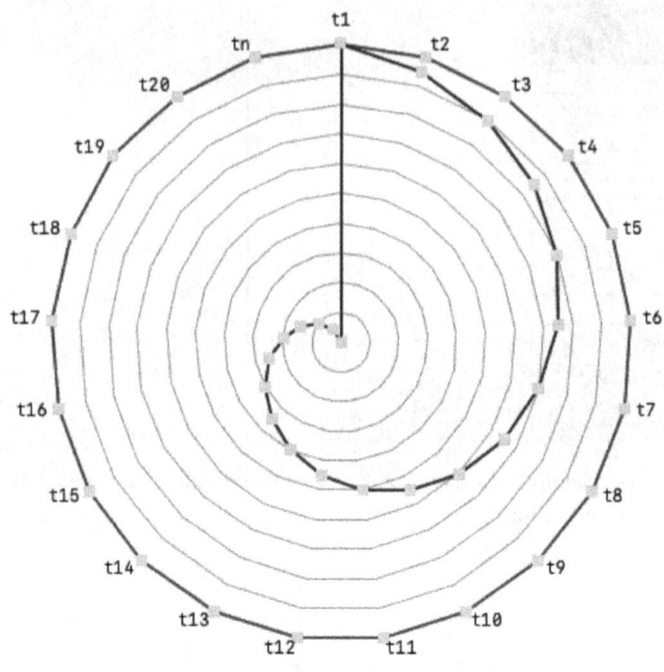

Figure 4. The process of economic systems sucking into the "underdevelopment whirlpool" from the positions of the theory of economic time.

considered system does not, thus lagging behind the sample system by the level of socio-economic development.

Then, at the moment of time t_3, the difference between the levels of socio-economic development of economic systems grows, etc. At the moment of time t*n* (bottom of "underdevelopment whirlpool"), the difference is too large within the current model of the economic system's development. The features and reasons for sucking into and overcoming the "underdevelopment whirlpool" and the tools of state administration of this process are shown in Table 1.

As shown in Table 1, the features indicating the sucking into the "underdevelopment whirlpool" are a decrease in GDP growth rate and a slow rate of growth of GDP per capita as compared to the sample; the features indicating overcoming the "whirlpool" are the increase in GDP

Table 1. Features and reasons for sucking into and overcoming the "underdevelopment whirlpool" and the tools of state administration of this process.

	Sucking into the "whirlpool"	Overcoming the "whirlpool"
Features	• Reduction of GDP growth rate • Slow growth rate of GDP per capita as compared to the sample	• Increase in GDP growth rate • Quick growth rate of GDP per capita as compared to the sample
Reasons	• Inability to adapt to new conditions in the external environment (technological progress, globalization) • Impact of internal destabilizing factors (decrease of business activity in the economy, growth of the shadow economy, and decrease of innovative activity in the economy)	• Increase of global competitiveness of the economy (development of export) • Growth of business activity in the economy • "De-shadowization" of the economy • Increase of innovative activity in the economy
Tools of management	• Increase of flexibility of state administration of the economy • Overcoming the internal (e.g., social) contradictions • Increase of investment attractiveness of the economy • Improvement of business climate and increase of trust between government and entrepreneurship • Stimulation of the economy's innovative development	

growth rate and quick rate of growth of GDP per capita as compared to the sample.

The reasons for sucking into an "underdevelopment whirlpool" are the economic system's inability to adapt to new conditions in the external environment (technological progress, globalization) and the impact of internal destabilizing factors (decrease of business activity[1] in the economy, growth of the shadow economy,[2] and decrease of innovative activity in economy). The prospective means of accelerating economic time in the economic system to overcome an "underdevelopment whirlpool" are the increase of global competitiveness of the economy, growth of business activity in the economy, "de-shadowization" of the economy, and an increase of innovative activity in the economy.

The tools of economic system management in the interests of accelerating economic time and overcoming an "underdevelopment whirlpool" are the increase of the flexibility of the state administration of the economy, overcoming of internal (e.g., social) contradictions, an increase of the economy's investment attractiveness, improvement of business climate and increase of trust between government and entrepreneurship, and the stimulation of the economy's innovative development.

Thus, the "underdevelopment whirlpool" is a manifestation of time disproportions in the development of economic systems; it is a whirlpool that sucks economic systems that are not able to develop "in tune with the times". "Underdevelopment whirlpool" is an elevator, in which the economic system can either go up or down between the levels of socio-economic development; it is a mechanism of the use of a "time machine" in the economy.

References

Ahmad, Y., Lo, M. C., & Staveley-O'Carroll, O. (2019). Nonlinearities in the real exchange rates: New evidence from developed and developing countries. *Applied Economics*, 51(25): 2731–2743.

Ashenfelter, O. C., Hosken, D. S., & Weinberg, M. C. (2013). The price effects of a large merger of manufacturers: A case study of maytag-whirlpool. *American Economic Journal: Economic Policy*, 5(1): 239–261.

[1] Business activity — the intensity of entrepreneurial activities.

[2] Shadow (unobservable, unofficial) economy — economic activities that are conducted with a violation of the laws. It is not considered by statistics and includes tax evasion.

Bacon, J. M. (2017). 'A lot of catching up', knowledge gaps and emotions in the development of a tactical collective identity among students participating in solidarity with the Winneme Wintu. *Settler Colonial Studies*, 7(4): 441–455.

Berta, N., Gautherat, E., & Gun, O. (2017). Transactions in the European carbon market: A bubble of compliance in a whirlpool of speculation. *Cambridge Journal of Economics*, 41(2): bew041, 575–593.

Bolotin, B. (2001). World Economy in 100 Years. *The World Economy and International Relations*, 9: 98.

Borup, J. (2017). Pizza, curry, skyr and whirlpool affect religious circulations between east and west. *International Studies in Religion and Society*, 29: 13–35.

Bulatov, A. (2014). The global problem of economic underdevelopment. *World and National Economy*, 2(29): 3.

Elida, L. (2018). Preliminary study: The dynamics of local cities in the whirlpool of the global economy in Medan-Siantar-Sibolga. *International Journal of Scientific and Technology Research*, 7(4): 241–245.

Grassetti, F., Mammana, C., & Michetti, E. (2018). Poverty trap, boom and bust periods and growth. A nonlinear model for non-developed and developing countries. *Decisions in Economics and Finance*, 41(2): 145–162.

Gurova, M. V. (2009). The role of intellectual property in overcoming economic underdevelopment. *Bulletin of the Orenburg State University*, 4(98): 64–68.

Hare, P. (2019). Growth and development-catching up. *Acta Oeconomica*, 69: 215–240.

Inshakov, O. V. & Frolov, D. P. (2002). *Institutionalism in Russian Economic Thought.* Volgograd: Volga State University Publishing House.

Karkoulian, S., Mukaddam, W., McCarthy, R., & Messarra, L. C. (2013). Job insecurity: A whirlpool of chronic powerlessness. *Education, Business and Society. Contemporary Middle Eastern Issues*, 6(1): 55–70.

Khavari, S. D., Momeni, F., & Mirjalili, S. H. (2016). Characterizing new structural economics to the explanation of the path of development and catching up a pattern for developing countries. *International Business Management*, 10(20): 4783–4793.

Kindzersky, Y. V. (2010). Features of the development of the institution of property in the system of measures to overcome industrial underdevelopment. *Scientific Works of Donetsk National Technical University. Series: Economic*, 1(38): 61–69.

Laptev, A. V. & Sozinova, A. A. (2018). Analysing "underdevelopment whirlpools" as a tool for managing innovations and the process of reorganization of enterprise structures. *Quality — Access to Success*, 19(S2): 3–7.

Li, Y., Dong, S., Zeng, Q., Zhang, C., Wang, T., & Wang, L. (2019). Development and application of a new type of catching periodic waterflooding technology.

Shiyou Huagong Gaodeng Xuexiao Xuebao/Journal of Petrochemical Universities, 32(1): 1–8.

Luo, Y., Zhang, H., & Bu, J. (2019). Developed country MNEs investing in developing economies: Progress and prospect. *Journal of International Business Studies*, 50(4): 633–667.

Nassif, A., Feijó, C., & Araújo, E. (2015). Structural change and economic development: Is Brazil catching up or falling behind? *Cambridge Journal of Economics*, 39(5): 1307–1332.

Popkova, E. G. (2004a). The spatio-temporal approach in the concept of a new quality of economic growth. *Economic Sciences*, 7: 33–40.

Popkova, E. G. (2004b). Interaction of the concepts of sustainable development and the new quality of economic growth. *Finance and Credit*, 25(163): 43–47.

Popkova, E. G. (2004c). Interaction of the concepts of sustainable development and the new quality of economic growth. *Economic Analysis: Theory and Practice*, 25: 43.

Popkova, E. G. (2005). Formation of the concept of a new quality of economic growth in the context of globalization. Dissertation for the Degree of Doctor of Economics, Penza.

Popkova, E. (2014). New prospects of economic growth in the context of underdevelopment whirlpools phenomena. *Applied Econometrics and International Development*, 14(1): 5–25.

Popkova, E. (2017a). Problem analysis of ‘underdevelopment whirlpools’ as an obstacle for economic growth in Asian countries. *International Journal of Business and Globalisation*, 19(2): 167–174.

Popkova, E. (2017b). Use of methodology of “underdevelopment whirlpools” with analysis of problems and perspectives of economic growth in Asian countries. *Journal of Entrepreneurship in Emerging Economies*, 9(1), DOI:10.1108/JEEE-07-2016-0027.

Popkova, E., Gornostaeva, Z., & Tregulova, N. (2018). Role of innovations in the provision of competitiveness and innovational development of economy and overcoming of “underdevelopment whirlpools” in Russia and countries of Eastern Europe. *Journal of Entrepreneurship in Emerging Economies*, 10(3): 511–523.

Safronov, A. (2009). The comprador bourgeoisie and the problem of “economic underdevelopment”. *Free Thought*, 12(1607): 77–92.

Schuh, G. E. (2003). Can lagging countries catch up? *Agrekon*, 42(2): 95–105.

Semenov, A. S. & Derunov, V. A. (2016). Mathematical substantiation of economic growth in the conditions of the country falling into the “underdevelopment whirlpools”. *Bulletin of the Saratov University. New series. Series: Economics Control Law*, 16(3): 288–293.

Shakhovskaya, L. S. & Popkova, E. G. (2004). New quality of economic growth in the context of modern globalization. *Finance and Credit*, 23(16): 71–77.

Younsi, M. & Nafla, A. (2019). Financial stability, monetary policy, and economic growth: Panel data evidence from developed and developing countries. *Journal of the Knowledge Economy*, 10(1): 238–260.

Zabrodotsky, Y. (2006). Anatomy of underdevelopment and corruption. *Economic Strategies*, 8.7(49): 42–47.

Chapter 13

Methodology for Studying and Measuring "Underdevelopment Whirlpools": Time Is Measurable

The great science to live happily is to live in the present.

Pythagoras of Samos, ancient Ionian Greek philosopher

This chapter states that time is a tool for the analysis of the global economy.

This chapter considers the following topics:

- scientific and methodological approaches to measuring economic time (Figure 1);
- depth as a static parameter of "underdevelopment whirlpool";
- speed of sucking or overcoming as a dynamic parameter of "underdevelopment whirlpool".

Time is the decisive factor of human life, and thus the issues related to measuring it were always a subject of serious attention. At first, humans used the Sun to measure time during the day and observed the movement of stars in the sky to measure time during longer periods (week, month, and year).

In Ancient Egypt, there were astrological observatories, the main task of which was measuring time. Ancient Greeks used a sun clock, which allowed determining time by the position of a wand's shadow on a semisphere. Also, people invented and used the sand clock, fire clock, and water clock, until the mechanical clock was invented in the 18th century.

Figure 1. Time is measurable.

Source: Photo by scholar and photographer Elena Popkova, https://www.saatchiart.com/account/artworks/1599809.

At present, mechanical clocks are gradually being ousted by an improved alternative, an electronic watch, which is built into various technical devices. Thus, the problem of measuring astronomical time has been successfully solved, but the problem of measuring economic time remains.

When solving this problem, it is necessary to answer two questions.

The first question is, "What is time in economics?" Modern economic science usually applied the theory of innovation when answering this question. For example, at the level of the global economy, this theory is used to determine the current technological mode and the corresponding technologies, which are used by most economic systems. As of 2019, the third technological mode dominated the economy, within which digital technologies of non-intellectual automatization of labour are used (PCs and Internet).

When we consider a country's economic activities if the technologies of the third mode have been used, we state that the country is in the present time. If the technologies of the previous technological mode (pre-digital) are used, then the country is considered to be in the past time. If the economy uses the technologies of the next (fourth) technological mode (Industry 4.0) and the intellectual automatization of labour based on robots, the Internet of Things, and artificial intelligence is implemented, then the country is in the present time; if technologies of Industry 4.0 (machine learning, robots, technologies of virtual and augmented reality, unmanned transport) are used, the economy is considered to be in the future time.

Measuring of economic time through the lens of technological mode is performed in the works of Inshakov & Frolov (2005), Inshakov & Mitrofanova (2007), Inshakov *et al.* (2008, 2014, 2015), Inshakov & Fesyun (2014a, 2014b), Inshakov & Inshakova (2015, 2016), and Inshakov & Kryukova (2015).

The second question is, "What is the speed of economic time?" It is a more difficult question to answer since the course of astronomical time is always the same and is determined by the speed of the Earth's rotation around its axis and around the Sun, which, does not change — though fundamental studies in the sphere of physics draw the connection between the *speed of time* and its density. The psychological perception of the *speed of time* depending on the intensity of thoughts and events in a person's life cannot be measured in terms of economics.

When analyzing the *speed of time* (dynamics characteristic) in economics, as well as determining its current value (static characteristic), we usually use the theory of innovation, in particular, technological revolutions. The shorter the period between the previous and current industrial revolutions, the faster the technological progress and, therefore, the faster the economic time.

Measuring the speed of economic time through the lens of the speed of change of technological modes (beginning of industrial revolutions) is performed in the works of Shakhovskaya & Popkova (2004), Popkova (2004a, 2004b, 2004c, 2005, 2019), Zabrodotsky (2006), Gurova (2009), Safronov (2009), Kindzersky (2010), Bulatov (2014), Semenov & Derunov (2016), Allen (2019), Kellyand Ó Gráda (2019), Lojanica *et al.* (2019), Nagano (2019), and Singhal & Singhal (2019).

As shown in Figure 2, the First Industrial Revolution took place in the 18th/early 19th centuries. It led to the establishment of industry. The Second Industrial Revolution took place in the late 19th/early 20th

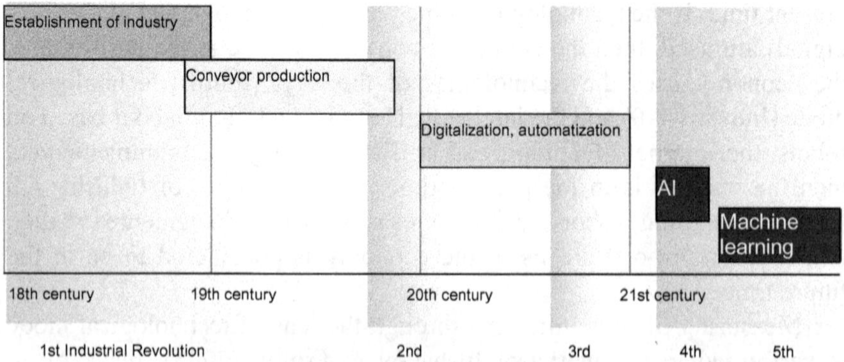

Figure 2. Chronogram of the economy through the lens of the speed of the change of technological modes (beginning of industrial revolutions).

centuries. It led to the development of conveyor production. The Third Industrial Revolution took place in the late 20th century. It ensured digitalization and automatization. The Fourth Industrial Revolution began in 2011 and continues until now. Its most important manifestation is the creation and dissemination of AI and cyber-physical systems that function based on AI (e.g., the Internet of Things).

The periods between industrial revolutions are not constant. The period from the First to the Second Industrial Revolution is designated as t_1; from the Second to the Third Industrial Revolution — t_2. Since $t_1 > t_2$, economic time slowed down in the 20th century. The period between the Third and Fourth Industrial Revolutions is designated as t_3. Since $t_3 < t_2$, economic time accelerated in the 21st century.

A serious drawback in the determination of the current time and measuring of the speed of economic time with the help of the theory of innovation is low precision. The process of determining the technological mode is always subjective. In addition to this, the comparison of economic systems that belong to the same technological mode is complicated, since in practice the level and rate of their socio-economic and innovative development could be very different.

This drawback is overcome during the determination of current time and measuring the speed of economic time with the help of the theory of economic cycles. In this case, the process of measuring economic time is closer to the process of measuring astronomical (physical) time, since the course of time is cyclical, not linear (as within the theory of innovation).

The economic system's being at a certain phase of the economic cycle determines its current time, and the frequency of repetition of the economic cycle shows the speed of economic time. Measuring the speed of economic time through the lens of an increase in the frequency of repetition of the economic cycle is performed in the works of Chian *et al.* (2007), Dini (2015), Botero (2016), Wong *et al.* (2016), Calderón Villarreal & Hernández Bielma (2017), and van Giesen & Pieters (2019). According to these works, the chronogram of the economy is shown in Figure 3.

As shown in Figure 3, the frequency of repetition of the cyclical fluctuations of the world GDP in 1960–2018 constantly decreases, $t_3 < t_2 < t_1$, which is a sign of the acceleration of economic time. Though the precision of determining economic time and its speed is higher when relying on the methodology of the Theory of Economic Cycles, the informative value of the analysis results is low due to the impossibility to compare different economic systems.

For example, the economic system's being in the phase of decline does not mean that the level of its socio-economic and innovative development is lower than the system that is in the phase of rise — a

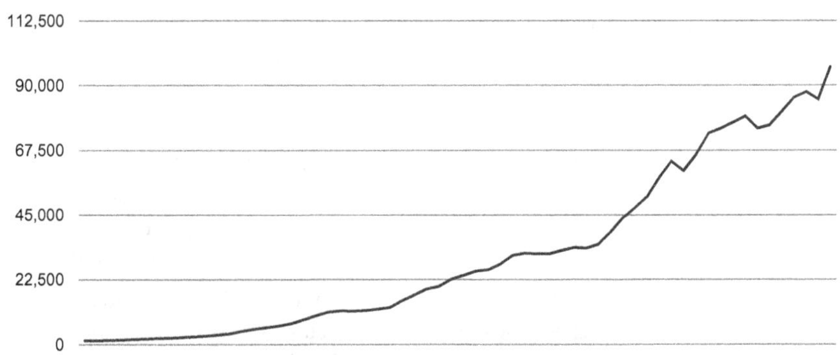

Figure 3. The chronogram of the economy through the lens of its cyclical fluctuations by the example of the dynamics of world GDP in 1960–2018, USD trillion in current prices.

Source: Based on World Bank (2023).

directly opposite situation is possible in practice. Similarly, the acceleration of the cyclical fluctuations of an economic system is not direct proof of either the increase or decrease of the level of its socio-economic and innovative development as compared to other systems.

The drawbacks of both approaches (innovative and cyclical) are overcome within the offered new approach to measuring economic time — conical ("cone-shaped") — which allows for the simultaneous achievement of high precision of analysis and high informativeness of its results. The comparative analysis of the existing and offered (new) approaches to measuring economic time is performed in Table 1.

Table 1. Comparative analysis of the existing and offered (new) approaches to measuring economic time.

	Innovative approach	**Cyclical approach**	**Conical approach**
Theoretical and methodological basis	Theory of innovation	Theory of economic cycles	Theory of economic growth
View at a course of time	Linear	Cyclical	Linear
Object of analysis	Technological progress	Economic cycle	Economic growth
Object of analysis	Technological mode	Phase of the economic cycle	Gross domestic product per capita (GDP per capita)
Method of analysis	Comparative analysis	Trend analysis	Analysis of "under-development whirlpools"
Method of determining the current time	Comparison of the technological mode of the considered system with the average for the world	Determination of the current phase of the system's economic cycle	Calculation of the depth of "under-development whirlpool" by comparing the GDP per capita of the system and the sample

Table 1. (*Continued*)

	Innovative approach	Cyclical approach	Conical approach
Method of determining the *speed of time*	Comparison of the periods between industrial revolutions	Evaluation of the frequency of the change of economic cycles	Calculation of the speed of sucking into or over-coming of "underdevelop-ment whirlpool" by comparing its current and past depths
Precision of analysis and informativeness of its results	Low precision due to the subjectivity of analysis, high informativeness due to the possibility to compare different systems	High precision due to the objectivity of analysis, low informative-ness due to the impossibility to compare different systems	High precision due to the objectivity of analysis, high informativeness due to the possibility to compare different systems

As shown in Table 1, according to the conical ("cone-shaped") approach, which is based on the theory of economic growth, the course of time is considered to be linear. The logic of this provision, which is the basis of the conical ("cone-shaped") approach, is as follows: economic growth is always forward-oriented, i.e., it is oriented at the future: stops and declines (crises) do not change the general growing linear tendency. The object of the analysis is GDP per capita as the main indicator of economic growth.

The advantage of using this indicator during the analysis is the compatibility of the data of various economic systems (unlike GDP, during the analysis of which there's a need for classification of systems by the scale of the economy). The analysis method is the analysis of "underdevelopment whirlpools". A method of determining the current time of the economic system is the calculation of the depth of the "underdevelopment whirlpool" by comparing the GDP per capita of the system and the sample.

The method of determining the *speed of time* is a calculation of the speed of sucking into or overcoming an "underdevelopment whirlpool" by comparing its current and past depth. This allows for high precision due to the objectivity of analysis and high informativeness due to the possibility to compare different systems. The parameters for measuring "underdevelopment whirlpools" are shown in Figure 4.

As shown in Figure 4, an "underdevelopment whirlpool" has two parameters:

- *Depth* (*D*): Static parameter of "underdevelopment whirlpool" (measured in years);
- *Speed of sucking into or overcoming* (*S*): Dynamic parameter of "underdevelopment whirlpool" (measured in years per one year).

Let us consider the algorithm for calculating "underdevelopment whirlpools". A preliminary (zero) stage envisages the determination of the considered economic system (α) and the sample economic system (β),

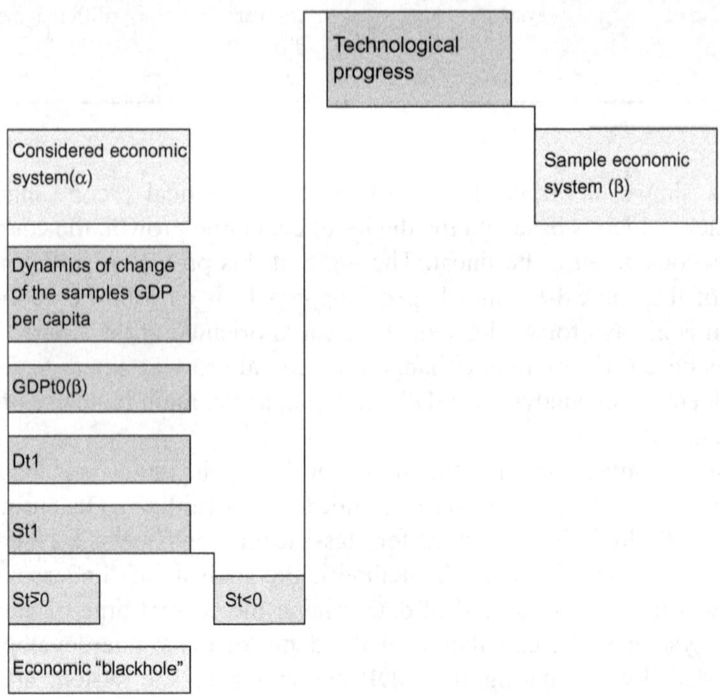

Figure 4. Parameters for measuring "underdevelopment whirlpools".

which should exceed the considered system by the level and rate of socio-economic and innovative development. In the first stage, the dynamics of change of GDP per capita of the sample economic system during several recent decades is determined (the higher the better).

In the second stage, the period of time ($\text{GDP}t_{1(\circledR)}$) in which the sample economic system has the same level of GDP per capita as with the considered economic system at the moment of time t_1 ($\text{GDP}t_{1(()}$) is determined, at which ($\text{GDP}t_{1(\circledR)}$) $\geq$ ($\text{GDP}t_{1(()}$). In the third stage, the difference between the current year (t_1) and $\text{GDP}t_{1(\circledR)}$ is calculated — this is the depth of the "underdevelopment whirlpool" ($\text{D}t_1$). In the fourth stage, the difference between the depth of the "underdevelopment whirlpool" in the current year ($\text{D}t_1$) and the previous year ($\text{D}t_0$) is calculated, which is the speed of sucking into the "underdevelopment whirlpool" ($\text{S}t_1$). If $\text{S}t_1 > 0$, the system is sucked into the "underdevelopment whirlpool". If $\text{S}t_1 < 0$, the system overcomes the "underdevelopment whirlpool". If $\text{S}t_1 = 0$, the "underdevelopment whirlpool" remains unchanged.

The scientific and methodological recommendations on measuring the speed of economic time through the lens of "underdevelopment whirlpools" and examples of their calculation based on the experience of the modern economic systems are provided in the works of Popkova (2014, 2017a, 2017b), and Popkova *et al.* (2018). According to the conical ("cone-shaped") approach, the chronogram of the economy is shown in Table 2.

Table 2. Chronogram of the economy through the lens of "underdevelopment whirlpools": the time asymmetry of economic development.

Depth of "underdevelopment whirlpool"	**Depth of "underdevelopment whirlpool" by years**				
	t_0	t_1	t_2	t_3	t_n
0	$\text{D}t_0 = 0$				
1		$\text{D}t_1 = 1$ $\text{S}t_1 = 1$			
2					$\text{D}t_n = 2$ $\text{S}t_n = -2$
3			$\text{D}t_2 = 3$ $\text{S}t_2 = 2$		
+n				$\text{D}t_3 = \text{n}$ $\text{S}t_3 = 1$	

As shown in Table 2, the chronogram of the economy through the lens of "underdevelopment whirlpools" is a time asymmetry of economic development. At the initial period (t_0), the depth of the "underdevelopment whirlpool" is zero ($Dt_0=0$). In the next period (t_1), "underdevelopment whirlpool" increased by 1 year ($Dt_1=1$), and the speed of sucking into the "underdevelopment whirlpool" was 1 year per 1 year ($St_1=Dt_1-Dt_0=1-0=1$). Then, in the period (t_2), the "underdevelopment whirlpool" further increased ($Dt_2=3$), and the speed of sucking into the "whirlpool" increased up to 2 years per 1 year ($St_2=Dt_2-Dt_1=3-1=2$). Then, in the period ($t_{\ldots 3}$), the "underdevelopment whirlpool" further increased ($Dt_3=\mathrm{n}$), and the speed of sucking into the "whirlpool" reduced down to 1 year per 1 year ($St_3=Dt_3-Dt_2=3-1=2$). In the final period (t_{n}), the depth of the "underdevelopment whirlpool" was reduced to 2 years ($Dt_{\mathrm{n}}=2$), and the speed of overcoming the "underdevelopment whirlpool" was 2 years per 1 year ($St_{\mathrm{n}}=Dt_{\mathrm{n}}-Dt_3=n-2=-2$).

Thus, time is a tool for analyzing the structure of the global economy (determining its disproportions) and analyzing the dynamics of economic systems' development and their position in the global economy. Economic time could and should be measured — but it is more difficult to do this as compared to astronomical time. The existing scientific and methodological approaches to measuring economic time do not fully conform to the needs of modern science, do not ensure high precision, and do not allow comparing economic systems by their economic time.

These drawbacks could be overcome with the help of the conical ("cone-shaped") approach, which envisages the calculation of "underdevelopment whirlpools". This allows for a precise determination of the underrun of one economic system from another (sample) in years (depth of the "underdevelopment whirlpool" as an answer to the question "what is the time in the economy?") and for the determination of the dynamics of the underrun (speed of sucking into or overcoming of the "underdevelopment whirlpool" as an answer to the question: "what is the *speed of time* in the economy?").

References

Allen, R. C. (2019). Class structure and inequality during the industrial revolution: Lessons from England's social tables, 1688–1867. *Economic History Review*, 72(1): 88–125.

Botero, D. I. R. (2016). Bolivia: From the economic crisis to the "Rebel Cycle", 2000–2005. *Anuario Colombiano de Historia Social y de la Cultura*, 43(1): 295–322.

Bulatov, A. (2014). The global problem of economic underdevelopment. *World and National Economy*, 2(29): 3.

Calderón Villarreal, C. & Hernández Bielma, L. (2017). Economic integration, economic crises, and business cycles in Mexico. *Contaduria y Administracion*, 62(1): 64–84.

Chian, A. C.-L., Rempel, E. L., & Rogers, C. (2007). Crisis-induced intermittency in non-linear economic cycles. *Applied Economics Letters*, 14(3): 211–218.

Dini, F. (2015). Economic cycle and crisis among Kuznets, Piketty, and the Geography. *Rivista Geografica Italiana* 122(4): 611–620.

Gurova, M. V. (2009). The role of intellectual property in overcoming economic underdevelopment. *Bulletin of the Orenburg State University*, 4(98): 64–68.

Inshakov, O. V. & Fesyun, A. V. (2014a). Impact of Russia's accession to the WTO on the development of the national nano industry. In *Modernization of the Economic System of the Southern Macroregion in the Conditions of the WTO: A Collective Monograph*. Moscow: Volgograd State University, pp. 9–28.

Inshakov, O. V. & Fesyun, A. V. (2014b). The industry as a form of establishment, distribution and domination of the economic structure in the economy. *Bulletin of the Volgograd State University. Series 3: Economics. Ecology*, 2(1): 44–53.

Inshakov, O. V. & Frolov, D. P. (2005). Institutional factions in modern society. In *Institutional Man*. Volgograd: Russian Academy of Sciences, Department of Social Sciences, Southern Scientific Center of the Russian Academy of Sciences, Volgograd State University, pp. 37–59.

Inshakov, O. V. & Inshakova, E. I. (2015). Reconstruction of RF nano industry institutions in an unfavourable global environment. *Bulletin of the Volgograd State University. Series 3: Economics. Ecology*, 4(1): 7–17.

Inshakov, O. V. & Inshakova, E. I. (2016). Development of the world and Russian nano industry: Results and problems. *Economic Science of Modern Russia*, 4(1): 65–78.

Inshakov, O. V. *et al.* (2008). *Modernization of the Economy of the South of Russia. Problems, Priorities, Projects*. Moscow: Russian Academy of Sciences, Southern Scientific Center.

Inshakov, O. V., Inshakova, E. I., & Kryukova, E. V. (2014). Special economic zones as an institution for the development of the nano industry: Essence, structure, improvement. *Bulletin of the Volgograd State University. Series 3: Economics. Ecology*, 6(1): 81–95.

Inshakov, O. V., Inshakova, E. I., & Fesyun, A. V. (2015). Nanoindustrialization as a stage in the formation of a new economic order in Russia. Grant research and educational activities. In *Goals, Technologies, Results: Collective*

Monograph in 9 Volumes. Limited Liability Company International Research Center "Scientific Cooperation", Rostov-on-Don. pp. 76–106.

Inshakov, O. V. & Kryukova, E. V. (2015). Special economic zones as an institution for the development of the nano industry: Failures, problems and prospects. *Bulletin of the Volgograd State University. Series 3: Economics. Ecology*, 1(1): 6–17.

Inshakov, O. V. & Mitrofanova, I. V. (2007). The modern look of the economic complex in the south of Russia. *Regional Economy: Theory and Practice*, 11(1): 3–14.

Kelly, M. & Ó Gráda, C. (2019). Speed under sail during the early industrial revolution (1750–1830). *Economic History Review*, 72(2): 459–480.

Kindzersky, Y. V. (2010). Features of the development of the institution of property in the system of measures to overcome industrial underdevelopment. *Scientific Works of Donetsk National Technical University. Series: Economic*, 1(38): 61–69.

Lojanica, V., Colic-Damjanovic, V.-M., & Jankovic, N. (2019). The housing of the future: Housing design of the fourth industrial revolution. *Proceedings of the 2018 5th International Symposium on Environment-Friendly Energies and Applications*, EFEA 2018, 8617094.

Nagano, A. (2019). Thinking about industrial revolutions in systems theory — Moving towards the fourth industrial revolution. *ACM International Conference Proceeding Series*, Part F148155, pp. 470–471.

Popkova, E. G. (2004a). The spatio-temporal approach in the concept of a new quality of economic growth. *Economic Sciences*, 7: 33–40.

Popkova, E. G. (2004b). Interaction of the concepts of sustainable development and the new quality of economic growth. *Finance and Credit*, 25(163): 43–47.

Popkova, E. G. (2004c). Interaction of the concepts of sustainable development and the new quality of economic growth. *Economic Analysis: Theory and Practice*, 25: 43.

Popkova, E. G. (2005). Formation of the Concept of a New Quality of Economic Growth in the Context of Globalization. Dissertation for the degree of Doctor of Economics, Penza.

Popkova, E. (2014). New prospects of economic growth in the context of underdevelopment whirlpools phenomena. *Applied Econometrics and International Development*, 14(1): 5–25.

Popkova, E. (2017a). Problem analysis of 'underdevelopment whirlpools' as an obstacle for economic growth in Asian countries. *International Journal of Business and Globalisation*, 19(2): 167–174.

Popkova, E. (2017b). Use of methodology of "underdevelopment whirlpools" with analysis of problems and perspectives of economic growth in Asian countries. *Journal of Entrepreneurship in Emerging Economies*, 9(1): DOI:10.1108/JEEE-07-2016-0027.

Popkova, E. G. (2019). Preconditions of formation and development of industry 4.0 in the conditions of the knowledge economy. *Studies in Systems, Decision and Control*, 169: 65–72.

Popkova, E., Gornostaeva, Z., & Tregulova, N. (2018). Role of innovations in the provision of competitiveness and innovational development of economy and overcoming of "underdevelopment whirlpools" in Russia and countries of Eastern Europe. *Journal of Entrepreneurship in Emerging Economies*, 10(3): 511–523.

Safronov, A. (2009). The comprador bourgeoisie and the problem of "economic underdevelopment". *Free Thought*, 12(1607): 77–92.

Semenov, A. S. & Derunov, V. A. (2016). Mathematical substantiation of economic growth in the conditions of the country falling into the "trap of underdevelopment". *Bulletin of the Saratov University. New series. Series: Economics. Control. Law*, 16(3): 288–293.

Shakhovskaya, L. S. & Popkova, E. G. (2004). New quality of economic growth in the context of modern globalization. *Finance and Credit*, 23(16): 71–77.

Singhal, K. & Singhal, J. (2019). Technology and manufacturing in China before the industrial revolution and glimpses of the future. *Production and Operations Management*, 28(3): 505–515.

Van Giesen, R. I. & Pieters, R. (2019). Climbing out of an economic crisis: A cycle of consumer sentiment and personal stress. *Journal of Economic Psychology*, 70: 109–124.

Wong, S. S.-L., Puah, C.-H., Abu Mansor, S., & Liew, V. K.-S. (2016). Measuring business cycle fluctuations: An alternative precursor to economic crises. *Economic Computation and Economic Cybernetics Studies and Research*, 50(4): 235–248.

World Bank. (2023). GDP (current US$). https://data.worldbank.org/indicator/NY.GDP.MKTP.CD. Accessed: 05 January 2023.

Zabrodotsky, Y. (2006). Anatomy of underdevelopment and corruption. *Economic Strategies*, 8.7(49): 42–47.

Chapter 14

“Underdevelopment Whirlpools” as a Tool for Macroeconomic Analysis: Time Is a Method of Creation and Destruction

Even as we speak, time speeds swiftly away.

Horace, Roman lyric poet

This chapter states that time is a tool for managing the global economy’s development.

This chapter considers the following topics:

- substantiating the advantages of the dynamic cone-shaped model of an economy’s development;
- calculating the “underdevelopment whirlpool” in the modern Russian economy;
- three-dimensional modelling of the process of the modern Russian economy’s sucking into the “underdevelopment whirlpool” (Figure 1).

The history of mankind had numerous economic collapses; many of the greatest economic systems were destroyed and forgotten. The most vivid examples are overwhelming economic crises, which led to the abandonment of the economic systems of Maya (Indian civilization in Central America), Easter Island (an island in the South-East Pacific, the modern territory of Chile), Pueblo (Indian settlement in the South-West of the modern USA), Indus Civilization (valley of the Indus River, the modern territory of India), Mesopotamia (territory divided by the modern Iraq and Syria), and the Mycenaean civilization (Ancient Greece).

Figure 1. Time is a method of creation and destruction.

Source: Photo by scholar and photographer Elena Popkova, https://www.saatchiart.com/account/artworks/1599809.

In all these examples, the economies reached their peak but collapsed over time. Their experience could be useful during the research of the process of the modern economic systems' development under the influence of the time factor. "Underdevelopment whirlpools" could be a tool for macroeconomic analysis. Their advantages are determined by the author of this book in cooperation with Sokolov (Ph.D.), a business consultant for the European Bank for Reconstruction and Development.

First, "underdevelopment whirlpools" allow taking into account the impact of the time factor on the development of economic systems, acknowledging its indirect role. The national economy is dynamic, i.e., it is in constant movement. This is stated in the works of Semenov & Derunov (2016), Eke *et al.* (2018), Wei & Yang (2018), Wei & Yu (2018), Xu *et al.* (2018), and Aydin & Esen (2019).

That's why time is not a feature that directly determines the dynamics of the economy. It determines economic development only indirectly, through the participation of time characteristics in the formula of such indicators as speed. The indicator of "density of time" is actually very close to the speed. Such a parameter as "speed" is very close to reflecting the dynamic characteristics of the economy.

The methodology of "underdevelopment whirlpools" allows measuring the time of economic systems' development (speed of sucking into a "whirlpool"), due to which it reflects not just their change in time (as during the traditional — e.g., horizontal or trend — macroeconomic analysis) but their change under the impact of the time factor. That is, during the calculation of "underdevelopment whirlpools", time is not a parameter but a factor, due to which the calculation and analysis of "underdevelopment whirlpools" is not just a tool of the theory of economic growth but also a tool of the Theory of Time in economics.

Second, the methodology of "underdevelopment whirlpools" allows for determining the dynamics of change of the considered economic system's positions as to the sample one (not only as to itself) and interpreting graphically the results of the analysis for the convenience of their qualitative treatment. The linear model with the use of speed indicators is not convenient due to noncompactness. This is confirmed in the following works: Zabrodotsky (2006), Safronov (2009), Vitlinskyy *et al.* (2012), Oliveira *et al.* (2016), West (2017), and Sørensen (2018). That's why a model of a whirlpool with constant rotation is preferable. Such a model allows setting the angular rate of rotation as a parameter that reflects the dynamic characteristics of the economy. In physics, angular rate characterizes the speed of an item's rotation and is measured in radians per second.

Besides, the whirlpool envisages the dependence of the diameter of rotation on the angular rate or the dependence of the angular rate on diameter. That's why a more powerful and dynamic economy in the whirlpool is located closer to its centre, having a large angular rate. In this model, GDP per capita is used as the main indicator. Of course, this indicator does not fully reflect the dynamic processes in the economy, but it allows an understanding of the model. The most developed economies are located closer to the centre of the whirlpool, which envisages the largest angular rate of rotation.

Third, the methodology of "underdevelopment whirlpools" allows using various characteristics of time (static and dynamic), "tuning" the dynamic model of the economic system's development to perform its necessary analysis. In the dynamic model of rotation, it could take place at various levels of the whirlpool, i.e., at various radiuses and with various speeds. The time spent at a certain level could be unlimited and is determined by the dynamics. The higher the dynamics, the longer the period of change of GDP per capita in a certain direction and the more probable either centripetal or axifugal transition in the whirlpool.

The economy, which has organic (by means of internal capabilities) growth, possesses centripetal dynamics. This conclusion is confirmed by the results of the studies of Gurova (2009), Kindzersky (2010), Bulatov (2014), Balakrishnan *et al.* (2017), Borozan (2017), Recio *et al.* (2018), and Panshak *et al.* (2019).

However, "all dynamically developing economies are dynamic", so a centre that is constantly moving increases its angular rate and thus sets it as a normative structure and dynamics of the system on the whole. This determines the general dynamics of the whole model, which is constantly moving. The indicators of growth, which coincide with the general world dynamics, determine a stable position of the considered economic system concerning the sample system and a stable level of rotation or radius, in the whirlpool. This is stability, which is "relative from the point of view of dynamics". In this state, an economy, which functions stably, could occupy its place for a very long time. That's why the indicator of time is secondary.

Fourth is the methodology of "underdevelopment whirlpools" which opens a possibility for multi-dimensional macroeconomic analysis. Professor Oleg V. Inshakov notes in his works the close interconnection between spatial and time characteristics of economic systems. As an example, we could consider the work of Inshakov and Frolov (2005). According to the works, an "underdevelopment whirlpool" is a tool for determining economic chronotopes — regularities of time-space development of economic systems. This allows for a systemic study of economic systems' development: in time and space.

The works of Popkova (2004a, 2004b, 2004c, 2005), Shakhovskaya & Popkova (2004), and Popkova *et al.* (2011) suggest a classification of "underdevelopment whirlpools" by a range of qualitative and quantitative criteria (Table 1).

As shown in Table 1, the volatile "whirlpools" (less dangerous) have a short (no more than 10 years) duration of an economic system's being in the "underdevelopment whirlpool". The institutional reason for the

Table 1. Classification of "underdevelopment whirlpools".

	Volatile "whirlpools"	**Structural "whirlpools"**
Duration of the economic system's being in the "underdevelopment whirlpool"	Short (less than 10 years)	Long (10+ years) with a risk of emergence of an economic "black hole"
Institutional reason for emergence of "underdevelopment whirlpools"	Distortion of the work of certain markets' mechanisms (separate "institutional traps")	Systemic problems in an economy (multiple "institutional traps")
Perspectives of the market overcoming "under-development whirlpools"	Wide	Limited
Method of overcoming "underdevelopment whirlpools"	Improvement of the work of certain market mechanisms	Change of technological mode (industrial revolution)
Social consequences of "underdevelopment whirlpools"	Temporary (reversible) moderate reduction of quality of life	Critical reduction of quality of life, risk of a social crisis

Source: Based on Popkova *et al.* (2011).

emergence of "underdevelopment whirlpools" is the distortion of the mechanism of work of certain markets (separate "institutional traps"). The perspectives of the market overcoming "underdevelopment whirlpools" are wide. A method of overcoming the "underdevelopment whirlpools" is the improvement of the work of market mechanisms. The social consequences of "underdevelopment whirlpools" are connected to a temporary (reversible) reduction of quality of life.

Structural "whirlpools" (more dangerous) have a larger (10+ years) duration of an economic system's being in the "underdevelopment whirlpool" with a risk of emergence of an economic "black hole". The institutional reason for the emergence of "underdevelopment whirlpools" is the systemic problems in the economy (multiple "institutional traps"). The perspectives of the market overcoming "underdevelopment whirlpools" are limited. A method of overcoming "underdevelopment whirlpools" is the change of the technological mode (industrial revolution). The social consequences of "underdevelopment whirlpools" include a critical reduction of quality of life and a risk of a social crisis.

Let us use the methodology of "underdevelopment whirlpools" for the macroeconomic analysis of the impact of the time factor on the development of one of the most progressive modern economic systems, Russia (2% in the structure of world GDP in 2022). The sample economic system is the leader by the share in the world GDP (23%), the USA. The dynamics of the US GDP per capita in 1960–2021 are given in Table 2.

Table 2. Dynamics of the US GDP per capita in 1960–2021.

Year	GDP per capita, $ trillion	Year	GDP per capita, $ trillion	Year	GDP per capita, $ trillion
1960	3,007.12	1981	13,976.11	2002	37,997.76
1961	3,066.56	1982	14,433.79	2003	39,490.27
1962	3,243.84	1983	15,543.89	2004	41,724.63
1963	3,374.52	1984	17,121.23	2005	44,123.41
1964	3,573.94	1985	18,236.83	2006	46,302.00
1965	3,827.53	1986	19,071.23	2007	48,050.22
1966	4,146.32	1987	20,038.94	2008	48,570.05
1967	4,336.43	1988	21,417.01	2009	47,194.94
1968	4,695.92	1989	22,857.15	2010	48,650.64
1969	5,032.14	1990	23,888.60	2011	50,065.97
1970	5,234.30	1991	24,342.26	2012	51,784.42
1971	5,609.38	1992	25,418.99	2013	53,291.13
1972	6,094.02	1993	26,387.29	2014	55,123.85
1973	6,726.36	1994	27,694.85	2015	56,762.73
1974	7,225.69	1995	28,690.88	2016	57,866.74
1975	7,801.46	1996	29,967.71	2017	59,907.75
1976	8,592.25	1997	31,459.14	2018	62,823.31
1977	9,452.58	1998	32,853.68	2019	65,120.39
1978	10,564.95	1999	34,515.39	2020	63,530.63
1979	11,674.18	2000	36,329.96	2021	70,248.63
1980	12,574.79	2001	37,133.62		

Source: Based on World Bank (2019).

Based on the data from Table 2, we determine the values of GDPt(β) in Table 2, in which the calculation of "underdevelopment whirlpools" of Russia is performed. The period of calculation is very wide (as the statistical data allow) and covers all stages of the formation of the modern Russian economy:

- soviet stage (1988–1990);
- stage of the market reformation of the economy (1991–2004), including the default in 1992 and 1999;
- stage of digital modernization and transition to the Fourth technological mode (2005–2021), including the crisis of the Russian economy under the impact of the Great Recession in 2008–2010, as well as the COVID-19 global economic crisis.

Table 3. Calculation of "underdevelopment whirlpools" in Russia in 1988–2021.

t	Year	GDP$t_{(\alpha)}$, $ billion	GDP$t_{(\beta)}$	Dt, years	St, years per 1 year
t_0	1988	3,777.24	1965	23	—
t_1	1989	3,428.76	1964	25	2
t_2	1990	3,492.71	1963	27	2
t_3	1991	3,490.45	1963	28	1
t_4	1992	3,098.80	1960	32	4
t_5	1993	2,930.67	1960	33	1
t_6	1994	2,662.10	1960	34	1
t_7	1995	2,665.78	1960	35	1
t_8	1996	2,643.93	1960	36	1
t_9	1997	2,737.57	1960	37	1
t_{10}	1998	1,834.86	1960	38	1
t_{11}	1999	1,330.76	1960	39	1
t_{12}	2000	1,771.59	1960	40	1
t_{13}	2001	2,100.35	1960	41	1
t_{14}	2002	2,377.53	1960	42	1
t_{15}	2003	2,975.13	1960	43	1
t_{16}	2004	4,102.36	1966	38	−5
t_{17}	2005	5,323.46	1970	35	−3

(*Continued*)

Table 3. (*Continued*)

t	Year	$GDPt_{(\alpha)}$, $ billion	$GDPt_{(\beta)}$	Dt, years	St, years per 1 year
t_{18}	2006	6,920.19	1973	33	−2
t_{19}	2007	9,101.25	1977	30	−3
t_{20}	2008	11,635.27	1979	29	−1
t_{21}	2009	8,562.81	1976	33	4
t_{22}	2010	10,675.00	1978	32	−1
t_{23}	2011	14,311.08	1982	29	−3
t_{24}	2012	15,420.88	1983	29	0
t_{25}	2013	15,974.64	1983	30	1
t_{26}	2014	14,095.65	1982	32	2
t_{27}	2015	9,313.01	1977	38	6
t_{28}	2016	8,704.90	1976	40	2
t_{29}	2017	10,720.33	1978	39	−1
t_{30}	2018	11,287.36	1979	39	0
t_{31}	2019	11,536.25	1979	40	1
t_{32}	2020	10,169.09	1978	42	2
t_{33}	2021	12,194.78	1980	41	−1

Source: Based on World Bank (2023).

Let us consider an example of calculations in Table 3. In 1988, Russia's GDP was $3,77.24 billion. That is, $t_0 = 1988$, $GDPt_{0(\alpha)} = \$3,777.24$ billion. The US GDP's value slightly exceeded $GDPt_{0(\alpha)}$ in 1965 ($3,827.53 billion), i.e., $GDPt_{0(\beta)} = 1965$. This allows calculating the depth of "underdevelopment whirlpools": $Dt_0 = t_0 - GDPt_{0(\beta)} = 1988 - 1965 = 23$ years.

In 1989, Russia's GDP was $3,428.76 billion. That is, $t_1 = 1989$ г., $GDPt_{1(\alpha)} = \$3,428.76$ billion. The US GDP's value slightly exceeded the value of $GDPt_{1(\alpha)}$ in 1964 ($3,573.94 billion). i.e., $GDPt_{1(\beta)} = 1964$. This allows calculating the depth of "underdevelopment whirlpool": $Dt_1 = t_1 - ВДНt_{1(\beta)} = 1989 - 1964 = 25$ years. The speed of the Russian economy's sucking in the "underdevelopment whirlpool" in 1989 was as follows: $St_1 = Dt_1 - Dt_0 = 25 - 23 = 2$ years per 1 year. Further on, calculations are performed similarly. The chronogram of the Russian economy through the lens of "underdevelopment whirlpools" as a time asymmetry of its economic development is reflected in Figure 2.

Figure 2. Chronogram of the economy through the lens of "underdevelopment whirlpools": the time asymmetry of economic development.

For clarity, the depth of "underdevelopment whirlpools" is shown with a negative sign, for the "whirlpool" to deepen down, and its overcoming to be reflected by a rise. As shown in Figure 2, the largest depth of "underdevelopment whirlpools" was observed in 2003 (43 years), and the smallest in 1988 (23 years). Since the duration of the Russian economic system's being in the "underdevelopment whirlpool" is not less than 10 years, namely 31 years, the "whirlpool" is structural. Dynamics of the depth of Russia's "underdevelopment whirlpools" in 1988–2021 are shown in Figure 3.

As shown in Figure 3, the dynamics of the depth of Russia's "underdevelopment whirlpools" in 1988–2021 conform to the cone-shaped form, which is a sign of the Russian economic system's sucking into the "whirlpool". The three-dimensional graph of the development of the Russian economy from the positions of the time, GDP, and depth of the "whirlpool" in 1988–2021 is presented in Figure 4.

It should be noted that despite the growth of the Russian GDP, the "whirlpool" continues to deepen in many cases. For example, in 1990, Russia's GDP grew from $3,428.76 billion to $3,492.71 billion, but its level continued to conform to the US GDP in 1960, due to which the depth of "underdevelopment whirlpool" grew from 25 years (1989–1964) to 27 years (1990–1963).

Similarly, in 1997, Russia's GDP grew from $2,643.93 billion to $2,737.57 billion, but its level continued to conform to the US GDP in 1960, due to which the depth of the "underdevelopment whirlpool" grew from 36 years (1996–1960) to 37 years (1997–1960). The process of the

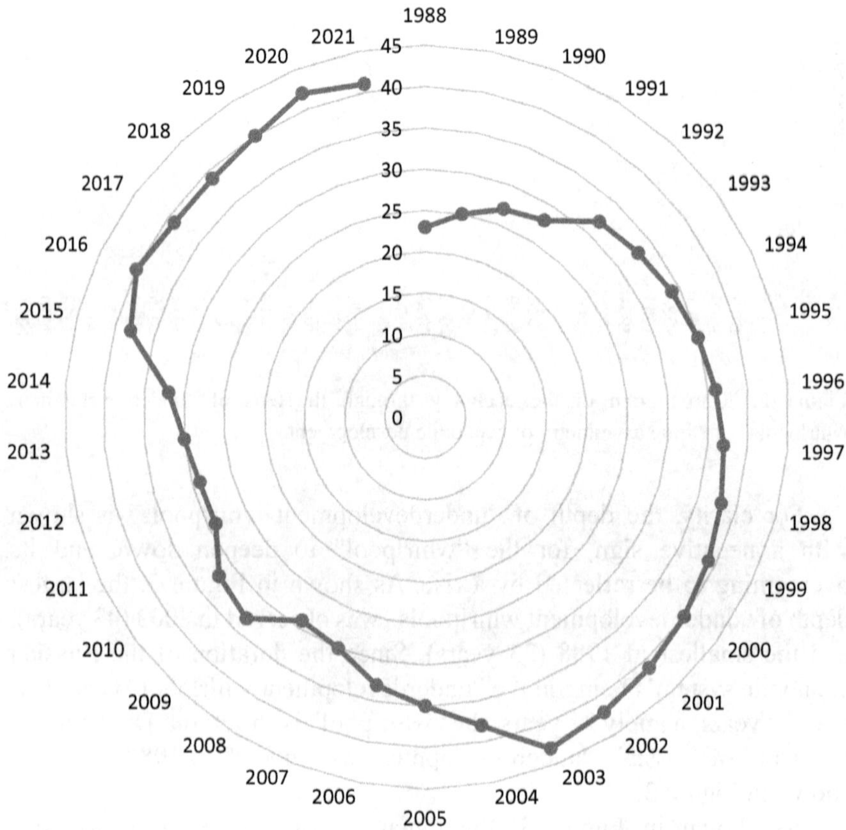

Figure 3. The process of the Russian economic system's sucking into the "underdevelopment whirlpool" from the positions of the theory of economic time.

Russian economy's sucking in the "underdevelopment whirlpool" could be compared to a sinking ship (Figure 4).

It is possible to conclude that time in the economy is a means of creation and destruction of economic systems. Some economic systems prosper, while others fall into decay, but all of them are subject to changes under the influence of the time factor. The methodology of "underdevelopment whirlpools" is a tool of macroeconomic analysis, the spectrum of which is rather wide.

It has been shown — by the example of macroeconomic analysis of modern Russia — that this methodology allows, first, forming a

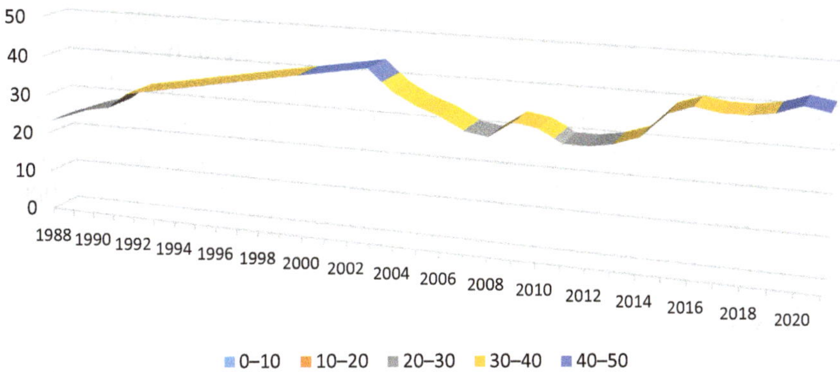

Figure 4. Three-dimensional graph of development (chronotop) of the Russian economy from the positions of the time, GDP, and depth of the "whirlpool" in 1988–2021.

Figure 5. Time is a method of creation and destruction.

Source: Photo by scholar and photographer Elena Popkova, https://www.saatchiart.com/account/artworks/1599809.

chronogram of an economy, determining the time asymmetries of economic development and, second, analyzing the process of an economic system's sucking into the "underdevelopment whirlpool" from the positions of the theory of economic time and then building a three-dimensional graph of the economy's development from the positions of the time, GDP, and the depth of the "whirlpool" (economic chronotope) (Figure 5).

References

Aydin, C. & Esen, Ö. (2019). Does too much government spending depress the economic development of transition economies? Evidence from dynamic panel threshold analysis. *Applied Economics*, 51(15): 1666–1678.

Balakrishnan, P., Das, M., & Parameswaran, M. (2017). The internal dynamic of Indian economic growth. *Journal of Asian Economics*, 50: 46–61.

Borozan, D. (2017). Internal migration, regional economic convergence, and growth in Croatia. *International Regional Science Review*, 40(2): 141–163.

Bulatov, A. (2014). The global problem of economic underdevelopment. *World and National Economy*, 2(29): 3.

Eke, P. O., Okoye, L. U., & Evbuomwan, G. O. (2018). A dynamic analysis of the nexus between entrepreneurship, human capital development and financial deepening: Evidence from selected African economies. *Journal of Applied Economic Sciences*, 13(5): 1344–1356.

Gurova, M. V. (2009). The role of intellectual property in overcoming economic underdevelopment. *Bulletin of the Orenburg State University*, 4(98): 64–68.

Inshakov, O. V. & Frolov, D. P. (2005). Economic space and spatial economics. Reflection on a new economic journal. *Economic Science of Modern Russia*, 4(1): 174–180.

Kindzersky, Y. V. (2010). Features of the development of the institution of property in the system of measures to overcome industrial underdevelopment. *Scientific works of Donetsk National Technical University. Series: Economic*, 1(38): 61–69.

Oliveira, C., Coelho, D., & Antunes, C. H. (2016). Coupling input-output analysis with multiobjective linear programming models for the study of economy-energy-environment-social (E3S) trade-offs: A review. *Annals of Operations Research*, 247(2): 471–502.

Panshak, Y., Civcir, I., & Ozdeser, H. (2019). Explaining Nigeria's economic growth: Balance of payments constrained growth approach with external and internal imbalances. *South African Journal of Economics*, 2(1): 35–46.

Popkova, E. G., Shakhovskaya, L. S., & Mitrakhovich, T. N. (2011). "Underdevelopment whirlpools" in the modern economy. Spoleczenstwo

Sieci — Gospodarka Sieciowa w Europie Srodkowej i Wschodniej. 1, Katolicki University Lubelski Jana Pawla II. In Partyckiego, S. (ed.) *Lublin*, pp. 377–381.

Popkova, E. G. (2004a). The spatio-temporal approach in the concept of a new quality of economic growth. *Economic Sciences*, 7: 33–40.

Popkova, E. G. (2004b). Interaction of the concepts of sustainable development and the new quality of economic growth. *Finance and Credit*, 25(163): 43–47.

Popkova, E. G. (2004c). Interaction of the concepts of sustainable development and the new quality of economic growth. *Economic Analysis: Theory and Practice*, 25: 43.

Popkova, E. G. (2005). Formation of the Concept of a New Quality of Economic Growth in the Context of Globalization. Dissertation for the degree of Doctor of Economics, Penza.

Recio, L. Á. H., Montero, P. A., & Hailer, A. M. (2018). Internal trade imbalances and economic growth in the Euro zone. *Revista de Economia Mundial*, 2(1): 48–57.

Safronov, A. (2009). The comprador bourgeoisie and the problem of "economic underdevelopment". *Free Thought*, 12(1607): 77–92.

Semenov, A. S. & Derunov, V. A. (2016). Mathematical substantiation of economic growth in the conditions of the country falling into the "trap of underdevelopment". *Bulletin of the Saratov University. New series. Series: Economics. Control. Law*, 16(3): 288–293.

Shakhovskaya, L. S. & Popkova, E. G. (2004). New quality of economic growth in the context of modern globalization. *Finance and Credit*, 23(16): 71–77.

Sørensen, P. B. (2018). From the linear economy to the circular economy: A basic model. *FinanzArchiv*, 74(1): 71–87.

Vitlinskyy, V., Kolyada, Y., & Tukalo, V. (2012). Research of synergetic models of the non-linear economy. In *Proceedings of the 2012 4th International Conference "Problems of Cybernetics and Informatics"*, 6486482.

Wei, L. & Yang, Y. (2018). Development trend of sharing economy in big data era based on duplication dynamic evolution game theory. *Cluster Computing*, 22(Suppl 5): 13011–13019, https://doi.org/10.1007/s10586-018-1832-9.

Wei, R. & Yu, Z. (2018). Sci-tech innovation, financial development and economy growth-empirical analysis based on static and dynamic panel data. *MATEC Web of Conferences*, 227: 02014.

West, K. D. (2017). Hansen and Sargent's recursive models of dynamic linear economies: A review. *Journal of Economic Literature*, 55(1): 173–181.

World Bank. (2019). Indicators: GDP per capita. https://data.worldbank.org/indicator/NY.GDP.PCAP.CD?most_recent_value_desc=true&view=chart. Accessed: 07 November 2019.

World Bank. (2023). GDP per capita (current US$). https://data.worldbank.org/indicator/NY.GDP.PCAP.CD?view=chart. Accessed: 05 January 2023.

Xu, H., Guo, H., Zhang, J., & Dang, A. (2018). Facilitating dynamic marketing capabilities development for domestic and foreign firms in an emerging economy. *Journal of Business Research*, 86: 141–152.

Zabrodotsky, Y. (2006). Anatomy of underdevelopment and corruption. *Economic Strategies*, 8.7(49): 42–47.

Part III

"Underdevelopment Whirlpools" as a Manifestation of Time Disproportions in the Development of the Modern World Economy: How Time Manifests Itself in the Economy

This part states that time in economics is manifested differently than in physics. Economic time is not a derivative of space but depends on the specifics of the economic system's socio-economic activities. A methodological tool for measuring and considering the differences in economic time of economic systems is "underdevelopment whirlpools". Calculation of "whirlpools" could be performed for determining the time lag of emerging economies from advanced economies in the aspect of studying the balance of the world economic system. "Underdevelopment whirlpools" could also be used for determining and measuring the disproportions in the system of advanced economies and the system of emerging economies. "Underdevelopment whirlpools" are a universal method of the Theory of Time in Economics, which allows — with high precision and correctness — measuring the differences in the current economic time of economic systems (with the help of a statistical indicator — the "whirl-pool's" depth) and the speed of their economic time (with the help of a dynamic indicator — the speed of sucking into the "whirlpool" or its overcoming).

It is necessary to note another feature of time, both physical (introduced by Anisov in 2019) and economic, universality. Time influences advanced and emerging economies, though they are located in different economic times, and the flow of time is different.

Chapter 15

"Underdevelopment Whirlpools" as the Indicator of the Time Lag Between Emerging and Advanced Economies: Time Is a Measure of Development

Horsepower sells cars, torque wins races.

Enzo Ferrari, Italian engineer, entrepreneur and race car driver. The founder of the "Ferrari" car manufacturer and the car racing team.

This chapter states that time is the criterion of comparison of economic systems with each other and the tool for analyzing the structure of the world economy.

This chapter considers the following topics:

- "underdevelopment whirlpools" in emerging economies as a manifestation of their underrun from advanced economies: a world overview;
- calculation of "underdevelopment whirlpools" of emerging economies and their underrun from advanced economies in regions of the world;
- 3D modelling of the process of emerging economies' sucking into an "underdevelopment whirlpool";
- comparative analysis of time disproportions in the development of regions of the modern world economy (Figure 1).

The modern view of time emphasizes its large value. The philosophy of capitalism is reflected in a widely known expression "time is money", which shows that time is a valuable resource, which has to be saved.

Figure 1. Sustainable development.

Source: Photo by scholar and photographer Elena Popkova, https://www.saatchiart.com/account/artworks/1599809.

Under the influence of globalization, there formed a perception of time as an epoch — a long period, characterized by a certain tendency and logically deriving from the previous period.

The limits of the epoch are usually set according to the dominating technological mode. The preconditions to the establishment of the modern approach to determining and measuring economic time were formed by the scientific and philosophical ideas of Marx (change of economic formations) and the works of Kuhn (the change of scientific paradigm is predetermined by scientific revolutions). According to this, the sequence of epochs (and the models of socio-economic systems that are implemented in them) could be described in the following way (Figure 2).

As shown in Figure 2, at present (21st century), the digital age has already started, under the influence of the Fourth Industrial Revolution. It is dominated by the digital economy, which, in its turn, is dominated by Industry 4.0 — hi-tech production based on the Internet of Things, robots, artificial intelligence (smart technologies), and other leading digital

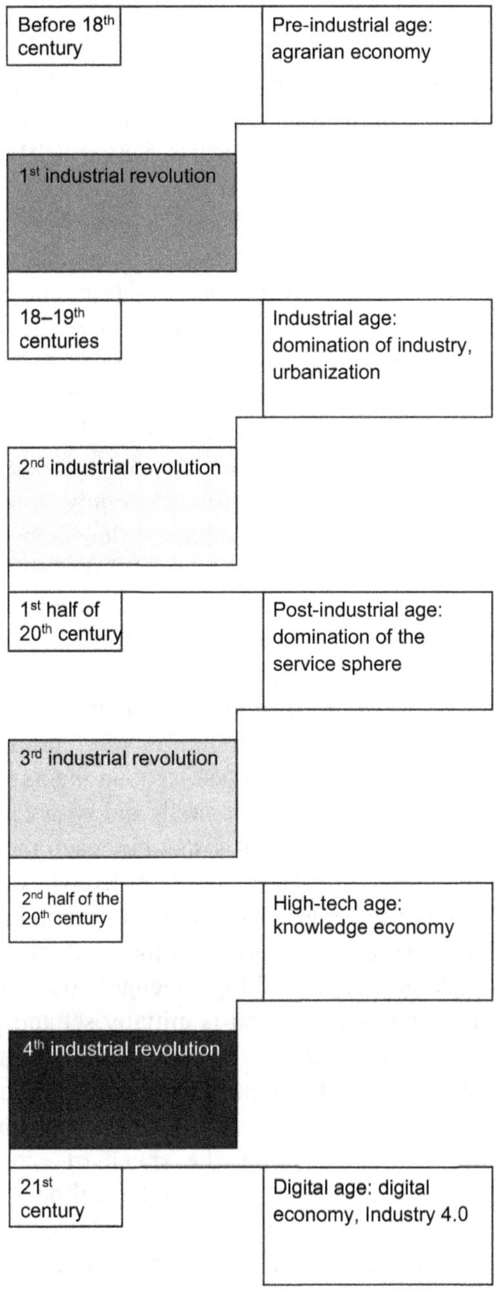

Figure 2. The modern view of economic time: Change of epochs under the impact of technological revolutions.

technologies. The process of transition to the modern age through the lens of the Fourth Industrial Revolution is described in the works of Sukhodolov *et al.* (2018) and Sozinova (2019). The characteristics of the digital age are given in the works on the topic of the digital economy and Industry 4.0 by Popkova (2019), Popkova & Sergi (2019), Popkova *et al.* (2019), and Sergi *et al.* (2019).

It should be noted that the time factor is actively studied and taken into account in modern economic science. In particular, attention should be paid to the scientific report "Categories of time and complexities in macro-financial models" by Moiseev, the head of the laboratory for macro-financial research and forecasting of the Institute of Economic Forecasting of the Russian Academy of Sciences, which was presented in Financial University under the Government of the Russian Federation on December 18, 2019. The report reconsiders the essence of money and substantiates that money performs its functions only in time. The author reconsiders, through the lens of the time factor, the essence of the process of the economy's slowdown and the speed of the creation of money (Moiseev, 2019). The report of Moiseev allowed for reflection on the category of time in the financial sphere; however, this category is not clearly defined in economics on the whole.

To understand the spirit of the modern age better, let us imagine a car race. In a car race, the importance of time is very significant, since the racer values each second. Racers compete against themselves, striving at the same time to fully realize their potential, and with each other, trying to overtake their rivals. The time that is spent by each racer for covering the set route can be clearly measured and is objective, which allows for comparing the results of different racers and determining the winner.

A very similar situation is observed in the modern world economy. The imaginary track is markets of high technologies and innovations. Unlike the regular racing track, which is initially set and predetermined, it becomes longer in the course of technological progress. The race of technologies determines different technological modes of modern economic systems, i.e., their location in different economic times. The speed of modernization determines the speed of economic time in the economy, and the current level of technological development — the position of an economic system at a conventional racing track of the world economy and its global competitiveness — time in relation to other countries.

To measure the level of technological development of modern economic systems, various derivative indicators are used; they are used as the basis of global ratings of countries. As an example, it is possible to consider the Global Competitiveness Ranking, the Innovative Development Ranking, and the Global Digital Competitiveness Ranking.

Though this allows comparing economic systems to each other by the criterion of the current level of their technological development and even considering the process of this development in the dynamics of a range of years, the existing indicators and rankings, which are compiled on their basis, do not allow determining the economic time of modern economic systems in the absolute (*speed of time*, differences over time) or relative (time in relation to each other, differences in current time) expression, due to the following drawbacks:

- Most of the indicators are qualitative (obtained based on surveys and expert evaluations) and thus are subjective (imprecise and incorrect). An example is the Global Competitiveness Index and the Global Competitiveness Ranking (World Economic Forum).
- A lot of indicators characterize the technological mode in a fragmentary way (only from one of many sides). Examples are the Global Innovation Index (WIPO) and the share of hi-tech export in the structure of GDP and the structure of export (World Bank).
- A short period of calculation of indices and compilation of rankings and/or frequent change of their structure and methodology, as well as incomplete coverage of the world economy. An example is the World Digital Competitiveness Ranking (IMD), which has been calculated since 2013 (covering 63 countries in 2013).

These drawbacks are a sign of the inexpedience of measuring economic time in the current (digital) age from the positions of the level of digital technologies' use since scientific measuring is difficult. Instead, taking into account that the main goal and the key manifestation of technological progress is socio-economic development (which embodies economic growth and increase of living standards), it is expedient to use such an indicator as GDP per capita when measuring economic time.

The advantages of this indicator are its universality (availability of data for all countries of the world), sufficient database (data since 1980 are available), objectivity (statistical indicator — precise and correct), and systemic reflection of economic time (from the positions of result, not process). This is stated in the works of Zabrodotsky (2006), Gurova (2009), Safronov (2009), Kindzersky (2010), Bulatov (2014), and Semenov & Derunov (2016).

This emphasizes the preference for using the methodology of "underdevelopment whirlpools" to study economic time. Using this methodology, let us determine the time lag between emerging economies and advanced economies. The theoretical and methodological issues of calculation of "underdevelopment whirlpools" are studied in the works of Popkova (2004a, 2004b, 2004c, 2005), and Shakhovskaya & Popkova (2004).

Let us consider the situation in the world. As a sample economic system, we shall use the leader by the share in the world GDP (23%) — the USA (advanced economy). The dynamics of GDP per capita of the USA in 1960–2021 are presented in Table 1.

Table 1. Dynamics of US GDP per capita in 1960–2021.

Year	GDP per capita, $ trillion	Year	GDP per capita, $ trillion	Year	GDP per capita, $ trillion
1960	3,007.12	1981	13,976.11	2002	37,997.76
1961	3,066.56	1982	14,433.79	2003	39,490.27
1962	3,243.84	1983	15,543.89	2004	41,724.63
1963	3,374.52	1984	17,121.23	2005	44,123.41
1964	3,573.94	1985	18,236.83	2006	46,302.00
1965	3,827.53	1986	19,071.23	2007	48,050.22
1966	4,146.32	1987	20,038.94	2008	48,570.05
1967	4,336.43	1988	21,417.01	2009	47,194.94
1968	4,695.92	1989	22,857.15	2010	48,650.64
1969	5,032.14	1990	23,888.60	2011	50,065.97
1970	5,234.30	1991	24,342.26	2012	51,784.42
1971	5,609.38	1992	25,418.99	2013	53,291.13
1972	6,094.02	1993	26,387.29	2014	55,123.85
1973	6,726.36	1994	27,694.85	2015	56,762.73
1974	7,225.69	1995	28,690.88	2016	57,866.74
1975	7,801.46	1996	29,967.71	2017	59,907.75
1976	8,592.25	1997	31,459.14	2018	62,823.31
1977	9,452.58	1998	32,853.68	2019	65,120.39
1978	10,564.95	1999	34,515.39	2020	63,530.63
1979	11,674.18	2000	36,329.96	2021	70,248.63
1980	12,574.79	2001	37,133.62		

Source: Based on World Bank (2023).

As the objects for research (emerging economies), the most progressive and dynamically developing countries of BRICS (typical examples of emerging economies) are considered: Brazil (located in South America), Russia (most parts of the territory and the capital are located in Europe), India, China (both located in Asia), and South Africa (located in Africa). This will allow covering all geographical regions of the world economy, thus considering the spatial aspects of its development in addition to the time aspect (reflecting this process in a systemic way). A systemic view of the time-space development of the economy is presented in the work of Inshakov & Frolov (2005). The results of the calculation of "underdevelopment whirlpools" are given in Table 2.

Let us consider an example of calculations in Table 2. In 1988, GDP per capita in Russia equalled \$3,777.24, i.e., t_0 = 1988. GDP per capita $t_{0(\alpha)}$ = \$3,777.24. GDP per capita in the USA acquired a value that slightly exceeded the value of GDP per capita $t_{0(\alpha)}$, in 1965 (\$3,827.53), i.e., GDP per capita $t_{0(\beta)}$ = 1965. This allows calculating the depth of the "underdevelopment whirlpool": $Dt_0 = t_0 -$ GDP per capita $t_{0(\beta)}$ = 1988−1965 = 23 years.

In 1998, Russia's GDP per capita equalled \$1,834.86. That is, t_1 = 1998, GDP per capita $t_{1(\alpha)}$ = \$1,834.86. The US GDP per capita acquired a value that slightly exceeded the value of GDP per capita $t_{1(\alpha)}$, in 1960 (\$3,007.12), i.e., GDP per capita $t_{1(\beta)}$ = 1960. This allows calculating the depth of the "underdevelopment whirlpool": $D_{t1} = t_1$ - GDP per capita $t_{1(\beta)}$ = 1998−1960 = 38 years. The speed of the Russian economy's sucking into the whirlpool in 1998 is as follows: $St_1 = Dt_1 - Dt_0$ = (23−38)/10 = 1.50 years per 1 year.

In 2008, Russia's GDP per capita equalled \$11,635.7, i.e., t_1 = 1998, GDP per capita $t_{1(\alpha)}$ = \$1,635.7. GDP per capita of the USA acquired a value that slightly exceeded the value of GDP per capita $t_{1(\alpha)}$, in 1979 (\$11,674.19), i.e., GDP per capita $t_{1(\beta)}$ = 1979. This allows calculating the depth of the "underdevelopment whirlpool": $Dt_1 = t_1$ - GDP per capita $t_{1(\beta)}$ = 2008−1979 = 29 years. The speed of the Russian economy's sucking into the "underdevelopment whirlpool" in 2008 is as follows: $St_1 = Dt_1 - Dt_0$ = (38 − 29)/10 = 0.90 years per 1 year.

In 2008, Russia's GDP per capita equalled \$11,288.9, i.e., t_1 = 1998, GDP per capita $t_{1(\alpha)}$ = \$11,288.9. GDP per capita of the USA acquired a value that slightly exceeded the value of GDP per capita $t_{1(\alpha)}$, in 1979 (\$11,674.19), i.e., GDP per capita $t_{1(\beta)}$ = 1979. This allows calculating the depth of the "underdevelopment whirlpool": $Dt_1 = t_1$ - GDP per capita $t_{1(\beta)}$ = 2018 − 1979 = 39 years. The speed of the Russian economy's

Table 2. "Underdevelopment whirlpools" as the indicator of the time lag of BRICS countries from the USA (advanced economy).

Characteristics of the "whirlpool" year (t)	**Indicator**	**Brazil (America)**	**Russia (Europe)**	**India (Asia)**	**China (Asia)**	**South Africa (Africa)**
1988 (t_0)	GDP per capita $t_{(\alpha)}$, $	2,300.38	3,777.24	354.15	283.54	3,371.18
	GDP per capita $t_{(\beta)}$	1960	1965	1960	1960	1963
	Dt, years	28	23	28	28	25
1998 (t_1)	GDP per capita $t_{(\alpha)}$, $	5,087.15	1,834.86	413.3	828.58	3,154.01
	GDP per capita $t_{(\beta)}$	1970	1960	1960	1960	1962
	Dt, years	28	38	38	38	36
	St, years per 1 year	0.00	1.50	1.00	1.00	1.10
2008 (t_3)	GDP per capita $t_{(\alpha)}$, $	8,831.02	11,635.7	998.52	3,468.3	5,760.81
	GDP per capita $t_{(\beta)}$	1977	1979	1960	1964	1972
	Dt, years	31	29	48	44	36
	St, years per 1 year	0.30	−0.90	1.00	0.60	0.00
2018 (t_4)	GDP per capita $t_{(\alpha)}$, $	8,920.76	11,288.9	2,015.59	9,770.85	6,339.57
	GDP per capita $t_{(\beta)}$	1977	1979	1960	1978	1973
	Dt, years	41	39	58	40	45
	St, years per 1 year	1.00	1.00	1.00	−0.40	0.90
2021 (t_4)	GDP per capita $t_{(\alpha)}$, $	7,507.16	12,194.78	2,256.59	12,556.33	7,055.04
	GDP per capita $t_{(\beta)}$	1,974	1,980	1,960	1,980	1,973
	Dt, years	47	41	61	41	48
	St, years per 1 year	2	0.66	1	0.33	1

sucking into the "underdevelopment whirlpool" in 2008 is as follows: $St_1 = Dt_1 - Dt_0 = (39 - 29)/10 = 1$ year per 1 year. For other countries, the calculations are conducted similarly.

The chronogram of the economy of the BRICS countries through the lens of "underdevelopment whirlpools" as a time asymmetry of their economic development and the process of their economies' sucking into the "underdevelopment whirlpool" from the positions of the theory of economic time is shown in Figure 3.

For illustration purposes, the depth of the "underdevelopment whirlpools" is shown with an opposite sign, for the "whirlpool" to deepen downward and its overcoming to be reflected by the rise. As shown in Figure 2, the largest depth of the "underdevelopment whirlpool" is observed in India (58 years in 2018). It increased substantially as compared to 1988 (28 years). The depth of India's "underdevelopment whirlpools" in 1988 was 38 years and in 2008 was 48 years. In 2018, the speed of sucking into the "whirlpool" was 1 year per 1 year (high).

The second position belongs to South Africa whose "underdevelopment whirlpool" was 45 years in 2018 (the speed of sucking into the whirlpool: 0.90 years per 1 year). It increased substantially as compared to 1988 (25 years). The depth of South Africa's "underdevelopment whirlpools" was 36 years in 1998, and in 2008 it was also 36 years. The third position belongs to Brazil whose "underdevelopment whirlpool" was 41 years in 2018 (the speed of sucking into the whirlpool: 1 year per 1 year). It grew substantially as compared to 1988 (28 years). The depth of Brazil's "underdevelopment whirlpool" was 28 years in 1998, and 31 years in 2008.

The fourth position belongs to China whose "underdevelopment whirlpool" was 40 years in 2018 (the speed of sucking into the whirlpool: 0.40 years per 1 year). It grew substantially as compared to 1988 (28 years). The depth of China's "underdevelopment whirlpool" was 38 years in 1988, and 44 years in 2008. The fifth position belongs to Russia whose "underdevelopment whirlpool" was 39 years in 2018 (the speed of sucking into the whirlpool: 1 year per 1 year). It grew substantially as compared to 1988 (23 years). The depth of Russia's "underdevelopment whirlpool" was 38 years in 1998, and 29 years in 2008.

Since the duration of the stay of the economic systems of BRICS countries in the "underdevelopment whirlpool" exceeds 10 years (it is 30 years), the "whirlpools" are systemic. Dynamics of the depth of the "underdevelopment whirlpools" of BRICS countries in 1988–2018 corresponds to a funnel shape, which is a sign of their economic systems' sucking into the "whirlpool". To clarify the spatial specifics of the time

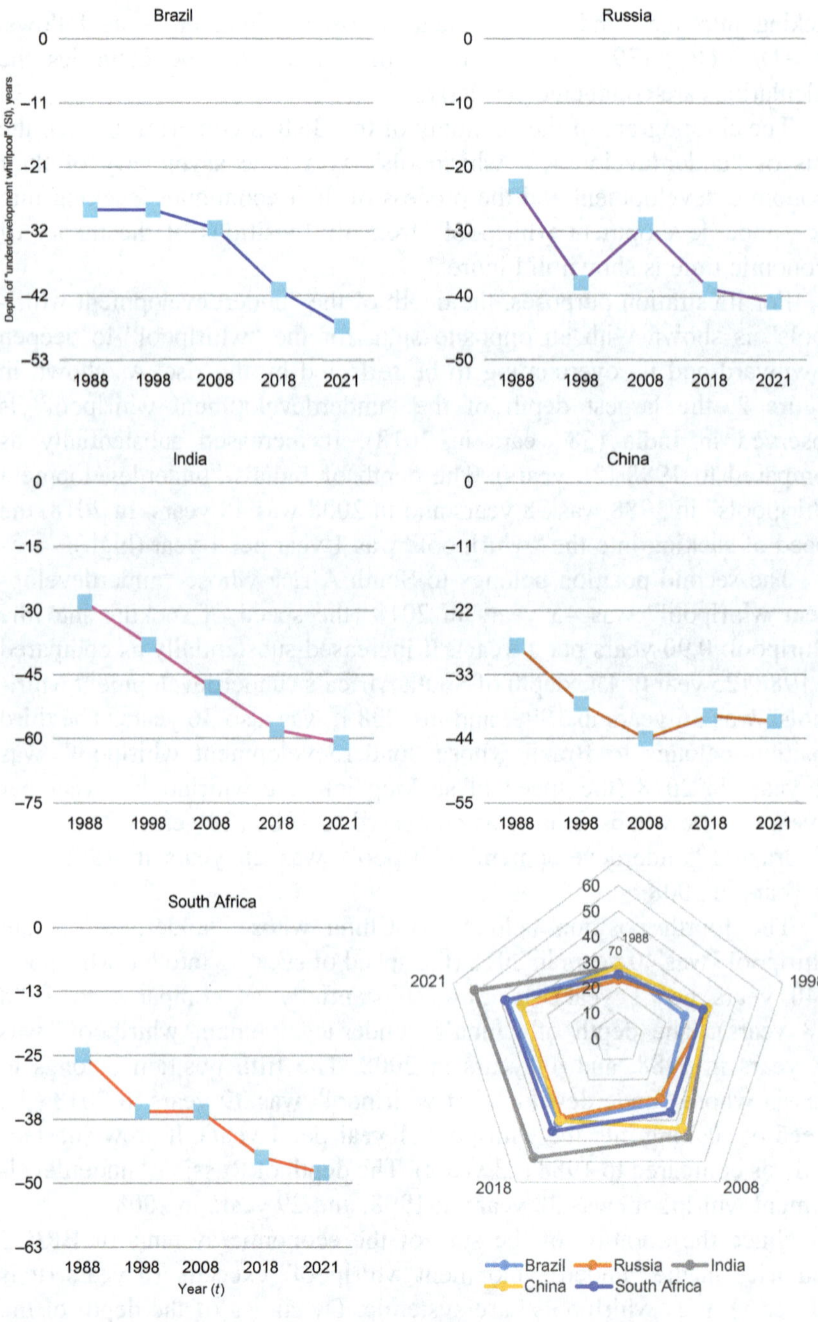

Figure 3. Chronogram of economies of the BRICS countries and the process of their sucking into the "underdevelopment whirlpool" from the positions of the theory of economic time.

lag of emerging economies from advanced economies, let us determine the "underdevelopment whirlpools", which are peculiar to different geographical regions of the world.

In America, the USA is the most notable sample — Brazil's "underdevelopment whirlpool" (Brazil's underrun from the USA) was already calculated in Table 1. Only two emerging economies are available for Africa, which does not allow for performing the necessary calculations. In Europe, the most notable sample is Germany. It is the most progressive country with a developed economy and was the first to start and implement the transition to the digital economy (and Industry 4.0). Germany

Table 3. Dynamics of Germany's GDP per capita in 1960–2021.

Year	GDP per capita, $	Year	GDP per capita, $	Year	GDP per capita, $
1960*	645.00	1981	10,170.45	2002	25,205.16
1961*	745.68	1982	9,876.23	2003	30,359.95
1962*	862.06	1983	9,827.02	2004	34,165.93
1963*	996.62	1984	9,277.93	2005	34,696.62
1964*	1,152.17	1985	9,393.89	2006	36,447.87
1965*	1,332.00	1986	13,410.90	2007	41,814.82
1966*	1,539.90	1987	16,614.41	2008	45,699.20
1967*	1,780.25	1988	17,863.44	2009	41,732.71
1968*	2,058.11	1989	17,697.16	2010	41,785.56
1969	2,379.35	1990	22,219.57	2011	46,810.33
1970	2,750.72	1991	23,269.38	2012	44,065.25
1971	3,180.06	1992	26,333.54	2013	46,530.91
1972	3,795.57	1993	25,488.52	2014	48,142.83
1973	5,027.66	1994	27,087.56	2015	41,394.66
1974	5,617.74	1995	31,729.70	2016	42,443.47
1975	6,212.76	1996	30,564.25	2017	44,681.08
1976	6,609.75	1997	27,045.72	2018	48,195.58
1977	7,653.88	1998	27,340.67	2019	46,793.68
1978	9,446.17	1999	26,795.99	2020	46,772.82
1979	11,238.34	2000	23,718.75	2021	51,203.55
1980	12,092.38	2001	23,687.32		

Source: Based on World Bank (2023).

demonstrates the highest level of GDP per capita. The dynamics of the US GDP per capita in 1960–2021 are given in Table 3.

The calculation of Russia's "underdevelopment whirlpool" (Russia's underrun from Germany) is performed in Table 4. The World Bank's data on Russia are available only from 2000.

The chronogram of the Russian economy through the lens of the "underdevelopment whirlpools", as a time asymmetry of their economic

Table 4. The "underdevelopment whirlpool" in Europe as the indicator of the time lag between Russia and Germany (advanced economy).

t (year)		GDP per capita $t_{(\alpha)}$, $	GDP per capita $t_{(\beta)}$	Dt, years	St, years per 1 year
t_0	2000	1,771.60	1967	33	—
t_1	2001	2,100.36	1969	32	−1
t_2	2002	2,377.54	1969	33	1
t_3	2003	2,975.13	1971	32	−1
t_4	2004	4,102.37	1973	31	−1
t_5	2005	5,323.47	1974	31	0
t_6	2006	6,920.19	1977	29	−2
t_7	2007	9,101.26	1978	29	0
t_8	2008	11,635.27	1980	28	−1
t_9	2009	8,562.81	1978	31	3
t_{10}	2010	10,675.00	1979	31	0
t_{11}	2011	14,351.21	1987	24	−7
t_{12}	2012	15,434.57	1987	25	1
t_{13}	2013	16,007.09	1987	26	1
t_{14}	2014	14,100.73	1987	27	1
t_{15}	2015	9,313.79	1978	37	10
t_{16}	2016	8,745.38	1978	38	1
t_{17}	2017	10,750.59	1979	38	0
t_{18}	2018	11,288.87	1980	38	0
t_{19}	2019	11,536.25	1980	39	1
t_{20}	2020	10,169.09	1979	41	2
t_{21}	2021	12,194.78	1980	41	0

Source: Based on World Bank (2023).

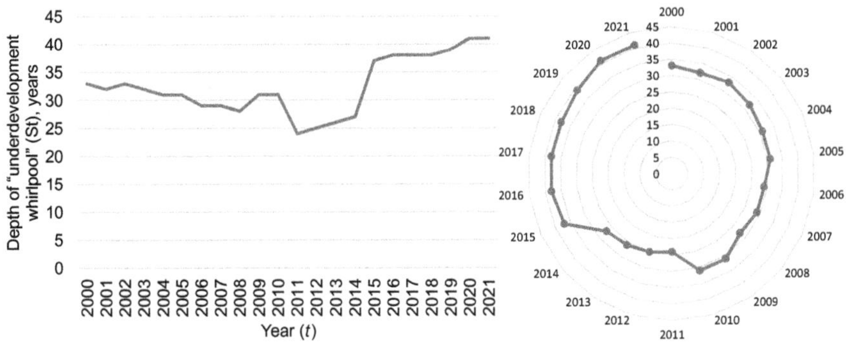

Figure 4. Chronogram of the Russian economy and the process of its sucking into the "underdevelopment whirlpool" (Russia's underrun from Germany) from the positions of the theory of economic time.

development, and the process of the Russian economy's sucking into the "underdevelopment whirlpool" (Russia's underrun from Germany) from the positions of the theory of economic time are shown in Figure 4.

As shown in Figure 3, the depth of the "underdevelopment whirlpool" was 39 years in 2018 (the speed of sucking into the whirlpool — 1 year per 1 year); it grew substantially compared to 2000 when it was 33 years.

In Asia, the most notable sample is Japan. It is the most progressive country with an advanced economy and was the first to start and implement the transition to the digital economy (and Industry 4.0), which demonstrates the highest level of GDP per capita. The dynamics of Japan's GDP per capita in 1960–2021 are shown in Table 5.

The calculation of the "underdevelopment whirlpools" between India/China and Japan is performed in Table 6 (World Bank data from 2000 are available).

Chronogram of India and China's economy through the lens of "underdevelopment whirlpools" as a time asymmetry of their economic development and the process of their economies' sucking into the "underdevelopment whirlpool", as compared to Japan, from the positions of the theory of economic time are shown in Figures 5 and 6.

Figure 5 shows that in 2018, China started overcoming the "underdevelopment whirlpool", while that continues to deepen in India.

Table 5. The dynamics of Japan's GDP per capita in 1960–2021.

Year	GDP per capita, $	Year	GDP per capita, $	Year	GDP per capita, $
1960	479.00	1981	10,361.32	2002	32,289.35
1961	563.59	1982	9,578.11	2003	34,808.39
1962	633.64	1983	10,425.41	2004	37,688.72
1963	717.87	1984	10,984.87	2005	37,217.65
1964	835.66	1985	11,584.65	2006	35,433.99
1965	919.78	1986	17,111.85	2007	35,275.23
1966	1,058.50	1987	20,745.25	2008	39,339.30
1967	1,228.91	1988	25,051.85	2009	40,855.18
1968	1,450.62	1989	24,813.30	2010	44,507.68
1969	1,669.10	1990	25,359.35	2011	48,168.00
1970	2,037.56	1991	28,925.04	2012	48,603.48
1971	2,272.08	1992	31,464.55	2013	40,454.45
1972	2,967.04	1993	35,765.91	2014	38,109.41
1973	3,997.84	1994	39,268.57	2015	34,524.47
1974	4,353.82	1995	43,440.37	2016	38,794.33
1975	4,659.12	1996	38,436.93	2017	38,331.98
1976	5,197.81	1997	35,021.72	2018	39,286.74
1977	6,335.79	1998	31,902.77	2019	40,458.00
1978	8,821.84	1999	36,026.56	2020	39,918.17
1979	9,105.14	2000	38,532.04	2021	39,312.66
1980	9,465.38	2001	33,846.47		

Source: Based on World Bank (2023).

As shown in Figure 6, the depth of the "underdevelopment whirlpool" in India was 49 years in 2018 (the speed of sucking into the "whirlpool": 1 year per 1 year), which has increased compared to 2000, when it was 28 years. The depth of the "underdevelopment whirlpools" in China was 35 years (the speed of overcoming the "whirlpool": 2 years per 1 year), which has increased compared to 2000, when it was 28 years.

The considered regional specifics and the global tendency of an increase of the time lag between emerging economies and advanced economies and their sucking into "underdevelopment whirlpools" allow compiling a model of the modern world economy's development from the

Table 6. The "underdevelopment whirlpool" in Asia as the indicator of the time lag between India/China and Japan (advanced economy).

		India				China			
t (year)		GDP per capita $t_{(\alpha)}$, \$	GDP per capita $t_{(\beta)}$	Dt, year	St, years per 1 year	GDP per capita $t_{(\alpha)}$,\$	GDP per capita $t_{(\beta)}$	Dt, years	St, years per 1 year
t_0	1988	354.15	1960	28	—	283.54	1960	28	—
t_1	1989	346.11	1960	29	1	310.88	1960	29	1
t_2	1990	367.56	1960	30	1	317.88	1960	30	1
t_3	1991	303.06	1960	31	1	333.14	1960	31	1
t_4	1992	316.95	1960	32	1	366.46	1960	32	1
t_5	1993	301.16	1960	33	1	377.39	1960	33	1
t_6	1994	346.10	1960	34	1	473.49	1960	34	1
t_7	1995	373.77	1960	35	1	609.66	1962	33	−1
t_8	1996	399.95	1960	36	1	709.41	1963	33	0
t_9	1997	415.49	1960	37	1	781.74	1964	33	0
t_{10}	1998	413.30	1960	38	1	828.58	1964	34	1
t_{11}	1999	442.00	1960	39	1	873.29	1965	34	0
t_{12}	2000	443.31	1960	40	1	959.37	1966	34	0
t_{13}	2001	451.57	1960	41	1	1,053.11	1966	35	1
t_{14}	2002	470.99	1960	42	1	1,148.51	1967	35	0
t_{15}	2003	546.73	1961	42	0	1,288.64	1968	35	0
t_{16}	2004	627.77	1962	42	0	1,508.67	1968	36	1
t_{17}	2005	714.86	1963	42	0	1,753.42	1970	35	−1
t_{18}	2006	806.75	1964	42	0	2,099.23	1971	35	0
t_{19}	2007	1,028.33	1966	41	−1	2,693.97	1972	35	0
t_{20}	2008	998.52	1966	42	1	3,468.3	1973	35	0
t_{21}	2009	1,101.96	1966	43	1	3,832.24	1973	36	1
t_{22}	2010	1,357.56	1968	42	−1	4,550.45	1975	35	−1
t_{23}	2011	1,458.10	1969	42	0	5,618.13	1977	34	−1
t_{24}	2012	1,443.88	1968	44	2	6,316.92	1977	35	1
t_{25}	2013	1,449.61	1968	45	1	7,050.65	1978	35	0
t_{26}	2014	1,573.88	1969	45	0	7,651.37	1978	36	1
t_{27}	2015	1,605.61	1969	46	1	8,033.39	1978	37	1

(*Continued*)

Table 6. (*Continued*)

	India				China			
t (year)	GDP per capita $t_{(\alpha)}$, \$	GDP per capita $t_{(\beta)}$	Dt, year	St, years per 1 year	GDP per capita $t_{(\alpha)}$,\$	GDP per capita $t_{(\beta)}$	Dt, years	St, years per 1 year
t_{28} 2016	1,729.27	1969	47	1	8,078.79	1978	38	1
t_{29} 2017	1,981.50	1970	47	0	8,759.04	1978	39	1
t_{30} 2018	2,015.59	1970	48	1	9,770.85	1981	37	−2
t_{31} 2019	2,047.23	1970	49	1	10,143.83	1981	38	1
t_{30} 2020	1,910.42	1969	51	2	10,408.67	1983	37	−1
t_{31} 2021	2,256.59	1971	50	1	12,556.33	1985	36	−1

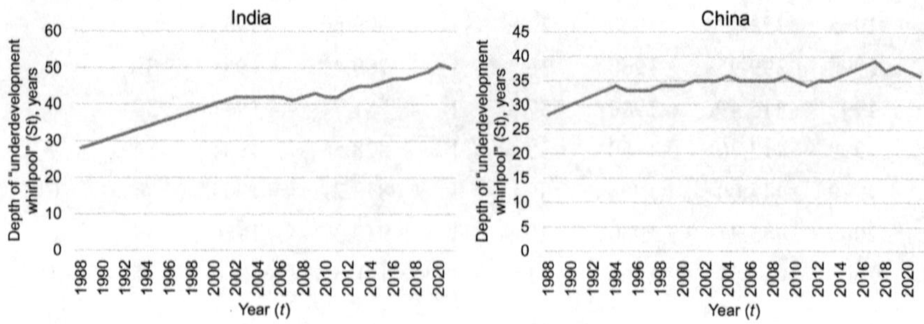

Figure 5. Chronogram of India and China's economy.

positions of the theory of economic time, which reflects systemically its space-time characteristics (Figure 7).

This research allows for the following conclusion: there is a vivid and growing time disproportion of the modern global economic system, which is a sign of the unequal development of this system and clear differentiation between advanced economies and emerging economies.

Drawing an analogy with a race track (Figure 5), which is represented by the development of the world economy under the influence of technological progress, it could be observed that the speed of economic systems' development is different. The leader of the world economy — the USA — is rushing forward in a racing car. Other advanced economies

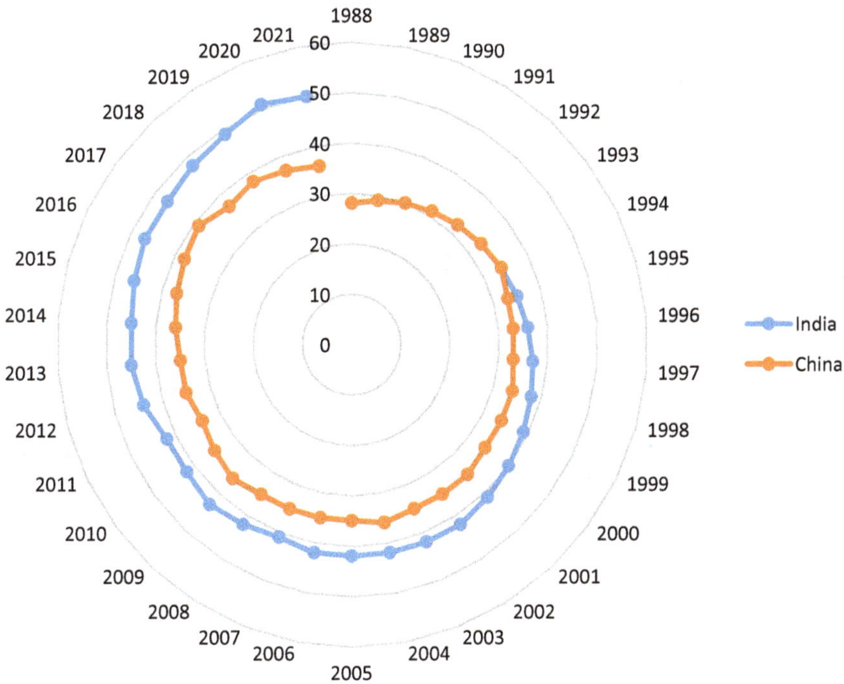

Figure 6. The process of the Indian and Chinese economies' sucking into the "underdevelopment whirlpool" (India and China's underrun from Japan) from the positions of the theory of economic time.

seem to be driving retro cars, and emerging economies drive carriages drawn by horses.

The differences between the participants of an international economic "race" are growing since the starting positions were different for them. Advanced economies start closer to the finish and are moving faster while emerging economies start far from the finish and are moving slowly. The spatial differences in the level and rate of economic development are also vivid. North America is the leader, it is followed by Western Europe, and the race's outsiders are other countries (Eastern Europe, South America, Asia, and Africa).

That's why time-space disproportions of the world economy's development increase its time and become constant and regular. Even in

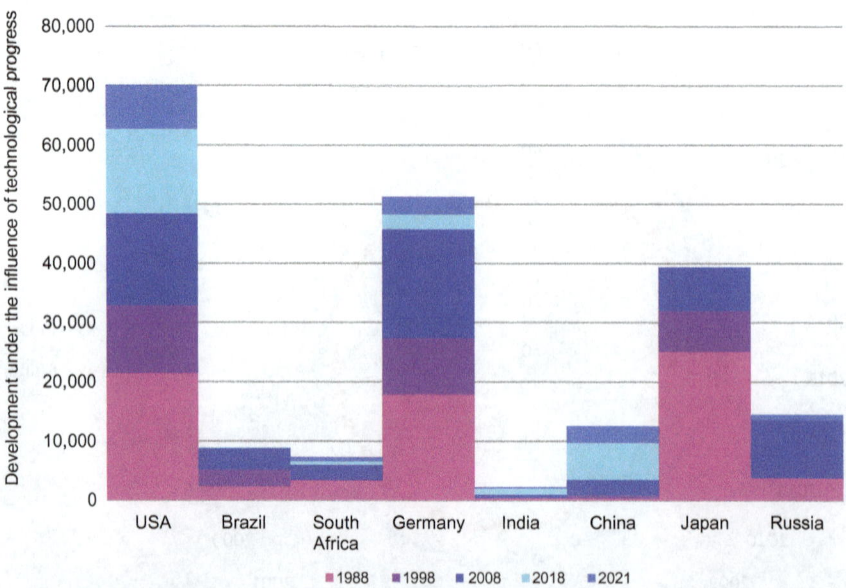

Figure 7. The model of the modern world economy's development from the positions of the theory of economic time.

Figure 8. Time is a measure of development.

Source: Photo by scholar and photographer Elena Popkova, https://www.saatchiart.com/account/artworks/1599809.

the period of a new technological (industrial) revolution, emerging economies cannot start closer to the finish. That's why the only possible way of overcoming the disproportions in the world economy's development is the change of "transport" — "putting emerging economies in fast cars" (Figure 8). Though this solution seems to be obvious, the issue of implementing it in practice remains open …

References

Bulatov, A. (2014). The global problem of economic underdevelopment. *World and National Economy*, 2(29): 3.

Gurova, M. V. (2009). The role of intellectual property in overcoming economic underdevelopment. *Bulletin of the Orenburg State University*, 4(98): 64–68.

Inshakov, O. V. & Frolov, D. P. (2005). Economic space and spatial economics. Reflection on a new economic journal. *Economic Science of Modern Russia*, 4(1): 174–180.

Kindzersky, Y. V. (2010). Features of the development of the institution of property in the system of measures to overcome industrial underdevelopment. *Scientific works of Donetsk National Technical University. Series: Economic*, 1(38): 61–69.

Moiseev, A. K. (2019). Scientific Report: Categories of Time and Complexity in Macro-financial Models. http://www.fa.ru/org/dep/det/News/2019-12-20-Time.aspx. Accessed: 28 December 2019.

Popkova, E. G. (2004a). The spatio-temporal approach in the concept of a new quality of economic growth. *Economic Sciences*, 7: 33–40.

Popkova, E. G. (2004b). Interaction of the concepts of sustainable development and the new quality of economic growth. *Finance and Credit*, 25(163): 43–47.

Popkova, E. G. (2004c). Interaction of the concepts of sustainable development and the new quality of economic growth. *Economic Analysis: Theory and Practice*, 25: 43.

Popkova, E. G. (2005). Formation of the Concept of a New Quality of Economic Growth in the Context of Globalization. Dissertation for the degree of Doctor of Economics, Penza.

Popkova, E. G. (2019). Preconditions of formation and development of Industry 4.0 in the conditions of the knowledge economy. *Studies in Systems, Decision and Control*, 169: 65–72.

Popkova, E. G. & Sergi, B. S. (2019). Will Industry 4.0 and other innovations impact Russia's development? In *Exploring the Future of Russia's Economy and Markets*. Bingley, UK: Emerald Publishing, pp. 34–42.

Popkova, E. G., Morozova, I. A., & Litvinova, T. N. (2019). Transformational processes in the media system under industry conditions 4.0: future outlines and perspectives. Reflections on the article by Alexander P. Sukhodolov, Doctor of Economics, Professor and Irina A. Kuznetsova, Ph.D. in Engineering, Associate Professor "Designing the mass media as a homeostatic system by means of automation engineering: Basic concepts, structure, components"). *Theoretical and Practical Issues of Journalism*, 7(1): 145–154.

Safronov, A. (2009). The comprador bourgeoisie and the problem of "economic underdevelopment". *Free Thought*, 12(1607): 77–92.

Semenov, A. S. & Derunov, V. A. (2016). Mathematical substantiation of economic growth in the conditions of the country falling into the "trap of underdevelopment". *Bulletin of the Saratov University. New series. Series: Economics. Control. Law*, 16(3): 288–293.

Sergi, B. S., Popkova, E. G., Bogoviz, A. V., & Ragulina J. V. (2019). Entrepreneurship and economic growth: The experience of developed and developing countries. In *Entrepreneurship and Development in the 21st Century*. Bingley, UK: Emerald Publishing Ltd, pp. 3–32.

Shakhovskaya, L. S. & Popkova, E. G. (2004). New quality of economic growth in the context of modern globalization. *Finance and Credit*, 23(16): 71–77.

Sozinova, A. A. (2019). Causal connections of formation of industry 4.0 from the positions of the global economy. *Studies in Systems, Decision and Control*, 169: 131–143.

Sukhodolov, A. P., Popkova, E. G., & Litvinova, T. N. (2018). Models of Modern Information Economy. In *Conceptual Contradictions and Practical Examples*. Bingley, UK: Emerald Publishing Limited, pp. 1–38.

World Bank. (2023). GDP per capita (current US$). https://data.worldbank.org/indicator/NY.GDP.PCAP.CD?view=chart. Accessed: 05 January 2023.

Zabrodotsky, Y. (2006). Anatomy of underdevelopment and corruption. *Economic Strategies*, 8.7(49): 42–47.

Chapter 16

"Underdevelopment Whirlpools" in the System of Advanced Economies: Time Is a Measure of Victory

Time and money are largely interchangeable terms.

Sir Winston Leonard Spencer Churchill, British statesman and politician, Prime Minister of Great Britain 1940–1945 and 1951–1955,

Nobel Prize winner in Literature

This chapter states that time is the indicator of deep differences among structural entities of the world economy — advanced economies.

This chapter considers the following issues:

- "underdevelopment whirlpools" in advanced economies as a manifestation of their heterogeneity by the example of G7 countries;
- creation and analysis of the chronograms of advanced economies;
- 3D modelling of the process of advanced economies' sucking into "underdevelopment whirlpools";
- comparative analysis of time disproportions among advanced economies.

In the second half of the 20th century, the modern scientific and philosophical view of the structure of the world economy was established. This view is expressed in the most precise and comprehensive way in Winston Churchill's statement: "Time and money are largely interchangeable terms". The economic sense of this phrase is that the measure of success is money, with the help of which it is possible to subdue (actually, buy) time itself (Figure 1).

Figure 1. Time is a measure of victory.

Source: Photo by scholar and photographer Elena Popkova, https://www.saatchiart.com/account/artworks/1599809.

Possessing the largest and most attractive financial resources, advanced economies are the leaders of technological progress, since they can afford the large-scale financing of science and education and the implementation of large technological innovative projects. Due to this, they achieve the highest living standards and quality of life. It is for this reason that they are considered the most progressive countries and drivers of the world economy. Figuratively speaking, they live in the future.

However, considering the process of these countries' development in detail, it is possible to see that they are in very tough competition. They could be compared to players in a stock exchange, which possess assets and try to invest them with the largest profit. For them, time decides everything. The player who is the first to realize the perspectives of the asset and to invest in it will be the one to obtain the largest profit.

Similarly, advanced economies are in a constant search for perspective innovative projects. Delay is not an option for them, because it could lead to a loss of leadership in the investment and hi-tech markets and a loss of competitive advantages. Similarly to a stock exchange, advanced economies accept a high level of risk in their striving to multiply their assets. When competition is high and each second counts, there are always those who are faster and more forward-looking and those who have invested with less profit or have suffered losses.

Similarly to a stock exchange, where there are more and fewer successful players, advanced economies are also heterogeneous and have a complex internal structure. To study it, let us dwell on the experience of countries within a certain category. One of the most widespread categories of advanced economies is that presented by the Organization of Economic Co-operation and Development (OECD). As of 2019, 36 countries belonged to this category, as well as several additional members (including Russia), and options for full inclusion are being actively discussed.

A detailed analysis of such a large category of countries is complicated and could be performed in a fragmentary manner (by the example of certain countries of the category), which will inevitably lead to a reduction of the results' prevision. That's why we shall consider an alternative — less widespread but generally recognized — category of advanced economies, which was introduced and is used by the International Monetary Fund (IMF) — Major advanced economies (G7). As can be seen from the title, this category includes seven countries: the USA (North America), Canada (North America), France (Western Europe), Germany (Western Europe), Italy (Western Europe), Japan (Eastern Asia), and the UK (Western Europe).

Let us use the methodology of "underdevelopment whirlpools" to study the economic time of advanced economies in the G7 category. Using this methodology, let us determine the time lag between advanced economies and the leader of this category by the level of GDP per capita in 2021 — the USA ($70,248.63). The dynamics of the US GDP per capita in 1960–2021 are given in Table 1.

The proprietary methodology of "underdevelopment whirlpools", which is described in detail in Chapters 12–14, is based on the scientific provision of the space-time approach. The most notable Russian representatives of this approach are Inshakov & Frolov (2005). In her early works, which include Popkova (2004a, 2004b, 2004c) and Shakhovskaya & Popkova (2004), Doctor of Economics, Professor Elena G. Popkova, develops the provisions of the space-time approach and, based on them, develops a concept of the new quality of economic growth as well as the methodology of "underdevelopment whirlpools", which has become one of the main scientific results in her doctoral thesis (Popkova, 2005).

Table 1. Dynamics of GDP per capita of the USA in 1960–2021.

Year	GDP per capita, $	Year	GDP per capita, $	Year	GDP per capita, $
1960	3,007.12	1981	13,976.11	2002	38,023.16
1961	3,066.56	1982	14,433.79	2003	39,496.49
1962	3,243.84	1983	15,543.89	2004	41,712.80
1963	3,374.52	1984	17,121.23	2005	44,114.75
1964	3,573.94	1985	18,236.83	2006	46,298.73
1965	3,827.53	1986	19,071.23	2007	47,975.97
1966	4,146.32	1987	20,038.94	2008	48,382.56
1967	4,336.43	1988	21,417.01	2009	47,099.98
1968	4,695.92	1989	22,857.15	2010	48,466.82
1969	5,032.14	1990	23,888.60	2011	49,883.11
1970	5,234.30	1991	24,342.26	2012	51,603.50
1971	5,609.38	1992	25,418.99	2013	53,106.91
1972	6,094.02	1993	26,387.29	2014	55,032.96
1973	6,726.36	1994	27,694.85	2015	56,803.47
1974	7,225.69	1995	28,690.88	2016	57,904.20
1975	7,801.46	1996	29,967.71	2017	59,927.93
1976	8,592.25	1997	31,459.14	2018	62,641.01
1977	9,452.58	1998	32,853.68	2019	65,120.39
1978	10,564.95	1999	34,513.56	2020	63,530.63
1979	11,674.19	2000	36,334.91	2021	70,248.63
1980	12,574.79	2001	37,133.24		

Source: Based on World Bank (2023).

Among the recent works of Prof. Elena G. Popkova, in which the description and examples of the calculation of "underdevelopment whirlpools" are provided, are the following publications in English: Popkova (2014, 2017a, 2017b), and Popkova *et al.* (2018). Prof. Popkova's methodology is acknowledged and used by modern Russian scholars and researchers, among who are Laptev and Sozinova (2018). The issue of differences in the level and rate of socio-economic development of advanced economies is considered in the works of the following international scholars: Ahuja & Tandon (2010), Sarmiento Espinel *et al.* (2015), Popkova & Sergi (2019), and Sergi *et al.* (2019), as well as in the works of the following Russian authors.

Gurova (2009) emphasizes the important role of intellectual property in overcoming economic underdevelopment, in particular in the system of advanced economies. Kindzersky (2010) also notes the necessity for the development of the institution of property in the system of measures to overcome industrial underdevelopment. The scholars show that based on the development and realization of intellectual property there is a competitive struggle going on, and the transition of developed countries from the segment of underdeveloped (within their category) to the segment of advanced countries is taking place.

Zabrodotsky (2006) derives the notion of the "anatomy of underdevelopment" through the lens of corruption as a barrier on the path of socio-economic development of an economic system. The author acknowledges that underdevelopment could be peculiar not only for emerging economies but also for advanced economies within its category. Bulatov (2014) writes about the global problem of economic underdevelopment, pointing at the fact that underdevelopment could be peculiar also to advanced economies. Safronov (2009) studies the comprador bourgeoisie and the problem of "economic underdevelopment" and concludes that social structure largely determines economic development in an economic system. Semenov & Derunov (2016) provide a mathematical substantiation of economic growth in the conditions of the country's finding itself in an "underdevelopment whirlpool".

The performed literature review on the given topic has shown that the issue of economic underdevelopment is studied in detail in the existing research literature through the lens of spatial disproportions of the world economy. However, time disproportions, in particular in the category of advanced economies, are studied very poorly. The calculation of the "underdevelopment whirlpool" (Canada/France's underrun from the USA) is performed in Table 2.

The chronogram of the Canadian and French economy through the lens of "underdevelopment whirlpools" as a time asymmetry of their economic development and the process of their economies' sucking into the "underdevelopment whirlpool" (their underrun from the USA) from the positions of the Theory of Economic Time are shown in Figures 2 and 3.

Figure 2 shows that in 1998, 2001, and 2002, the Canadian economy was at the bottom of the "underdevelopment whirlpool", whose depth was

Table 2. The "underdevelopment whirlpool" as the indicator of Canada/France's time lag from the USA.

		Canada				France			
t (year)		GDP per capita $t_{(\alpha)}$, $	GDP per capita $t_{(\beta)}$	Dt, years	St, years per 1 year	GDP per capita $t_{(\alpha)}$, $	GDP per capita $t_{(\beta)}$	Dt, years	St, years per 1 year
t_0	1988	18,966.34	1986	2	—	18,326.78	1985	3	—
t_1	1989	20,763.52	1987	2	0	18,328.02	1985	4	1
t_2	1990	21,495.15	1988	2	0	22,600.46	1989	1	−3
t_3	1991	21,807.26	1989	2	0	22,524.41	1989	2	1
t_4	1992	20,915.03	1987	5	3	24,725.74	1991	1	−1
t_5	1993	20,145.56	1987	6	1	23,212.10	1990	3	2
t_6	1994	19,963.30	1986	8	2	24,398.14	1991	3	0
t_7	1995	20,641.54	1987	8	0	27,898.30	1994	1	−2
t_8	1996	21,257.09	1988	8	0	27,870.57	1994	2	1
t_9	1997	21,857.61	1988	9	1	25,167.00	1992	5	3
t_{10}	1998	20,975.14	1987	11	2	25,951.70	1992	6	1
t_{11}	1999	22,261.15	1989	10	−1	25,680.90	1992	7	1
t_{12}	2000	24,221.27	1991	9	−1	23,317.94	1990	10	3
t_{13}	2001	23,777.49	1990	11	2	23,342.09	1990	11	1
t_{14}	2002	24,210.04	1991	11	0	25,226.21	1992	10	−1
t_{15}	2003	28,242.19	1995	8	−3	30,808.71	1996	7	−3
t_{16}	2004	32,075.36	1998	6	−2	35,153.79	1999	5	−2
t_{17}	2005	36,315.73	2000	5	−1	36,209.52	2000	5	0
t_{18}	2006	40,441.77	2004	2	−3	37,900.03	2003	3	−2
t_{19}	2007	44,599.15	2005	2	0	43,155.50	2004	3	0
t_{20}	2008	46,660.87	2006	2	0	47,273.32	2006	2	−1
t_{21}	2009	40,831.10	2004	5	3	43,234.25	2005	4	2
t_{22}	2010	47,512.68	2007	3	−2	42,249.06	2005	5	1
t_{23}	2011	52,143.84	2012	−1	−4	45,430.28	2006	5	0
t_{24}	2012	52,577.39	2013	−1	0	42,333.09	2004	8	3
t_{25}	2013	52,494.13	2013	0	1	44,104.92	2005	8	0
t_{26}	2014	50,509.59	2011	3	3	44,413.12	2005	9	1
t_{27}	2015	43,349.62	2005	10	7	37,612.91	2001	14	5
t_{28}	2016	42,210.13	2005	11	1	38,127.65	2002	14	0
t_{29}	2017	43,611.26	2005	12	1	37,294.72	2001	16	2

(Continued)

Table 2. *(Continued)*

		Canada				France			
t (year)		GDP per capita $t_{(\alpha)}$, $	GDP per capita $t_{(\beta)}$	Dt, years	St, years per 1 year	GDP per capita $t_{(\alpha)}$, $	GDP per capita $t_{(\beta)}$	Dt, years	St, years per 1 year
t_{30}	2018	44,649.65	2005	13	1	38,087.37	2002	16	0
t_{31}	2019	46,328.67	2006	13	0	40,494.90	2004	15	−1
t_{32}	2020	43,258.26	2005	15	2	39,055.28	2003	17	2
t_{33}	2021	51,987.94	2012	9	−6	43,658.98	2005	16	−1

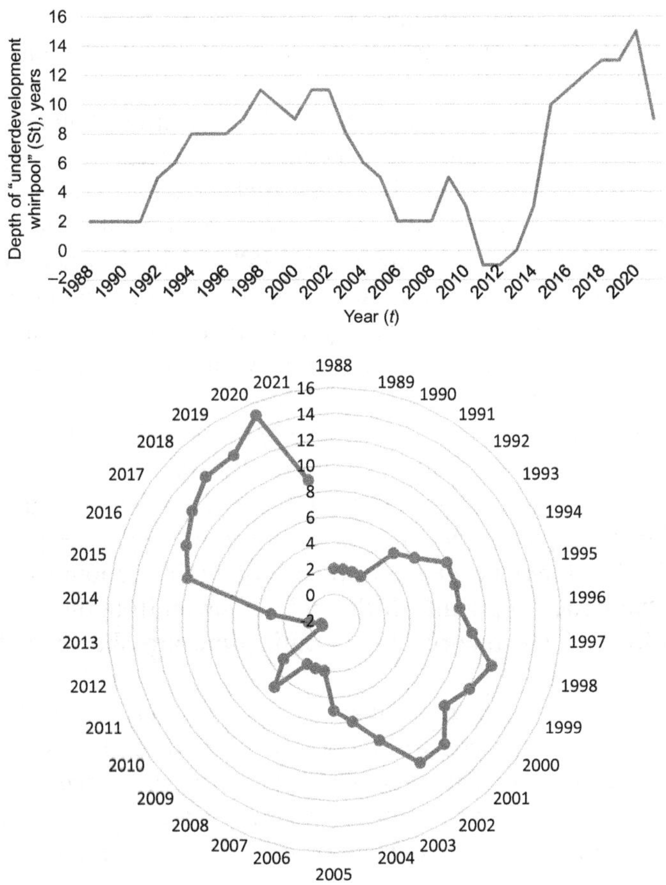

Figure 2. The chronogram of the Canadian economy and the process of its sucking into the "underdevelopment whirlpool" (underrun from the USA) from the positions of the theory of economic time.

11 years. Afterward, the “whirlpool” was overcome and in 2011–2012 the development of Canada exceeded that of the USA, but, starting from 2016, a new “whirlpool” of Canada’s underdevelopment emerged and started to quickly deepen, equalling 14 years in 2019. The speed of sucking into the “whirlpool” was 1 year per 1 year. The situation worsened significantly as compared to 1988–1991 when the depth of the “whirlpool” was only 2 years and the speed of sucking into it was 0.

Figure 3 shows that the French economy in 2001 was at the bottom of the “underdevelopment whirlpool”, whose depth was 11 years. Though the “whirlpool” was not fully overcome, its depth was reduced to 2 years in 2008. However, given the phase of the cycle of the world economy’s development during that time, the decrease of France’s underrun from the USA could be logically explained by the crisis and reduction of the rate of development of the American economy rather than the acceleration of France’s development.

Since 2015, the “whirlpool” of Canada’s underdevelopment started deepening again, reaching 16 years in 2019. However, the speed of sucking into the “whirlpool” is zero, which is a positive tendency as compared to 2017, when it was 2 years per 1 year. The situation worsened substantially as compared to 1988 and 1990, when the depth of the “whirlpool” was 3 years and 1 year, respectively, and the speed of sucking was negative (−3 years per 1 year), which promised the overcoming of the “underdevelopment whirlpool”, which was not eventually achieved.

The calculation of the “underdevelopment whirlpool” (Germany/Italy’s underrun from the USA) is performed in Table 3.

Chronogram of the German and Italian economies through the lens of “underdevelopment whirlpools” as a time asymmetry of their economic development and the process of their economies’ sucking into the “underdevelopment whirlpool” (underrun from the USA) from the positions of the theory of economic time are shown in Figures 4 and 5.

Figure 5 shows that the Italian economy is very cyclical and the Italian “underdevelopment whirlpool” is deep. In 2001, the depth of Italy’s “underdevelopment whirlpool” (underrun from the USA) was 14 years, in 2012, 13 years, and by 2019 it reached 23 years. The speed of sucking into the “underdevelopment whirlpool” is 1 year per 1 year. The

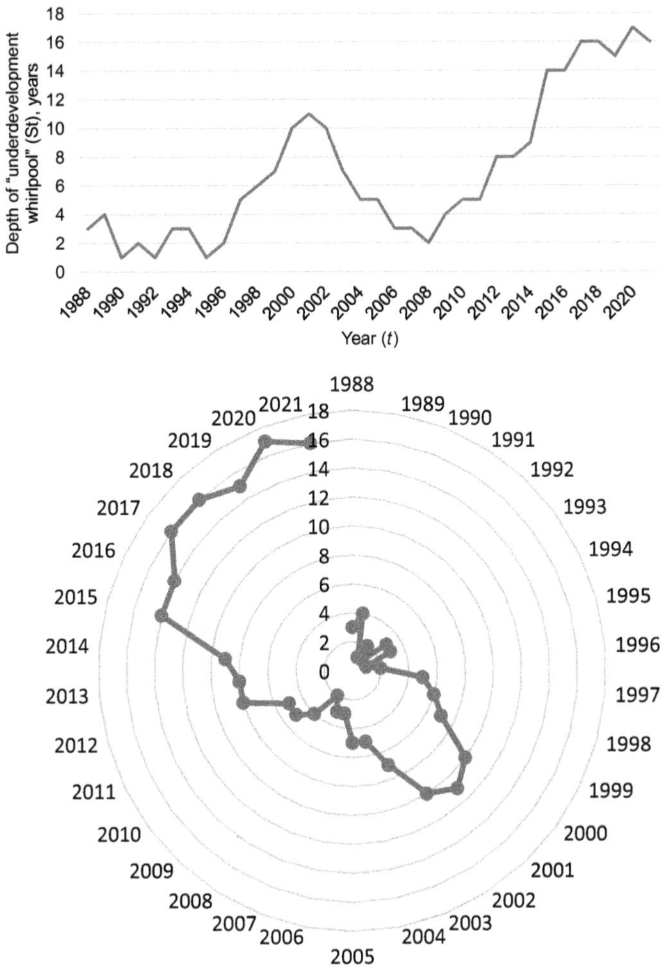

Figure 3. Chronogram of the French economy and the process of its "underdevelopment whirlpool" (France's underrun from the USA) from the positions of the theory of economic time.

situation worsened substantially as compared to 1992 when the depth of the "whirlpool" was just 2 years, and the speed of sucking into it was negative (−1 year per 1 year), which was a sign of the prospects of overcoming the "whirlpool" that were never realized.

Table 3. The "underdevelopment whirlpool" as the indicator of Germany/Italy's time lag from the USA.

		Germany				Italy			
t (year)		GDP per capita $t_{(\alpha)}$, $ billion	GDP per capita $t_{(\beta)}$	Dt, years	St, years per 1 year	GDP per capita $t_{(\alpha)}$, $	GDP per capita $t_{(\beta)}$	Dt, years	St, years per 1 year
t_0	1988	16,454.65	1984	4	—	15,966.45	1983	5	—
t_1	1989	16,174.32	1984	5	1	16,591.14	1984	5	0
t_2	1990	20,174.03	1987	3	−2	20,691.00	1987	3	−2
t_3	1991	23,371.61	1990	1	−2	21,844.14	1988	3	0
t_4	1992	26,441.80	1993	−1	−2	23,159.17	1990	2	−1
t_5	1993	25,569.63	1992	1	2	18,609.97	1985	8	6
t_6	1994	27,247.03	1994	0	−1	19,186.32	1986	8	0
t_7	1995	31,907.94	1997	−2	−2	20,609.06	1987	8	0
t_8	1996	30,744.89	1996	0	2	23,033.40	1990	6	−2
t_9	1997	27,257.16	1994	3	3	21,811.82	1988	9	3
t_{10}	1998	27,581.93	1994	4	1	22,283.57	1989	9	0
t_{11}	1999	27,054.59	1994	5	1	21,968.42	1988	11	2
t_{12}	2000	24,008.66	1991	9	4	20,116.62	1987	13	2
t_{13}	2001	23,949.76	1990	11	2	20,423.14	1987	14	1
t_{14}	2002	25,576.54	1992	10	−1	22,303.02	1989	13	−1
t_{15}	2003	30,785.60	1996	7	−3	27,527.38	1994	9	−4
t_{16}	2004	34,657.52	1999	5	−2	31,319.73	1997	7	−2
t_{17}	2005	35,239.90	2000	5	0	32,066.38	1998	7	0
t_{18}	2006	37,020.35	2001	5	0	33,486.01	1999	7	0
t_{19}	2007	42,531.38	2004	3	−2	37,890.20	2001	6	−1
t_{20}	2008	46,681.07	2006	2	−1	40,953.86	2003	5	−1
t_{21}	2009	42,576.34	2004	5	3	37,130.15	2001	8	3
t_{22}	2010	42,641.68	2004	6	1	35,969.19	1999	11	3
t_{23}	2011	46,853.22	2006	5	−1	38,379.31	2002	9	−2
t_{24}	2012	44,089.69	2005	7	2	34,918.74	1999	13	4
t_{25}	2013	46,545.09	2006	7	0	35,706.62	1999	14	1
t_{26}	2014	47,978.61	2007	7	0	35,456.70	1999	15	1
t_{27}	2015	41,197.41	2004	11	4	30,032.11	1996	19	4
t_{28}	2016	41,902.28	2004	12	1	30,507.18	1996	20	1
t_{29}	2017	41,243.88	2004	13	1	29,747.13	1996	21	1

(Continued)

Table 3. (*Continued*)

t (year)		Germany: GDP per capita $t_{(\alpha)}$, \$ billion	Germany: GDP per capita $t_{(\beta)}$	Germany: Dt, years	Germany: St, years per 1 year	Italy: GDP per capita $t_{(\alpha)}$, \$	Italy: GDP per capita $t_{(\beta)}$	Italy: Dt, years	Italy: St, years per 1 year
t_{30}	2018	42,196.07	2004	14	1	30,260.04	1996	22	1
t_{31}	2019	46,793.69	2006	13	−1	30,673.75	1996	23	1
t_{31}	2020	46,772.82	2006	14	1	31,911.04	1997	23	0
t_{31}	2021	51,203.55	2012	9	−5	35,657.50	2000	21	−2

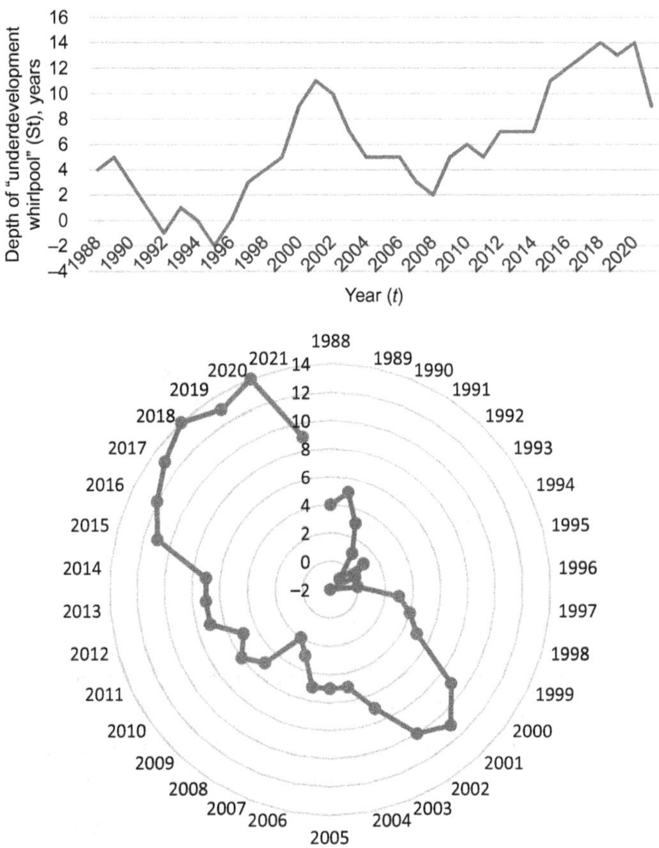

Figure 4. Chronogram of the German economy and the process of its sucking into the "underdevelopment whirlpool" (underrun from the USA) from the positions of the theory of economic time.

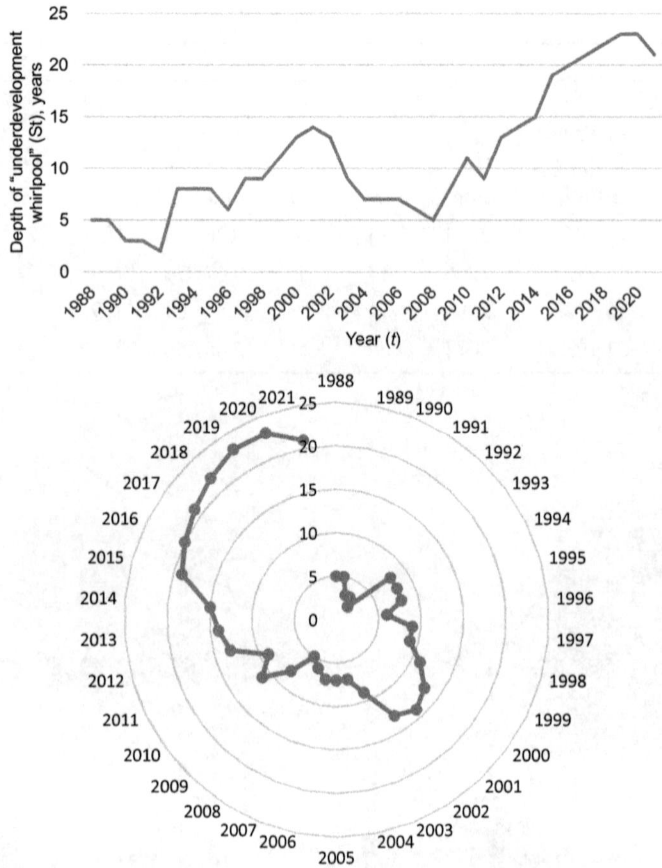

Figure 5. Chronogram of the Italian economy and the process of its sucking into the "underdevelopment whirlpool" (underrun from the USA) from the positions of the theory of economic time.

The calculation of Japan/UK's "underdevelopment whirlpool" (underrun from the USA) is performed in Table 4.

The chronogram of the Japanese and UK economies through the lens of "underdevelopment whirlpools" as a time asymmetry of their economic development and the process of their economies' sucking into the "underdevelopment whirlpool" (their underrun from the USA) from the positions of the theory of economic time is shown in Figures 6 and 7.

Table 4. "Underdevelopment whirlpool" as the indicator of Japan/UK's time lag from the USA.

		Japan				UK			
t (year)		GDP per capita $t_{(\alpha)}$, $	GDP per capita $t_{(\beta)}$	Dt, years	St, years per 1 year	GDP per capita $t_{(\alpha)}$, $	GDP per capita $t_{(\beta)}$	Dt, year	St, years per 1 year
t_0	1988	24,897.77	1991	−3	—	17,267.43	1984	4	—
t_1	1989	24,814.59	1991	−2	1	17,508.92	1984	5	1
t_2	1990	25,443.21	1992	−2	0	20,668.04	1987	3	−2
t_3	1991	28,910.25	1995	−4	−2	21,502.56	1988	3	0
t_4	1992	31,343.83	1997	−5	−1	22,119.10	1989	3	0
t_5	1993	35,802.93	1999	−6	−1	19,738.70	1986	7	4
t_6	1994	39,224.15	2003	−9	−3	21,098.89	1988	6	−1
t_7	1995	43,454.78	2004	−9	0	22,759.46	1989	6	0
t_8	1996	38,453.38	2002	−6	3	23,974.94	1990	6	0
t_9	1997	35,042.32	1999	−2	4	26,366.88	1993	4	−2
t_{10}	1998	35,912.46	1999	−1	1	27,769.02	1994	4	0
t_{11}	1999	31,931.07	1997	2	3	28,159.95	1995	4	0
t_{12}	2000	35,912.46	1999	1	−1	27,828.38	1994	6	2
t_{13}	2001	38,533.86	2002	−1	−2	27,296.67	1994	7	1
t_{14}	2002	33,860.45	1998	4	5	29,654.24	1996	6	−1
t_{15}	2003	32,301.30	1998	5	1	34,049.76	1999	4	−2
t_{16}	2004	34,844.66	2002	2	−3	39,871.03	2003	1	−3
t_{17}	2005	37,701.44	2001	4	2	41,566.63	2004	1	0
t_{18}	2006	37,228.23	2001	5	1	44,095.77	2005	1	0
t_{19}	2007	35,464.64	1999	8	3	49,973.92	2011	−4	−5
t_{20}	2008	39,453.50	2003	5	−3	46,890.22	2006	2	6
t_{21}	2009	41,014.19	2004	5	0	38,180.57	2002	7	5
t_{22}	2010	44,673.61	2005	5	0	38,737.56	2002	8	1
t_{23}	2011	48,168.81	2008	3	−2	41,259.50	2004	7	−1
t_{24}	2012	48,632.91	2008	4	1	41,683.67	2004	8	1
t_{25}	2013	40,490.16	2003	10	6	42,452.95	2005	8	0
t_{26}	2014	38,143.11	2002	12	2	46,478.84	2006	8	0

(Continued)

Table 4. (*Continued*)

		Japan				UK			
t (year)		GDP per capita $t_{(\alpha)}$, $	GDP per capita $t_{(\beta)}$	Dt, years	St, years per 1 year	GDP per capita $t_{(\alpha)}$, $	GDP per capita $t_{(\beta)}$	Dt, year	St, years per 1 year
t_{27}	2015	34,513.36	1999	16	4	43,976.42	2005	10	2
t_{28}	2016	38,917.29	2002	14	−2	40,095.95	2003	13	3
t_{29}	2017	38,281.58	2002	15	1	37,812.51	2001	16	3
t_{30}	2018	39,308.31	2003	15	0	38,254.40	2002	16	0
t_{31}	2019	40,458.00	2003	16	1	42,747.08	2004	15	−1
t_{31}	2020	39,918.17	2003	17	1	40,318.56	2003	17	2
t_{31}	2021	39,312.66	2003	18	1	46,510.28	2006	15	−2

As shown in Figure 6, the Japanese economy was at the bottom of the "underdevelopment whirlpool" in 1994–1995; the "whirlpool's" depth was nine years. Afterward, the "whirlpool" reduced significantly. Since 2013 (10 years), Japan's new "underdevelopment whirlpool" emerged and started to deepen — by 2019 it reached 16 years. The speed of sucking into the "whirlpool" was 1 year per 1 year. The situation worsened substantially as compared to 1993 when the "whirlpool's" depth was negative, and the speed of sucking into the "whirlpool" was also negative (−1 year per 1 year), which was a sign of Japan's opportunity to achieve leadership among advanced economies, which was never realized.

As shown in Figure 7, the UK economy was at the depth of an "underdevelopment whirlpool" in 1998, 2001, and 2002; the "whirlpool's" depth was 6 years. Afterwards, the "whirlpool" was overcome, but since 2015 (10 years) there emerged and deepened a new "underdevelopment whirlpool", which was 17 years in 2019. The speed of sucking into the whirlpool was 1 year per 1 year. The situation worsened substantially as compared to 2007 when the "whirlpool's" depth was 4 years, and the speed of sucking into it was negative (−5 years), which was a sign of the UK's opportunity to achieve leadership among advanced economies, which was not eventually realized.

The comparative analysis of time disproportions among advanced economies is presented in Figure 8.

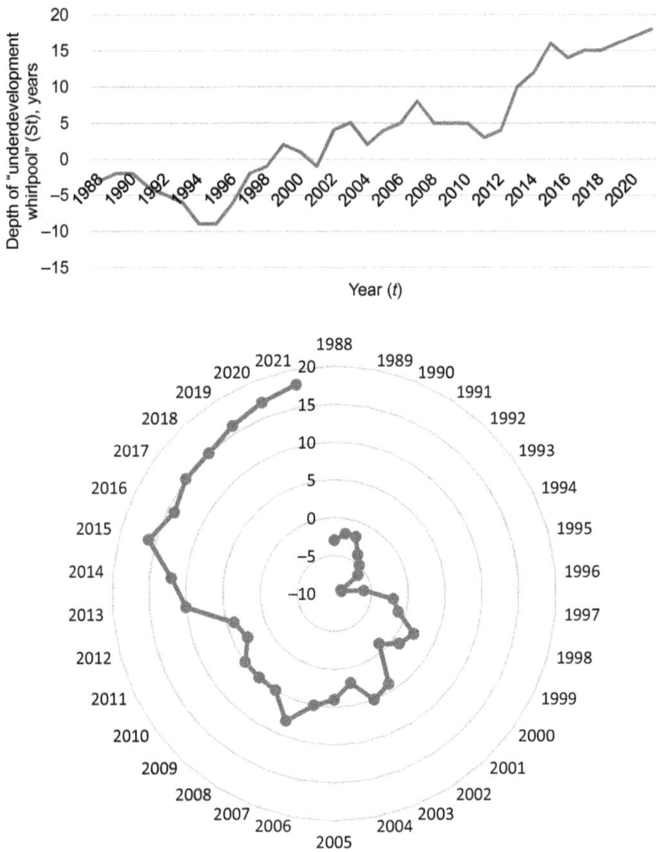

Figure 6. Chronogram of the Japanese economy and the process of its sucking into the "underdevelopment whirlpool" (underrun from the USA) from the positions of the theory of economic time.

As shown in Figure 8, as of 2021, the most successful players at a conventional stock exchange among advanced economies are Canada and Germany; their underrun from the USA is 9 years. They are followed by France and Japan and their underrun from the USA is 16 and 18 years, respectively. The underrun of the UK from the USA is 15 years. The most successful player at the conventional stock exchange among advanced economies in 2021 is Italy; its underrun from the USA is 21 years.

Thus, the structures of advanced economies, as a special category of the world economy, is not homogeneous; the level and rate of their development are much differentiated. During the studied period

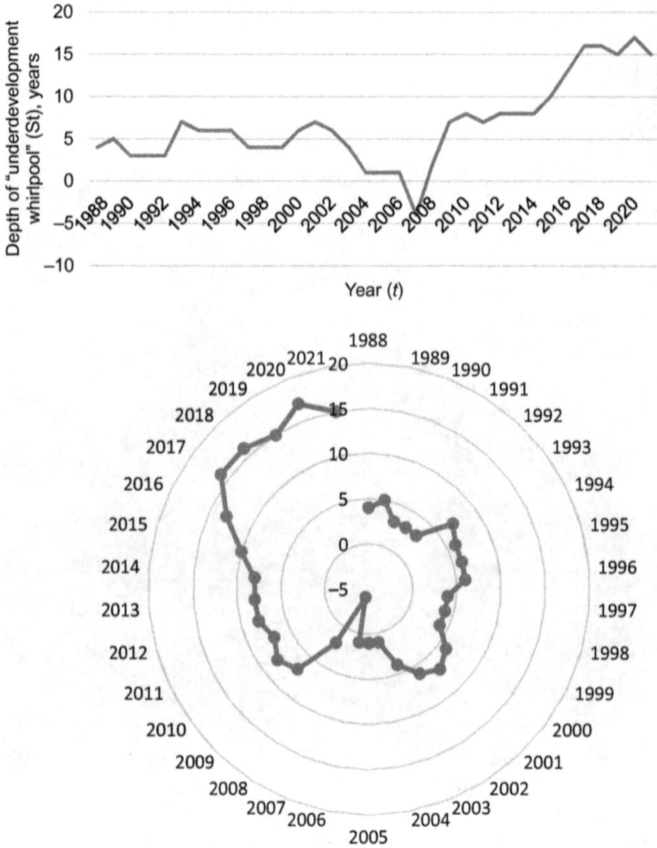

Figure 7. Chronogram of the UK economy and the process of its sucking into the "underdevelopment whirlpool" (underrun from the USA) from the positions of the theory of economic time.

(1988–2021), the countries of G7 demonstrated acceleration of socio-economic development (through the lens of GDP per capita) and were close to overcoming the USA. This could be compared to raising hands at the stock exchange — G7 countries were constantly starting prospective innovative projects faster than the USA.

However, since 2016, the leadership of the USA has been undisputable, which can be compared to this advanced economy's possessing privileged ("golden") shares, which guarantee it the advantage regardless of the situation at the stock exchange. However, in view of the cyclicity of the

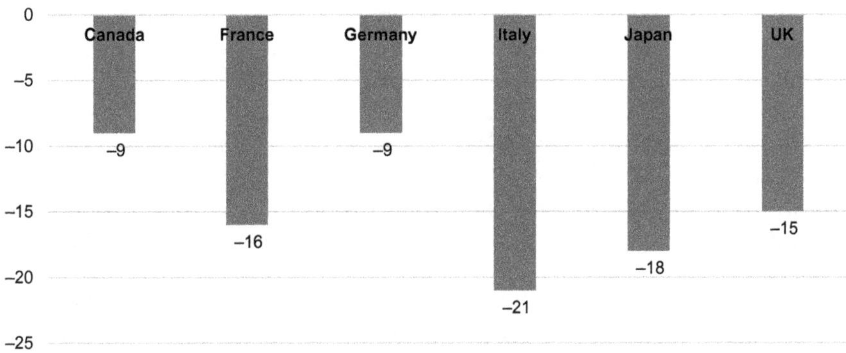

Figure 8. The comparative analysis of time disproportions among advanced economies in 2021.

development of the economy (and primarily stock exchange), it is logical to expect a change of balance of power in the category of advanced economies shortly.

References

Ahuja, V. & Tandon, R. K. (2010). Inflammatory bowel disease in the Asia-Pacific area: A comparison with developed countries and regional differences. *Journal of Digestive Diseases*, 11(3): 134–147.

Bulatov, A. (2014). The global problem of economic underdevelopment. *World and National Economy*, 2(29): 3.

Gurova, M. V. (2009). The role of intellectual property in overcoming economic underdevelopment. *Bulletin of the Orenburg State University*, 4(98): 64–68.

Inshakov, O. V. & Frolov, D. P. (2005). Economic space and spatial economics. Reflection on a new economic journal. *Economic Science of Modern Russia*, 4(1): 174–180.

International Monetary Fund (IMF) (2019). World Economic Outlook Database: Report for Selected Countries and Subjects. https://www.imf.org/external/pubs/ft/weo/2017/01/weodata/weorept.aspx?sy=1988&ey=2019&scsm=1&ssd=1&sort=subject&ds=%2C&br=0&pr1.x=50&pr1.y=3&c=156%2C158%2C132%2C112%2C134%2C111%2C136&s=NGDPDPC&grp=0&a=#cs1. Accessed: 02 November 2019.

Kindzersky, Y. V. (2010). Features of the development of the institution of property in the system of measures to overcome industrial underdevelopment. *Scientific Works of Donetsk National Technical University. Series: Economic*, 1(38): 61–69.

Laptev, A. V. & Sozinova, A. A. (2018). Study of disparities in the economic development of the Russian hotel services market using the analysis of “underdevelopment whirlpools”. *Economics and Management: Problems, Solutions*, 5, 3(75): 8–11.

Popkova, E. G. (2004a). The spatio-temporal approach in the concept of a new quality of economic growth. *Economic Sciences*, 7: 33–40.

Popkova, E. G. (2004b). Interaction of the concepts of sustainable development and the new quality of economic growth. *Finance and Credit*, 25(163): 43–47.

Popkova, E. G. (2004c). Interaction of the concepts of sustainable development and the new quality of economic growth. *Economic Analysis: Theory and Practice*, 25: 43.

Popkova, E. G. (2005). Formation of the Concept of a New Quality of Economic Growth in the Context of Globalization. Dissertation for the degree of Doctor of Economics, Penza.

Popkova, E. (2014). New prospects of economic growth in the context of underdevelopment whirlpools phenomena. *Applied Econometrics and International Development*, 14(1): 5–25.

Popkova, E. (2017a). Problem analysis of ‘underdevelopment whirlpools’ as an obstacle for economic growth in Asian countries. *International Journal of Business and Globalisation*, 19(2): 167–174.

Popkova, E. (2017b). Use of methodology of “underdevelopment whirlpools” with analysis of problems and perspectives of economic growth in Asian countries. *Journal of Entrepreneurship in Emerging Economies*, 9(1): DOI:10.1108/JEEE-07-2016-0027.

Popkova, E. G. & Sergi, B. S. (eds.) (2019). *Digital Economy: Complexity and Variety vs. Rationality*. Cham, Switzerland: Springer International Publishing.

Popkova, E., Gornostaeva, Z., & Tregulova, N. (2018). Role of innovations in the provision of competitiveness and innovational development of economy and overcoming of “underdevelopment whirlpools” in Russia and countries of Eastern Europe. *Journal of Entrepreneurship in Emerging Economies*, 10(3): 511–523.

Safronov, A. (2009). The comprador bourgeoisie and the problem of “economic underdevelopment”. *Free Thought*, 12(1607): 77–92.

Sarmiento Espinel, J. A., Silva Arias, A. C., & Van Gameren, E. (2015). Quality differences of higher education and its determinants in a less-developed country. *Journal of Higher Education Policy and Management*, 37(2): 204–221.

Semenov, A. S. & Derunov, V. A. (2016). Mathematical substantiation of economic growth in the conditions of the country falling into the “trap of underdevelopment”. *Bulletin of the Saratov University. New series. Series: Economics. Control. Law*, 16(3): 288–293.

Sergi, B. S., Popkova, E. G., Borzenko, K. V., & Przhedetskaya, N. V. (2019). Public-private partnerships as a mechanism of financing sustainable development. In Ziolo, M., & Sergi, B. S. (eds.) *Financing Sustainable Development: Key Challenges and Prospects*. Palgrave Macmillan, London. pp. 313–339. DOI:10.1007/978-3-030-16522-2_13.

Shakhovskaya, L. S. & Popkova, E. G. (2004). New quality of economic growth in the context of modern globalization. *Finance and Credit*, 23(16): 71–77.

World Bank. (2023). GDP per capita (current US$). https://data.worldbank.org/indicator/NY.GDP.PCAP.CD?view=chart. Accessed: 05 January 2023.

Zabrodotsky, Y. (2006). Anatomy of underdevelopment and corruption. *Economic Strategies*, 8.7(49): 42–47.

Chapter 17

"Underdevelopment Whirlpools" of Emerging Economies: Time Is a Means of Avoiding Defeat

Minutes, like frisky horses, fly,
You look around — the sunset is already close.

Al-Ma'arri, Arab poet, philosopher and philologist

This chapter states that time is the indicator of deep differences among structural entities of the world economy — emerging economies.

This chapter considers the following issues:

- "underdevelopment whirlpools" in emerging economies as a manifestation of their heterogeneity by the example of countries of BRICS;
- creation and analysis of the chronograms of emerging economies;
- 3D modelling of the process of emerging economies' sucking into "underdevelopment whirlpools";
- comparative analysis of time disproportions among emerging economies (Figure 1).

In an instant photo of "economy of present continuous", advanced economies look like a closed stock exchange for large investors, while emerging economies participate in an open marathon (running competition). They try to "catch and overtake" advanced economies by the level of socio-economic development. In the global "race", they do not drive race cars, as the advanced economies do. Instead, emerging economies run at their own rate, actively competing against each other and searching for their mechanisms of acceleration.

Figure 1. Time is a means of avoiding defeat.

Source: Photo by scholar and photographer Elena Popkova, https://www.saatchiart.com/account/artworks/1599809.

This is explained by the differences in economic time between advanced economies and emerging economies, which were shown in Chapter 1. The marathon of emerging economies might differ from the path that advanced economies have passed. Very often it is shorter — due to the experience of the latter.

For example, in case of a large difference in technological modes, when advanced economies form Industry 4.0, and the considered emerging economy is agrarian, it might be possible to skip the stages of industrialization and post-industrialization and to start the digital modernization of the agrarian economy and its initial industrialization based on the digital technologies of Industry 4.0.

Another variant of "shortcut", which envisages shortening its stages, is possible. For example, emerging economies might implement a quick post-industrialization (whose duration is several years, not decades) and then pass to the stage of neo-industrialization based on the digital economy and Industry 4.0. Thus, unlike advanced economies, which tend to walk (drive) a common way (but at different speeds), emerging economies walk (run) along different ways and at different speeds. The duality of differences predetermines the increased inclination of emerging economies towards the differentiation of socio-economic development.

Many scholars and researchers write of their underrun from advanced economies. Foreign authors include Coates (2015), Romano *et al.* (2019), Sergi (2018, 2019), and Sergi & Scanlon (2019). In Russian economic thought, the issue of emerging economies' underrun from advanced economies, as well as its measuring and overcoming, is an independent and well-elaborated direction of scientific research.

Prof. Oleg V. Inshakov actively studied the fundamental and applied aspects of using the evolutionary approach *n* strategic management and the parametric evaluation of the types of socio-economic development of meso-level economic systems by the example of Russia's regions (Inshakov, 2011; Inshakov & Shevandrin, 2007). Developing their ideas, Sagidov (2017) points out that self-motion in the development of the regions of the North Caucasus Federal District of the Russian Federation is a condition of taking the path of liquidating the underdevelopment.

Polterovich (2009) determines Russia's underrun from advanced economies by the level and rate of socio-economic development as an "underdevelopment whirlpool", noting that "Russia has a good chance to leave it". Drobot (2010) forms the problem of emerging economies' underdevelopment in the global political context. Rodionova and Monge (2014) note the problem of liquidating the socio-economic underdevelopment of emerging economies through the example of Tanzania.

Chepko and Shagiakhmetova (2017) determine the reasons for emerging economies' underrun from advanced economies, which include not only economic but also social ones (e.g., cultural specifics). Bozieva (2017) suggests the tools for dealing with Russia's innovative underdevelopment, noting that it is in the innovative sphere that Russia's underrun from advanced economies is the largest. Fenin (2018) performed a retrospective analysis of the state's influence on the Russian economy within the concept of economic underdevelopment.

The literature review has shown that emerging economies' underrun from advanced economies has been studied in detail and reflected in the existing publications. However, the disproportions in the system of emerging economies (differentiation of the level and rate of their socio-economic development) remain poorly studied and undefined by economic science. To study them, let us use the methodology of "underdevelopment whirlpools", which was developed by Prof. Elena G. Popkova in the works Popkova (2004a, 2004b, 2004c), and Shakhovskaya & Popkova (2004) and further developed in the later publications Popkova (2014, 2017a, 2017b), and Popkova *et al.* (2018). This methodology has been described in detail in Chapters 12–14 in this book.

The research objects are countries of BRICS — as the most typical example of emerging economies.[1] The comparative analysis of GDP per capita of the countries of this category has shown that the leader (by this indicator) in 2019 was Russia ($11,558.84, according to the IMF and $12,194.78 in 2021, according to the World Bank, 2023) so it shall be used as the sample. The dynamics of Russia's GDP per capita in 1992–2021 (the data are available since 1992) are presented in Table 1.

The chronogram of the Indian and Chinese economies through the lens of "underdevelopment whirlpools" as a time asymmetry of their economic development and the process of their economies' sucking into the "underdevelopment whirlpool" (underrun from Russia, see Table 2) from the positions of the theory of economic time are shown in Figures 2 and 3.

As shown in Figure 2, the Indian economy has a classic funnel-shaped form, which is a sign of its systematic and increasing underrun from Russia in terms of economic time. While in 1992 the depth of "underdevelopment whirlpool" was one year, it reached 25 years by 2019, though the speed of sucking into the "whirlpool" was zero.

---

[1]BRICS is a group of five countries with the emerging economies: Brazil, Russia, India, China (PRC — People's Republic of China), and South Africa (South Africa). The abbreviation BRIC was first proposed by the analyst Jim O'Neill in November 2001 in the Goldman Sachs' Building Better Global Economic BRICs policy brief. Until 2011, the abbreviation BRIC was used in relation to the organization.

Table 1. Dynamics of Russia's GDP per capita in 1992–2021.

Year	GDP per capita, $	Year	GDP per capita, $	Year	GDP per capita, $
1992	619.869	2002	2,556.64	2012	15,145.38
1993	1,330.054	2003	3,197.688	2013	15,558.8
1994	2,004.407	2004	4,408.374	2014	14,388
1995	2,271.31	2005	5,713.361	2015	9,521.081
1996	2,842.858	2006	7,420.484	2016	8,928.697
1997	2,944.467	2007	9,753.262	2017	10,885.48
1998	1,975.972	2008	12,468.38	2018	11,248.33
1999	1,432.661	2009	9,178.45	2019	11,536.25
2000	1,905.949	2010	11,445.13	2020	10,169.09
2001	2,259.023	2011	14,187.19	2021	12,194.78

Source: Based on World Bank (2023).

Table 2. "Underdevelopment whirlpool" as the indicator of India/China' time lag from Russia.

t (year)		India				China			
		GDP per capita $t_{(\alpha)}$, $	GDP per capita $t_{(\beta)}$	Dt, year	St, years per 1 year	GDP per capita $t_{(\alpha)}$, $	GDP per capita $t_{(\beta)}$	Dt, years	St, years per 1 year
t_0	1992	332.54	1991	1	—	423.03	1991	1	—
t_1	1993	315.42	1991	2	1	525.71	1991	2	1
t_2	1994	362.37	1991	3	1	472.65	1991	3	1
t_3	1995	391.25	1991	4	1	608.38	1992	3	0
t_4	1996	418.60	1991	5	1	708.58	1992	4	1
t_5	1997	434.74	1991	6	1	780.84	1992	5	1
t_6	1998	432.23	1991	7	1	827.64	1992	6	1
t_7	1999	462.13	1991	8	1	872.22	1992	7	1
t_8	2000	463.12	1991	9	1	958.56	1992	8	1
t_9	2001	471.31	1991	10	1	1,053.15	1992	9	1
t_{10}	2002	492.23	1991	11	1	1,150.21	1993	9	0
t_{11}	2003	572.30	1991	12	1	1,293.13	1993	10	1

(*Continued*)

Table 2. (*Continued*)

	India				China			
t (year)	GDP per capita $t_{(\alpha)}$, \$	GDP per capita $t_{(\beta)}$	Dt, year	St, years per 1 year	GDP per capita $t_{(\alpha)}$, \$	GDP per capita $t_{(\beta)}$	Dt, years	St, years per 1 year
t_{12} 2004	657.52	1992	12	0	1,512.62	1993	11	1
t_{13} 2005	748.85	1992	13	1	1,765.72	1993	12	1
t_{14} 2006	839.93	1992	14	1	2,110.57	1994	12	0
t_{15} 2007	1,080.89	1993	14	0	2,703.00	1995	12	0
t_{16} 2008	1,053.44	1993	15	1	3,467.03	2003	5	−7
t_{17} 2009	1,159.06	1993	16	1	3,837.90	2003	6	1
t_{18} 2010	1,429.60	1993	17	1	4,524.06	2004	6	0
t_{19} 2011	1,497.40	1993	18	1	5,582.89	2005	6	0
t_{20} 2012	1,470.73	1993	19	1	6,329.46	2005	7	1
t_{21} 2013	1,475.17	1993	20	1	7,080.83	2006	7	0
t_{22} 2014	1,594.32	1993	21	1	7,701.69	2006	8	1
t_{23} 2015	1,615.79	1993	22	1	8,166.76	2006	9	1
t_{24} 2016	1,723.30	1993	23	1	8,113.26	2006	10	1
t_{25} 2017	1,850.23	1993	24	1	8,480.65	2006	11	1
t_{26} 2018	1,998.26	1993	25	1	9,146.85	2007	11	0
t_{27} 2019	2,047.23	1991	28	3	10,143.83	2010	9	−2
t_{28} 2020	1,910.42	1993	27	−1	10,408.67	2010	10	1
t_{29} 2021	2,256.59	1995	26	−1	12,556.33	2010	11	1

As shown in Figure 3, in 1992 the Chinese economy was one year behind the Russian economy by GDP per capita, and by 2005 the depth of the "underdevelopment whirlpool" reached 12 years. In 2008, there was observed vivid progress — the "whirlpool's" depth reduced to 5 years, but then it continued growing, reaching 12 years in 2019, and the speed of sucking into the "whirlpool" was 1 year per 1 year.

The calculation of Brazil/South Africa's "underdevelopment whirlpool" (underrun from Russia) is presented in Table 3.

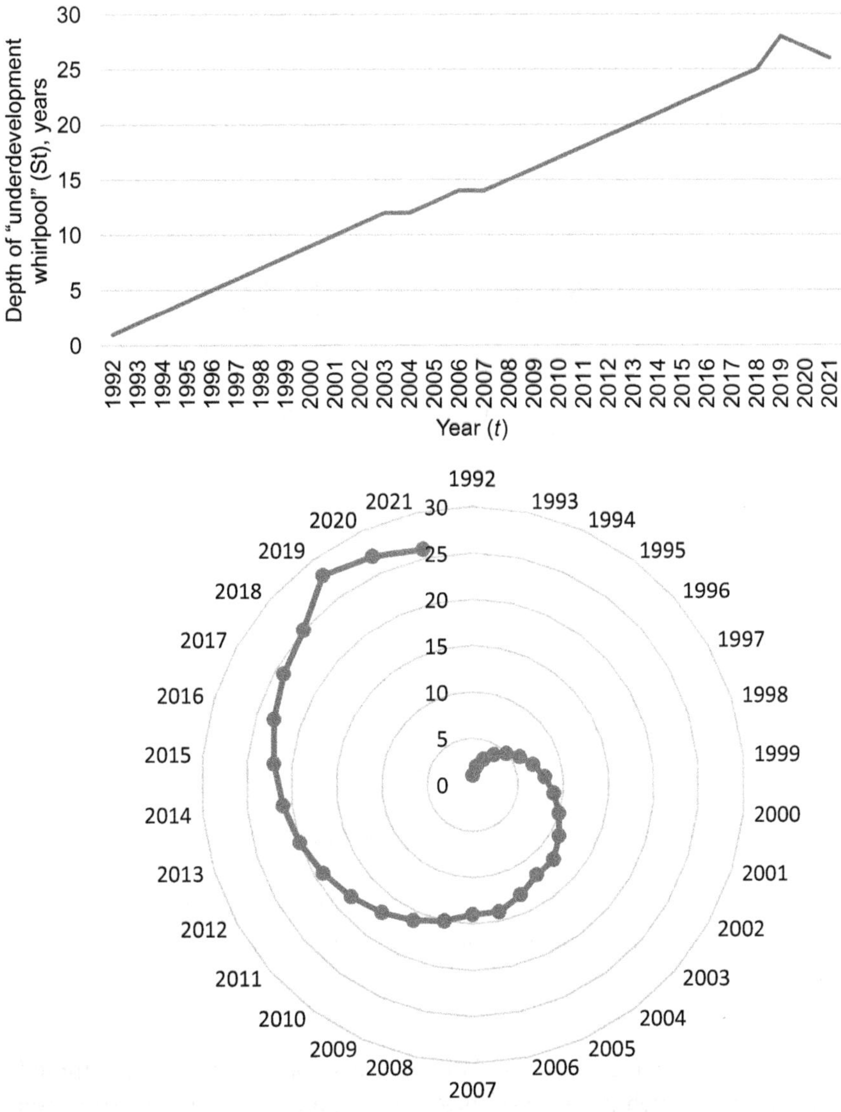

Figure 2. Chronogram of the Indian economy and the process of its sucking into the "underdevelopment whirlpool" (underrun from Russia) from the positions of the theory of economic time.

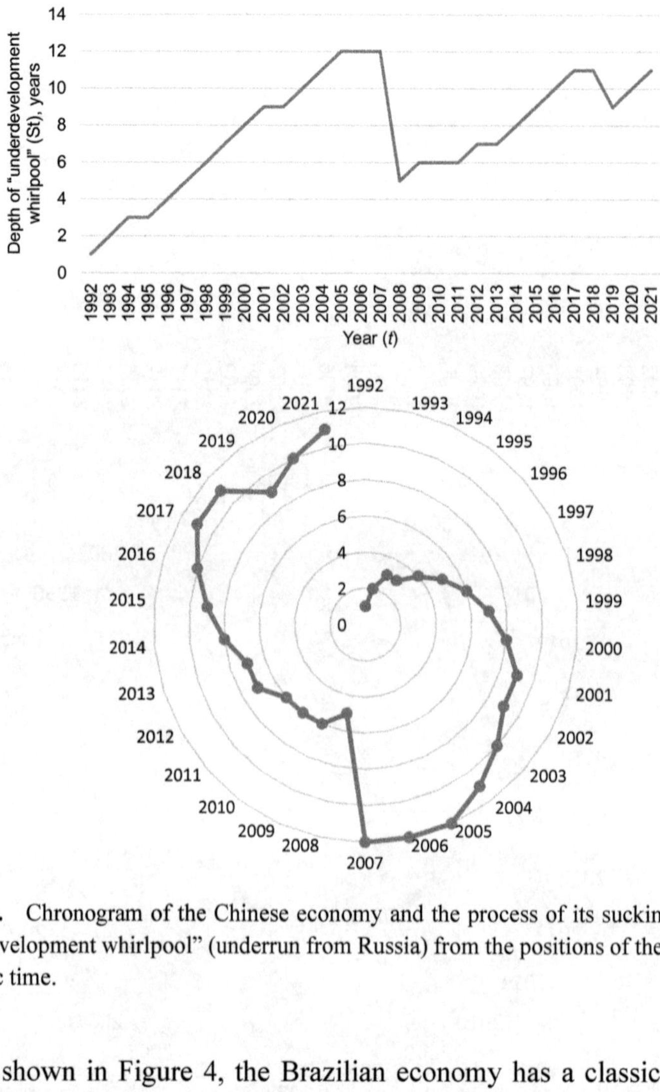

Figure 3. Chronogram of the Chinese economy and the process of its sucking into the "underdevelopment whirlpool" (underrun from Russia) from the positions of the theory of economic time.

As shown in Figure 4, the Brazilian economy has a classic funnel-shaped form, which is a sign of its systematic and growing underrun from Russia in terms of economic time. While in 1992 Brazil was 10 years ahead of Russia by GDP per capita, this difference reduced to zero by 2002, and 2004 marked the emergence of an "underdevelopment whirlpool", which reached 11 years by 2019, though the speed of sucking into the "whirlpool" was zero.

As shown in Figure 5, the South African economy has a classic funnel-shaped form, which is a sign of its systematic and growing underrun from Russia in terms of economic time. While in 1992 South Africa was 11 years ahead of Russia by GDP per capita, this advantage reduced to

Table 3. The "underdevelopment whirlpool" as the indicator of the time lag of Brazil and South Africa from Russia.

		Brazil				**South Africa**			
***t* (year)**		**GDP per capita $t_{(\alpha)}$, $**	**GDP per capita $t_{(\beta)}$**	**Dt, years**	**St, years per 1 year**	**GDP per capita $t_{(\alpha)}$, $**	**GDP per capita $t_{(\beta)}$**	**Dt, years**	**St, years per 1 year**
t_0	1992	2,633.39	2002	−10	—	3,481.42	2003	−11	—
t_1	1993	2,908.26	2003	−10	0	3,390.85	2003	−10	1
t_2	1994	3,569.46	2003	−9	1	3,446.84	2003	−9	1
t_3	1995	4,950.30	2004	−9	0	3,752.38	2003	−8	1
t_4	1996	5,273.89	2005	−9	0	3,500.03	2003	−7	1
t_5	1997	5,394.64	2005	−8	1	3,556.54	2003	−6	1
t_6	1998	5,197.03	2005	−7	1	3,160.84	2003	−5	1
t_7	1999	3,552.14	2003	−4	3	3,089.37	2003	−4	1
t_8	2000	3,778.97	2003	−3	1	3,042.43	2003	−3	1
t_9	2001	3,183.79	2003	−2	1	2,671.99	2002	−1	2
t_{10}	2002	2,859.60	2002	0	2	2,524.22	2002	0	1
t_{11}	2003	3,090.66	2003	0	0	3,775.56	2003	0	0
t_{12}	2004	3,659.10	2003	1	1	4,870.66	2004	0	0
t_{13}	2005	4,815.71	2004	1	0	5,412.37	2005	0	0
t_{14}	2006	5,912.55	2005	1	0	5,635.29	2005	1	1
t_{15}	2007	7,374.08	2006	1	0	6,117.19	2005	2	1
t_{16}	2008	8,854.16	2006	2	1	5,793.12	2005	3	1
t_{17}	2009	8,624.42	2006	3	1	5,914.14	2005	4	1
t_{18}	2010	11,297.84	2007	3	0	7,361.94	2006	4	0
t_{19}	2011	13,242.49	2008	3	0	8,058.91	2006	5	1
t_{20}	2012	12,367.14	2008	4	1	7,548.45	2007	5	0
t_{21}	2013	12,295.09	2008	5	1	6,898.48	2005	8	3
t_{22}	2014	12,112.57	2008	6	1	6,492.89	2005	9	1
t_{23}	2015	8,810.50	2006	9	3	5,721.15	2005	10	1
t_{24}	2016	8,726.90	2006	10	1	5,260.90	2005	11	1
t_{25}	2017	10,308.81	2007	10	0	5,588.96	2005	12	1
t_{26}	2018	10,699.60	2007	11	1	5,662.05	2005	13	1
t_{27}	2019	8,845.26	2006	13	2	6,688.79	2005	14	1
t_{27}	2020	6,794.49	2005	15	2	5,741.64	2005	15	1
t_{27}	2021	7,507.16	2006	15	0	7,055.04	2006	15	0

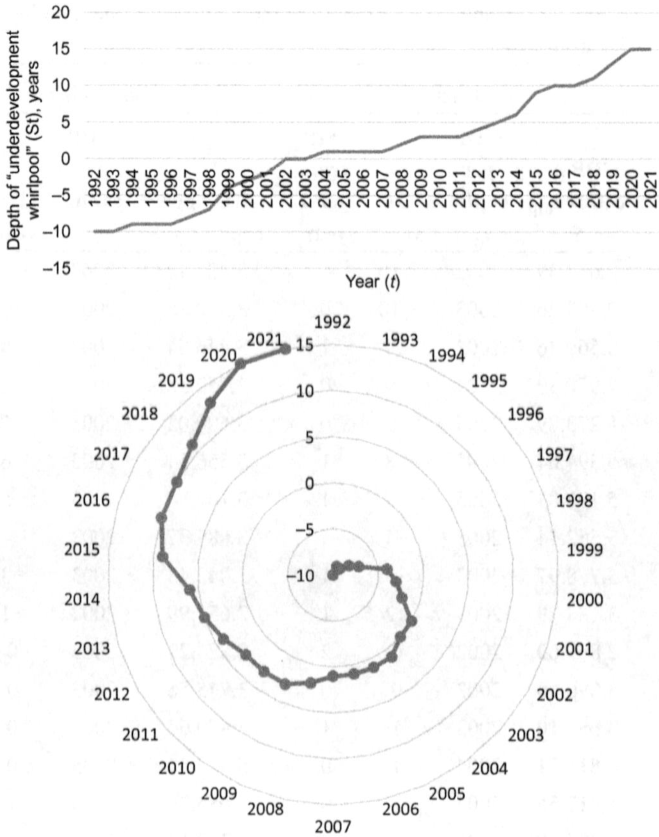

Figure 4. Chronogram of the Brazilian economy and the process of its sucking into the "underdevelopment whirlpool" (underrun from Russia) from the positions of the theory of economic time.

zero by 2002; 2006 marked the emergence of an "underdevelopment whirlpool", which reached 14 years by 2019, while the speed of sucking into the "whirlpool" is 1 year per 1 year.

The comparative analysis of time disproportions among emerging economies is presented in Figure 6.

As shown in Figure 6, BRICS countries are "running" at different speeds and on different tracks. Thus, South Africa, which was 11 years ahead of Russia by the level of GDP per capita in 1992, was ranked second among the countries of BRICS by the depth of "underdevelopment whirlpool" (underrun from Russia) in 2019 (14 years). South Africa was running on the longest track. On the contrary, China, which had the largest

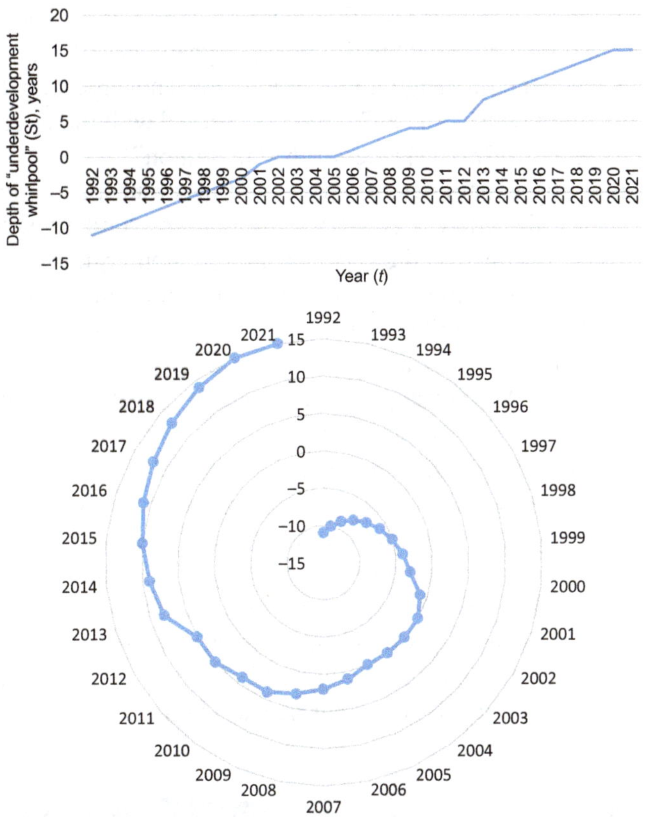

Figure 5. Chronogram of the South African economy and the process of its sucking into the "underdevelopment whirlpool" (underrun from Russia) from the positions of the theory of economic time.

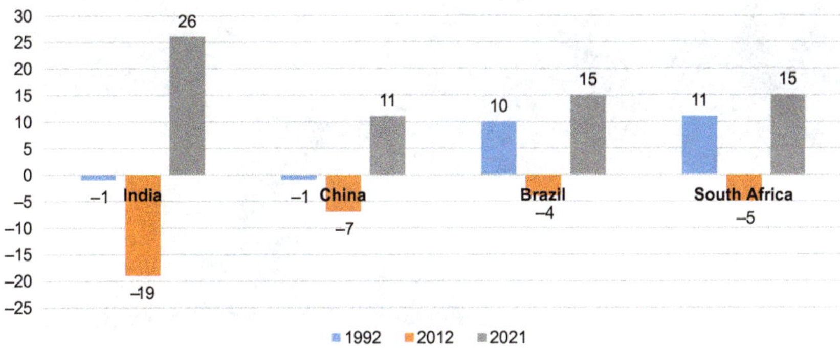

Figure 6. Comparative analysis of time disproportions among emerging economies in 1992, 2012 and 2021.

underrun from Russia (1 year) in 1992, became a country of BRICS with the smallest "underdevelopment whirlpool" (12 years) in 2019. This shows that China has reduced the length of its "marathon. The largest depth of the "underdevelopment whirlpool" in 2019 was observed with India (25 years), and the smallest, with Brazil (leader of the "marathon").

Thus, emerging economies do participate in a kind of marathon. As the experience of the BRICS countries has shown, "underdevelopment whirlpools" are peculiar for the most progressive emerging economies, which demonstrate the highest rate of socio-economic development (growth of GDP per capita). At present, all BRICS countries are developing a digital economy and performing a transition to Industry 4.0.

However, South Africa "skipped" the stage of industrialization, while Russia and China passed this stage very quickly. This caused substantial disproportions in the structure of the countries of BRICS. It should be noted that unlike advanced economies, in which "underdevelopment whirlpools" are relative and are frequently overcome, emerging economies are peculiar for classic "underdevelopment whirlpools", which are constantly deepening. This is a sign of much lower opportunities for emerging economies in overcoming the "underdevelopment whirlpools" and of the necessity to use a completely different approach for this — the one based not on just acceleration but acceleration and reduction of the marathon's length (Figure 7).

Figure 7. Time is a way of escaping defeat.

Source: Photo by scholar and photographer Elena Popkova, https://www.saatchiart.com/account/artworks/1599809.

References

Bozieva, I. A. (2017). Tools for overcoming Russian innovation underdevelopment. *Economics and Business: Theory and Practice*, 12: 51–54.

Chepko, K. V. & Shagiakhmetova, E. R. (2017). The reasons for the underdevelopment of developing countries from developed ones. *Axiom: Actual Aspects of the Humanities*, 2(6): 104–107.

Coates, H. (2015). Developing countries lag behind the US and UK in contributing to institutional repository literature. *Evidence-Based Library and Information Practice*, 10(2): 161–163.

Drobot, G. A. (2010). The problem of the underdevelopment of developing countries in the world political context. *Moscow University Bulletin. Series 12: Political Sciences*, 3: 53–66.

Fenin, K. V. (2018). Retrospective analysis of the influence of the state on the Russian economy within the framework of the concept of economic underdevelopment. *Humanitarian Scientific Journal*, 1(1): 8.

International Monetary Fund (IMF) (2019). World Economic Outlook Database: Report for Selected Countries and Subjects. https://www.imf.org/external/pubs/ft/weo/2017/01/weodata/weorept.aspx?sy=1988&ey=2019&scsm=1&ssd=1&sort=subject&ds=%2C&br=0&pr1.x=50&pr1.y=3&c=156%2C158%2C132%2C112%2C134%2C111%2C136&s=NGDPDPC&grp=0&a=#cs1. Accessed: 02 November 2019.

Inshakov, O. V. (2011). The potential of an evolutionary approach in the strategic management of mesoeconomic systems. *Regional Development Economics: Problems, Searches, Prospects*, 12: 111–126.

Inshakov, O. V. & Shevandrin, A. V. (2007). Applied aspects of parametric assessment of types of socio-economic development of regions. *Bulletin of the Volgograd State University. Series 3: Economics. Ecology*, 11: 67–78.

Polterovich, B. (2009). Scientific council. Underdevelopment trap: Russia has chances to get out of it. *Direct Investments*, 5(85): 8–11.

Popkova, E. G. (2004a). The spatio-temporal approach in the concept of a new quality of economic growth. *Economic Sciences*, 7: 33–40.

Popkova, E. G. (2004b). Interaction of the concepts of sustainable development and the new quality of economic growth. *Finance and Credit*, 25(163): 43–47.

Popkova, E. G. (2004c). Interaction of the concepts of sustainable development and the new quality of economic growth. *Economic Analysis: Theory and Practice*, 25: 43.

Popkova, E. G. (2005). Formation of the Concept of a New Quality of Economic Growth in the Context of Globalization. Dissertation for the Degree of Doctor of Economics, Penza.

Popkova, E. (2014). New prospects of economic growth in the context of underdevelopment whirlpools phenomena. *Applied Econometrics and International Development*, 14(1): 5–25.

Popkova, E. (2017a). Problem analysis of 'underdevelopment whirlpools' as an obstacle for economic growth in Asian countries. *International Journal of Business and Globalisation*, 19(2): 167–174.

Popkova, E. (2017b). Use of methodology of "underdevelopment whirlpools" with analysis of problems and perspectives of economic growth in Asian countries. *Journal of Entrepreneurship in Emerging Economies*, 9(1): DOI:10.1108/JEEE-07-2016-0027.

Popkova, E., Gornostaeva, Z., & Tregulova, N. (2018). Role of innovations in the provision of competitiveness and innovational development of economy and overcoming of "underdevelopment whirlpools" in Russia and countries of Eastern Europe. *Journal of Entrepreneurship in Emerging Economies*, 10(3): 511–523.

Rodionova, I. A. & Monge, E. (2014). The problem of overcoming the socio-economic underdevelopment of developing countries on the example of Tanzania. *Bulletin of the Peoples' Friendship University of Russia. Series: International Relations*, 2: 158–168.

Sagidov, Y. N. (2017). Self-movement in the development of the regions of the North Caucasus Federal District as a condition for becoming on the path of overcoming underdevelopment. *Regional Problems of Economic Transformation*, 10(84): 23–37.

Sergi, B. S. (ed.). (2018). *Exploring the Future of Russia's Economy and Markets: Towards Sustainable Economic Development*. Bingley, UK: Emerald Publishing Limited.

Sergi, B.S. (ed.). (2019). *Modeling Economic Growth in Contemporary Russia*. Bingley, UK: Emerald Publishing Limited.

Sergi, B. S. & Scanlon, C. C. (eds.) (2019). *Entrepreneurship and Development in the 21st Century*. Bingley, UK: Emerald Publishing Limited.

Shakhovskaya, L. S. & Popkova, E. G. (2004). New quality of economic growth in the context of modern globalization. *Finance and Credit*, 23(16): 71–77.

World Bank (2023). GDP per capita (current US$). https://data.worldbank.org/indicator/NY.GDP.PCAP.CD?view=chart. Accessed: 05 January 2023.

Part IV

Application of the Concept of "Underdevelopment Whirlpools" to Fill the Methodological Gaps of the Modern Theory of Innovation: How to Manage Time in Economy

This part states that economic time, unlike physical time, could be managed and requires management. Depending on the current economic time and the speed of its flow, various approaches to its management are needed. Advanced economies, which demonstrate time advance as compared to the average time in the world economy, could preserve a high quality of their economic growth by implementing investment and innovative projects. Emerging economies, which are peculiar for a time lag that is measured with the help of "underdevelopment whirlpools", can overcome them and increase the quality of their economic growth through the development of human potential, modernization, and integration. The prospects and ways of overcoming "underdevelopment whirlpools" depending on the level of time lag are offered. An economic calendar, as the indicator of economic systems' development in time in comparison with the existing technological mode, is compiled. The paradoxes of economic time are determined. Models of overcoming "underdevelopment whirlpools" in advanced and emerging economies through the lens of their time lag and economic calendar are developed.

It is necessary to pay attention to two properties of physical time, which are stated in Anisov (2019) and which also refer to economic time. The first one is irreversibility, and the second one is the absence of fixedness. The development of economic systems in time and their evolution leads to irreversible changes. Their future is variable and can go according to different scenarios, of which only one will take place in practice.

Chapter 18

Prospects and Ways to Overcome "Underdevelopment Whirlpools" Depending on the Degree of Time Lag: Time is the Object of Management

Money and time are the heaviest burdens of life, and... the unhappiest of all mortals are those who have more of either than they know how to use.

Samuel Johnson, English literary critic, lexicographer and poet of the 18th century

This chapter states that time is an object of management (Figure 1) and a customizable parameter, which allows changing the balance of powers in the world economy.

This chapter considers the following issues:

- factor analysis of "underdevelopment whirlpools" in developed and developing countries;
- overview of the ways of overcoming "underdevelopment whirlpools" in developed and developing countries;
- specifics of overcoming "underdevelopment whirlpools" in developed and developing countries;
- classification of the prospects of overcoming "underdevelopment whirlpools" by the criterion of complexity;
- the scale of overcoming "underdevelopment whirlpools" depending on the level of time lag.

Figure 1. Time is the object of management.

Source: Photo by scholar and photographer Elena Popkova, https://www.saatchiart.com/account/artworks/1599809.

The most important function of the Theory of Time in Economies is managing economic time in the interests of overcoming economic systems' underrun and reducing and eliminating the disproportions in the world economy's development. This necessity has been declared by the UN (2019) as one of the Sustainable Development Goals, which makes the Theory of Time in economics a scientific methodology, which stimulates the provision of sustainable development.

As the experience of developed countries (by the example of G7 countries), studied in Chapter 16, and the experience of developing countries (by the example of BRICS), studied in Chapters 15 and 17, has shown, the flow of economic time could be accelerated (as well as slowed down). This is an essential difference between economic and physical time since physical time only can be measured. The ideas of accelerating the Earth's rotation are connected to risks of biological catastrophes, belonging to the sphere of utopia. Economic time can be managed; moreover, its acceleration favourably influences the social mode and economic activities of humanity.

The economic time of an economic system is a customizable parameter, which allows changing the balance of powers in the world economy. The acceleration of economic time could be compared to the launch of a spaceship. The very idea of space flight was so innovative and popular that when the capabilities of technological progress in the second part of the 20th century allowed for its implementation in practice, a space race between the USSR and the USA started.

Orbital launches became the most significant ones in history. On October 4, 1957, the USSR launched the first artificial Earth satellite (Sputnik-1, rocket Sputnik 8K71PS, The Baikonur Cosmodrome) and on April 12, 1961, Yuri Gagarin became the first human to journey into outer space. Afterwards, on January 31, 1958, the USA launched its Earth satellite (Explorer 1, rocket Juno I) from the Cape Canaveral Missile Test Center, and on July 16, 1969, the American spaceship Apollo 1 took astronauts to the Moon.

These achievements are among the greatest in the history of humankind. They were a sign of a new era. A rocket engine develops incredible velocity, allowing covering large distances very quickly. In a conventional race (described in Chapter 16), the use of a rocket engine means phenomenal acceleration, which allows an economic system to overtake its rivals, even if they take shortcuts along the way.

Therefore, there's a need to search for an "economic recipe" for a rocket engine — means and ways to deal with "underdevelopment whirlpools". The necessity to overcome the disproportions in the structure of the world economy is noted by many modern scholars around the world, in particular Dudin & Frolova (2015), Solomou (1986), Sergi (2018, 2019), and Sergi & Scanlon (2019).

Russian researchers also pay close attention to the provision of the world economy's balance during the implementation of the Sustainable Development Goals. In particular, this issue is discussed in Inshakov & Shevandrin (2007), Inshakov (2011), Chernova (2012), Durdyeva (2014), Andreeva *et al.* (2015), Bragina (2016), and Endovitsky *et al.* (2018).

In view of the specifics of economic time, it cannot be studied through the lens of physical time. At the same time, its study requires a scientific and philosophical platform. One of the founders of the philosophy of time is Henri Bergson, a French philosopher of the early 20th century. In his paradigm work *Duration and Simultaneity: Bergson and the Einsteinian Universe* (Bergson, 1923), he reconsidered Einstein's theory of relativity and outlined a philosophical view of the interconnection between space and time. The peak of his ideas was the substantiation of the existence of "space-time" amalgam (the last, sixth, chapter "Four-dimensional Space-Time").

In economic theory, there is a phenomenon of amalgamation — the process of transnational corporations' monopolizing the global markets. This phenomenon was initially assigned to the age of imperialism. However, it remains topical now. According to Henri Bergson, amalgamation in physics leads to the merging of space and time, as a result of which a certain time is established (fixed) with a certain territory (space). In economics, this means institutionalization of the disproportions in the world economic system — advanced economies' establishment as the leaders, and emerging economies' establishment as outsiders.

Acknowledging the fact of institutionalization, it should be noted that, unlike the laws of physics, institutions could emerge as well as transform and disintegrate if they become "institutional traps" (losing their effectiveness). Thus, the Theory of Time in economics has to overcome "underdevelopment whirlpools" as the "institutional traps" of the global economy.

In cooperation with Sokolov (Ph.D., business consultant of the European Bank for Reconstruction and Development) the author of this book reconsidered the idea of what exactly could lead to a quick transition of the national economy to another (higher or lower) level of development — a new quality of economic growth. It is a quick change of the indicators of its dynamics, GDP, and GDP per capita. An example of such intensification is Chile's economy during the period of A. Pinochet's rule, South Korea, and other examples of an "economic miracle".[1] Examples of destructive consequences of the attempts of forced acceleration of economic growth rate are many. The recent ones are Venezuela, Baltic countries, and countries with "orange revolutions".

Thus, leaving a stability period determines the presence of a period of instability. There are two reasons for the transition to instability. The positive one is successful, revolutionary economic reforms (the condition of whose implementation would often be political reforms). The negative one is the destruction of the economy under the influence of the following:

- primarily internal factors (civil war);
- externally orchestrated internal factors ("orange revolutions").

[1]"Economic miracle" — Figurative title for a quickly developing economy of a country or region during a certain period of time.

It is possible to speak of positively or negatively oriented intensive influence on the economy, or "blow", as a necessary condition for taking it from the state of stability. A more attractive option is a positively oriented influence, which ensures intensification and centripetal development. The negative influence could lead to development according to two sub-models.

The "blow" and the transition to instability under the influence of internal factors will lead to the economy's movement to the periphery of the "whirlpool", and its further dynamics will be determined primarily by the same internal factors. It is interesting to consider an external "blow", i.e., external impact from countries with the most developed economies within the existing geopolitical tendencies for the preservation of the monopolar world order.

Under such a "blow", a country has only two options for development and must count only on its strength. Each of these options is determined by such factors as preservation or loss of not national but state and economic "authenticity", or independence. Striving for the preservation of independence leads to the economy's movement — under the impact of the "blow" — to the periphery of the "whirlpool", and it could stay there for a very long time (Cuba is a prime example).

The absence of a striving to preserve authenticity leads to the national economy's assimilation through full integration, not so much in the global economic system as — according to the world experience — in the economies of the most developed countries or, in other words, in the "global economic system" as a derivative of these economies. There are numerous tools for the implementation of this model (for example, the International Monetary Fund). In this case, the national economy ceases to exist from the point of view of authenticity, building into the most developed economies and losing its orbit, "falling into the whirlpool and dissolving in it" (Baltic countries are a vivid example).

The unattractiveness of the described model predetermines a need for an alternative model of using not external (managed by advanced economies) but own sources of the economic system's transition to a new quality of economic growth based on management of internal factors. This model is discussed in the works of Popkova (2004a, 2004b, 2004c, 2005, 2014, 2017a, 2017b), Shakhovskaya & Popkova (2004), and Popkova *et al.* (2018).

The most notable internal factors affecting the quality of economic growth are innovative activity, human development, foreign investments, and modernization. Taking into account the differences like "underdevelopment whirlpools" in advanced economies and emerging economies, a separate regression analysis of the influence of the above factors on the depth of "underdevelopment whirlpools" in these categories of countries is presented in Tables 1 and 2.

The results of the performed regression analyses are presented in Table 3.

Table 1. Depth of "underdevelopment whirlpools" and the internal factors of their emergence in advanced economies in 2021.

Country of G7 with an advanced economy	Depth of "underdevelopment whirlpool" (underrun from the USA (Dt)), years y_1	Global innovation index*, points 1–100 x_{11}	Human development index, shares 1 x_{12}	Volume of foreign direct investments, $ x_{13}	Digital competitiveness index*, points 1–100 x_{14}
Canada	−9	50.8	0.936	60,177.31	94.15
France	−16	55.0	0.903	88,427.62	81.42
Germany	−9	57.2	0.942	73,654.32	85.17
Italy	−21	46.1	0.895	14,327.30	68.33
Japan	−18	53.6	0.925	27,321.71	76.84
UK	−15	59.7	0.929	22,604.21	86.45
Arithmetic mean	−14.67	53.73	0.92	47,752.08	82.06
Standard deviation	4.84	4.82	0.02	30,485.55	8.85
Coefficient of variation, %	−33.03	8.97	2.03	63.84	10.78

Note: *data were taken from the 2022 rating as a result of 2021.

Source: Based on Cornell University, INSEAD, WIPO (2023), IMD (2023), UNDP (2023), World Bank (2023).

Table 2. Depth of "underdevelopment whirlpools" and the internal factors of their emergence in emerging economies in 2021.

Country of BRICS with emerging economy	**Depth of "underdevelopment whirlpool" (underrun from the USA (Dt), years**	**Depth of "underdevelopment whirlpool" (underrun from the regional sample (Dt), years**	**Depth of "underdevelopment whirlpool" (underrun from Russia (Dt), years**	**Innovations index*, points 1–100**	**Human development index, shares of 1**	**Volume of foreign direct investments, $**	**Digital competitiveness index*, points 1–100**
	y_2	y_3	y_4	x_{21}	x_{22}	x_{23}	x_{24}
India	−61	−50 (from Japan)	−26	36.6	0.633	44,727.28	63.93
China	−41	−36 (from Japan)	−11	55.3	0.768	333,979.03	86.42
Brazil	−47	—	−15	32.5	0.754	46,441.11	56.14
South Africa	−48	—	−15	29.8	0.713	40,450.00	51.24
Russia	−41	−41 (from Germany)	—	34.3	0.822	41,296.14	60.27**
Arithmetic mean	−47.60	−42.33	−16.75	37.70	0.74	101,378.71	63.60
Standard deviation	8.17	7.09	6.45	10.15	0.07	130,050.62	13.60
Coefficient of variation, %	−17.17	−16.76	−38.50	26.92	9.55	128.28	21.39

Notes: *data were taken from the 2022 rating as a result of 2021, **data for 2021 are presented due to the absence of the 2022 data.
Source: Based on Cornell University, INSEAD, WIPO (2023), IMD (2023), UNDP (2023), World Bank (2023).

Table 3. Characteristics of the regression dependence of the depth of "underdevelopment whirlpools" on the impact of the internal factors in advanced economies and emerging economies in 2021.

		Parameters of the function								
		Innovations index		Human development index		Volume of foreign direct investments		Digital competitiveness index		
Function	a	b, points	b, % of average	b, shares of 1	b, % of average	b, $	b, % of average	b, points	b, % of average	r^2, %
$y_1(x_{11}, x_{12}, x_{13}, x_{14})$	−169.03	−0.21	53.73	160.42	0.92	0	—	0.18	82.06	97.80
$y_2(x_{21}, x_{22}, x_{23}, x_{24})$	−45.88	−15.08	−40.00	72.94	9,883.29	0	—	7.37	11.59	99.99
$y_3(x_{21}, x_{22}, x_{23}, x_{24})$	−559.44	224.31	595.00	355.39	48,155.27	−0.01	0	−120.12	−188.87	99.99
$y_4(x_{21}, x_{22}, x_{23}, x_{24})$	112.50	−63.87	−169.42	28.39	3,846.93	0	—	33.00	51.88	99.99

Table 3 contains parameters of the models of multiple linear regression of the type $y = a + b_1 * x_1 + b_2 * x_2 + b_3 * x_3 + b_4 * x_{14}$: a are constant, b are the coefficients for each independent variable, and r^2 denotes coefficient of correlation. As can be seen, the volume of foreign direct investments is an insignificant factor in all obtained regression models.

Thus, an increase in the degree of time lag leads to complications in the means of its overcoming. The lowest degree of time lag is observed in the internal structure of advanced economies (the depth of "underdevelopment whirlpool" is 14.67 years on average, variation is moderate — 33.03%) and in the internal structure of emerging economies (the depth of "underdevelopment whirlpool" is 16.75 years on average, variation is high — 38.50%).

A method of overcoming the "underdevelopment whirlpool" between developed countries is the increase in innovative activities. Low variation of the innovations index in advanced economies (8.97%) allows for achieving the necessary effect even with minimum efforts, which predetermines the simplicity of the use of this method.

A method of overcoming the "underdevelopment whirlpool" between developing countries is an increase in the level of human development. Low variation of the innovations index in advanced economies (9.08%) allows for achieving the necessary effect even with the minimum efforts, which predetermines the simplicity of the use of this method. It should be noted that variation of the depth of "underdevelopment whirlpools" among emerging economies (38.50%) is much higher (by more than two times) than among advanced economies (33.03%) — 38.50/33.03 = 1.16 — therefore, emerging economies have to make greater efforts to overcome the "underdevelopment whirlpools" between emerging economies.

A method of overcoming the "underdevelopment whirlpool" between developing countries and regional leaders has not been found during the calculations. It might be caused by the impossibility of independent overcoming of regional "whirlpools" by emerging economies and by the necessity for their integration with each other and with regional samples — advanced economies.

A method of overcoming the "underdevelopment whirlpool" between developing countries and developed countries is digitalization (modernization) of the economy. The average variation of the innovations index in advanced economies (8.97%) allows for achieving the necessary effect with moderate efforts. Unlike innovations and human development, digitalization envisages the implementation of not separate initiatives but

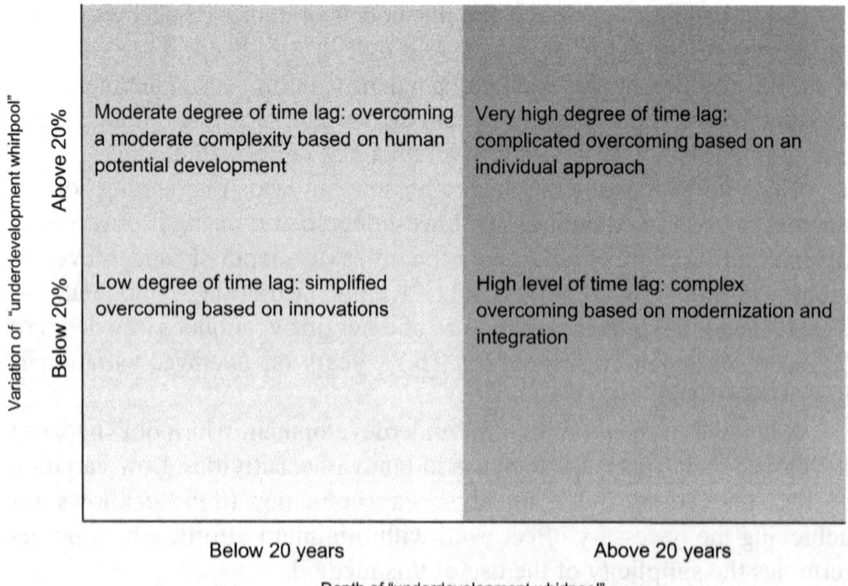

Figure 2. Scale for overcoming "underdevelopment whirlpools" depending on the degree of time lag.

systemic modernization, which predetermines a much higher complexity of using this method.

Based on the above, a scale of overcoming the "underdevelopment whirlpools" depending on the degree of time lag is presented (Figure 2); it reflects the logic of accelerating economic time depending on differences in it.

As shown in Figure 2, the presented scale allows classifying the prospects of overcoming the "underdevelopment whirlpools" by the criterion of their variation in the set totality of economies and by the criterion of the depth of "underdevelopment whirlpool" of the studied economy. In the case of low variation (below 20%) and small depth of the "whirlpool" (below 20 years) — lower left sector — a low degree of time lag is observed. In this case, the prospects of overcoming the "underdevelopment whirlpool" are the largest, and this process is simplified and connected to the implementation of innovative projects.

In case of a high variation (above 20%) but small depth of the "underdevelopment whirlpool" — upper left sector — a moderate degree of time lag is observed. In this case, the prospects of overcoming the "underdevelopment whirlpool" are smaller, and the process is complicated and connected to the development of human potential. In case of a low variation (below 20%) but large depth of the "underdevelopment whirlpool" (above 20 years) — lower right sector — a high degree of time lag is observed. In this case, the prospects of overcoming the "underdevelopment whirlpool" are very limited, and this process is peculiar for high complexity and is connected to modernization and integration.

In case of a high variation (above 20%) and the large depth of the "underdevelopment whirlpool" (above 20 years) — upper right sector — a very high degree of time lag is observed. In this case, the prospects of overcoming the "underdevelopment whirlpool" are minimal, and this process is peculiar for increased complexity and is conducted based on an individual approach. This means that in this case, it is impossible to offer a universal method of overcoming the "underdevelopment whirlpool", and there's a need for search and implementation of each economic system's capabilities.

Summing up the above, it should be noted that many countries have launched their rockets into space. Thus, the example of the USA and the USSR was followed by many emerging and advanced economies: France (1965), Italy (1967), Japan (1970), China (1970), the UK (1971), India (1980), Israel (1988), Russia (1992), Ukraine (1995), Iran (2009), Republic of Korea (2013), and New Zealand (2018). As the historical experience of the world has shown, each country used its launching area and used its resources. Similarly, during the increase in the quality of economic growth, it is necessary to take into account the specifics of the economic system's development and adaptation of basic models to these specifics.

It should also be noted that if only one race car uses a rocket engine, it has an advantage over the rivals; but if all participants of the race have race cars that use rocket engines, the advantage is eliminated. That's why it is obvious that overcoming "underdevelopment whirlpools" in the world economy envisages the whirlpools' countries obtaining unique (unreproducible by rivals) competitive advantages.

References

Andreeva, T. S., Ivanova, A. A., Potashev, A. V., & Potasheva, E. V. (2015). A study of the balance of a diversified economy using the Leontief model. *Scientific Review*, 15: 322–326.

Bergson, A. (1923). *Duration and Simultaneity (Concerning Einstein's Theory)*. Translation from French by A. A. Frankovsky. St. Petersburg: Academia.

Bragina, E. N. (2016). Analysis of the evolution of approaches to structuring the economy and assessing the balance of its development. *Society: Politics, Economics, Law*, 3: 95–98.

Chernova, O. A. (2012). The role of clusters in improving the balanced development of the economy of underdevelopment territories. *Regional Development Economics: Problems, Searches, Prospects*, 3: 162–168.

Cornell University, INSEAD, WIPO (2023). Global Innovation Index 2022: What Is the Future of Innovationdriven Growth? https://www.wipo.int/edocs/pubdocs/en/wipo-pub-2000-2022-section1-en-gii-2022-at-a-glance-global-innovation-index-2022-15th-edition.pdf. Accessed: 06 January 2023.

Dudin, M. N. & Frolova, E. E. (2015). The balanced scorecard as a basis for strategic company management in the context of the world economy transformation. *Asian Social Science*, 11(3): 282–288.

Durdyeva, D. A. (2014). On the issue of sustainability and socio-economic balance of the regional economy. *Business within the Law. Economic and Legal Journal*, 6: 176–179.

Endovitsky, D. A., Babicheva, N. E., & Lyubushin, N. P. (2018). Using the resource-based approach in assessing the systemic balance of the economy. *Economic Analysis: Theory and Practice*, 17, 12(483): 1298–1309.

IMD (2023). World Digital Competitiveness Rankings 2021-2022. https://www.imd.org/wcc/world-competitiveness-center-rankings/world-digital-competitiveness-rankings-2022/. Accessed: 06 January 2023.

Inshakov, O. V. (2011). The potential of an evolutionary approach in the strategic management of mesoeconomic systems. *Regional Development Economics: Problems, Searches, Prospects*, 12: 111–126.

Inshakov, O. V. & Shevandrin, A. V. (2007). Applied aspects of parametric assessment of types of socio-economic development of regions. *Bulletin of the Volgograd State University. Series 3: Economics. Ecology*, 11: 67–78.

Popkova, E. G. (2004a). The spatio-temporal approach in the concept of a new quality of economic growth. *Economic Sciences*, 7: 33–40.

Popkova, E. G. (2004b). Interaction of the concepts of sustainable development and the new quality of economic growth. *Finance and Credit*, 25(163): 43–47.

Popkova, E. G. (2004c). Interaction of the concepts of sustainable development and the new quality of economic growth. *Economic Analysis: Theory and Practice*, 25: 43.

Popkova, E. G. (2005). Formation of the Concept of a New Quality of Economic Growth in the Context of Globalization. Dissertation for the Degree of Doctor of Economics, Penza.

Popkova, E. (2014). New prospects of economic growth in the context of underdevelopment whirlpools phenomena. *Applied Econometrics and International Development*, 14(1): 5–25.

Popkova, E. (2017a). Problem analysis of 'underdevelopment whirlpools' as an obstacle for economic growth in Asian countries. *International Journal of Business and Globalisation*, 19(2): 167–174.

Popkova, E. (2017b). Use of methodology of "underdevelopment whirlpools" with analysis of problems and perspectives of economic growth in Asian countries. *Journal of Entrepreneurship in Emerging Economies*, 9(1): DOI:10.1108/JEEE-07-2016-0027.

Popkova, E., Gornostaeva, Z., & Tregulova, N. (2018). Role of innovations in the provision of competitiveness and innovational development of economy and overcoming of "underdevelopment whirlpools" in Russia and countries of Eastern Europe. *Journal of Entrepreneurship in Emerging Economies*, 10(3): 511–523.

Sergi, B. S. (ed.) (2018). *Exploring the Future of Russia's Economy and Markets: Towards Sustainable Economic Development*. Bingley, UK: Emerald Publishing Limited.

Sergi, B. S. (ed.) (2019). *Modelling Economic Growth in Contemporary Russia*. Bingley, UK: Emerald Publishing Limited.

Sergi, B. S. & Scanlon, C. C. (eds.) (2019). *Entrepreneurship and Development in the 21st Century*. Bingley, UK: Emerald Publishing Limited.

Shakhovskaya, L. S. & Popkova, E. G. (2004). New quality of economic growth in the context of modern globalization. *Finance and Credit*, 23(16): 71–77.

Solomou, S. (1986). Non-balanced growth and Kondratieff Waves in the world economy, 1850–1913. *The Journal of Economic History*, 46(1): 165–169.

United Nations (UN) (2019). Sustainable Development Goals. https://www.un.org/sustainabledevelopment/ru/sustainable-development-goals/. Accessed: 10 November 2019.

United Nations Development Programme (UNDP) (2023). Human Development Index 2021–2022. https://hdr.undp.org/data-center/human-development-index#/indicies/HDI. Accessed: 06 January 2023.

World Bank (2023). Foreign direct investment, net inflows (BoP, current US$). https://data.worldbank.org/indicator/BX.KLT.DINV.CD.WD?view=chart. Accessed: 06 January 2023.

Chapter 19

Models for Overcoming "Underdevelopment Whirlpools" in Emerging and Advanced Economies through the Lens of Their Time Lag and Economic Calendar: Time Is a Path of Development

It is man that makes truth great, not truth that makes man great.

Confucius, ancient Chinese thinker
and philosopher of the 5th century BC

This chapter states that time is a path of economic systems in the world economy (Figure 1).

This chapter considers the following issues:

- model of overcoming an "underdevelopment whirlpool" (underrun from the leader in a category) by emerging economies and its approbation by the example of BRICS countries;
- model of overcoming an "underdevelopment whirlpool" (underrun from the regional leader) by emerging economies and its approbation by the example of BRICS countries;
- model of overcoming an "underdevelopment whirlpool" (underrun from the global leader) by emerging economies and its approbation by the example of BRICS countries;

- model of overcoming an "underdevelopment whirlpool" (underrun from the global leader) by advanced economies and its approbation by the example of countries of G7;
- algorithm of levelling economic time in the modern world economic system: a roadmap for overcoming "underdevelopment whirlpools".

Figure 1. Time is a path of development.

Source: Photo by scholar and photographer Elena Popkova, https://www.saatchiart.com/account/artworks/1599809.

Under the influence of globalization, the development of economic systems is interdependent in the modern global economy. This allows — in a conventional manner — presenting economic time as a path of the economy's development. "To be in the spirit of the economic time" means to conform to the technological mode that is achieved in the world economy. Getting back to the abstraction of the world economy (Chapter 15) and presenting it in the form of a race track, it is possible to see that correspondence to the modern technological mode is a mandatory condition for levelling the speed of the "race's" participants, getting them in a line, and preventing a strong advance of some participants as compared to others, as well as a strong underrun of some participants.

In the terminology of modern economic science, this means the provision of the balance of the global economic system. It should be noted that this concept is contradictory. In case of a small influence of globalization on the economic system and the internal orientation of the social and business culture, the position in the world economy — the level of socio-economic development as compared to other countries, global competitiveness of entrepreneurship, and its role in the world markets — might be of small interest for the economic system.

This is proved by the fact that according to the authoritative international organization New Economic Foundation (2019), countries with the highest value of the happy planet index have relatively low values of the indicators of socio-economic development. Thus, for example, the leader of the happy planet index ranking — Costa Rica (44.7 points) — is ranked 74th ($12,026.5) in the ranking of the World Bank (2019) by GDP per capita. Mexico, which is ranked 2nd in the happy planet index ranking (40.7 points), is ranked 82nd ($9,698.1) by GDP per capita. Colombia is ranked 3rd in the happy planet index ranking (40.7 points) but is ranked 97th ($6,651.3) by GDP per capita.

Similarly, the leader of the ranking of World Bank (2019) by GDP per capita — Luxembourg ($144,340.5) — is ranked last but one (139th) in the ranking of New Economic Foundation (2019) by the happy planet index (13.2 points). This means that the socio-economic position of an economic system does not determine the level of happiness and well-being of its population. However, most of the modern countries with emerging economies are interested in improving their position in the international arena and overcoming their underrun from advanced economies, which predetermines the large importance of the concept of provision of the global economic system's balance.

As practical experience shows, the achievement of the leading technological order is a necessary but insufficient condition for implementing this concept. It is not possible to overtake a race car in a horse carriage, but two race cars could also have different speeds, depending on the drivers. The same holds good in the economy — a digital technological order creates opportunities but does not guarantee the overcoming of "underdevelopment whirlpools", which confirms their presence among advanced economies, whose technological order is similar.

At present, the model of "rapid development" is the most popular one; it envisages the use of the leader's experience to "copyi" its success. The theoretical and applied issues of implementing this model are given in the works of foreign authors: Dunford (2018), Nassif *et al.* (2015), Sergi (2018, 2019), Sergi & Scanlon (2019), and Russian scholars: Bagdasaryan (2017), Zolotareva (2018), Imanov (2019), Pluzhnikov (2018), Polterovich (2016), Spitsyn (2013), Tsiteladze (2018), and Shumakova & Kutavina (2018).

In her works, the author of this book, Prof. Elena G. Popkova points to the imperfection of the "rapid development" model and offers recommendations for a more effective overcoming of "underdevelopment whirlpools". This is studied in the works of Popkova (2004a, 2004b, 2004c, 2005, 2014, 2017a, 2017b), Shakhovskaya & Popkova (2004), and Popkova *et al.* (2018), and Prof. Oleg V. Inshakov also criticized the model of "rapid development" in the works of Inshakov and Shevandrin (2007) and Inshakov (2011).

This experience could be used conventionally or reconsidered through the experience of an economic system and adapted to its specifics. In both cases, the difference in economic time of the "overtaking" and the sample economic system is preserved. While the "overtaking" economic system takes the path in the wake of the sample system, the sample system continues to drift away from it, clearing a path forward. As a result, the "overtaking" economic system moves forward, but its underrun is preserved.

In addition to this, this model is considered universal and is used for overcoming any underrun. However, as the analysis of underrun (Chapter 15) has shown, it could be different, for it depends on different factors and, therefore, requires differentiated models of management. That's why there is a need for a range of new models for overcoming the "underdevelopment whirlpools" in emerging and advanced economies through the lens of their time lag and an economic calendar, which would allow taking into account the specifics of their economic time.

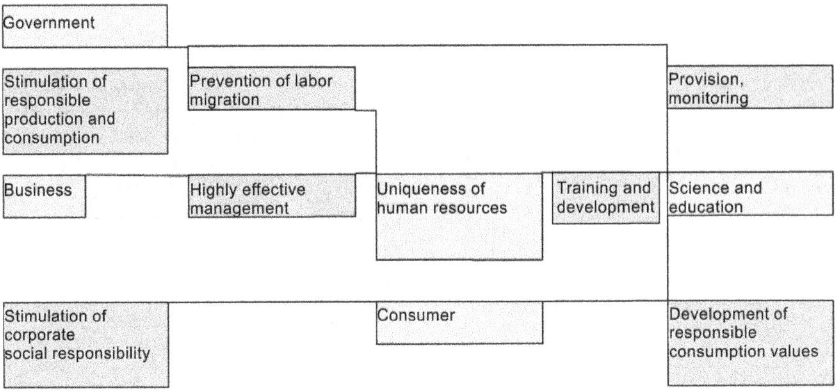

Figure 2. Model for overcoming the "underdevelopment whirlpools" in emerging economies to reduce the underrun from the leader in a category.

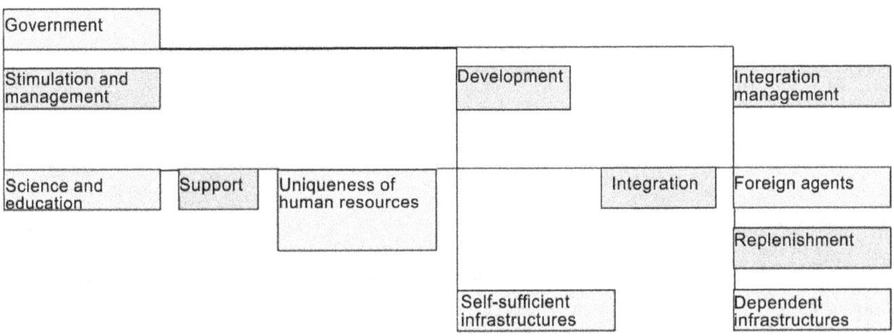

Figure 3. The model for overcoming the "underdevelopment whirlpools" in emerging economies to reduce the underrun from a regional leader.

These models should be based on the emphasis on the uniqueness of an economic system. Its economic time (path of development) should be treated as special and unique. It is necessary to refuse the very idea of "rapid development" and use own experience. This chapter offers four models, each of which is oriented to its type of time underrun (Figures 2–5).

As shown in Figure 2, to reduce the underrun from the leader in a category, it is recommended to pay attention primarily to the provision of human resources' uniqueness. This envisages the development of the rate and value of competencies, which allow producing special goods, which are in high demand in the international markets. Also, it is offered to

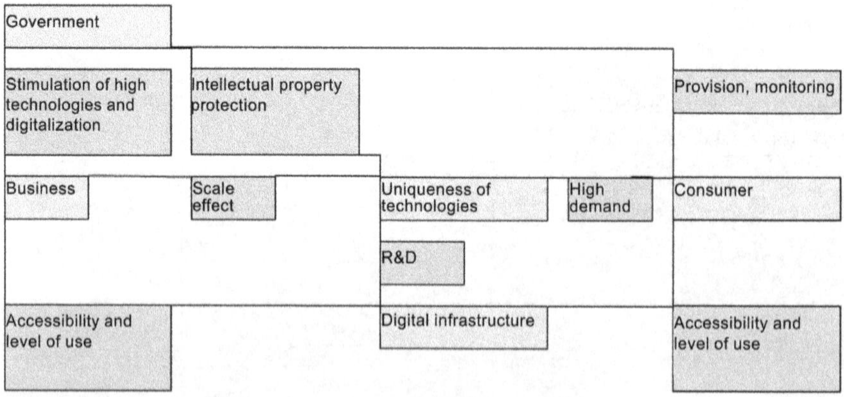

Figure 4. The model for overcoming the "underdevelopment whirlpools" in emerging economies to reduce the underrun from the global leader.

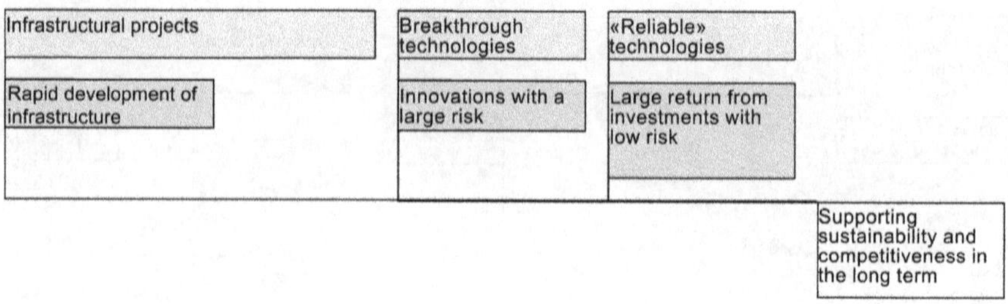

Figure 5. The model for overcoming the "underdevelopment whirlpools" in advanced economies to reduce the underrun from the global leader.

support the specific character of national culture. State regulators stimulate responsible production and consumption, as well as the balance of standardization and flexibility of the system of science and education.

Due to this, entrepreneurship uses human resources with much effectiveness. Corporate social responsibility is additionally stimulated by consumers. In the system of science and education, human resources are trained and developed, and the level of consumer awareness is raised through the teaching and development of responsible consumption values. In view of the compiled economic calendar (Chapter 19), emerging economies, in particular India, China, Brazil, and South Africa, need to overcome the "underdevelopment whirlpools" between them and Russia — to start, as quickly as possible, the implementation of the corresponding initiatives, so the results from them coincide — in time — with the "effect" from the transition to a new technological mode and the synergetic effect appears, which would multiply the advantages from the implementation of these initiatives.

This synergetic effect will allow overcoming the disproportions in the structure of the BRICS countries from as early as 2021. The most prospective initiatives are as follows:

- increase of affordability of education, in particular, based on the development of the remote education system;
- increase of quality of education;
- stimulation of continuation of education (life-long learning);
- provision of social justice in the labour market;
- stimulation of the value of education in entrepreneurship.

As shown in Figure 3, to reduce the underrun from a regional leader, it is necessary to pay attention primarily to the provision of entrepreneurship's uniqueness. Here, we speak of the formation, strengthening, and preservation of a country's competitive advantages, which cannot be copied by foreign rivals. An important role here belongs to infrastructural provision. Components of the infrastructure in which quantity and quality are sufficient are developed by the government, and components of the infrastructure that face deficit are replenished through integration with foreign rivals.

Integration could take any form, including the creation of transnational economic clusters, the formation of international innovative networks and technological parks, and the creation of special economic zones. Government regulators stimulate integration and ensure its implementation in the interests of domestic entrepreneurship with the preservation of its uniqueness. In this case, integration in the form of mergers and acquisitions, at which domestic companies cease their existence creating a platform for foreign rivals entering domestic markets, is unacceptable.

Given the compiled economic calendar, emerging economies, in particular, countries of BRICS, have to develop highly effective integration until 2023. This will allow joining the advantage of integration with the "effect" of transition to a new technological mode and will create a synergetic effect, due to which the underrun from regional leaders, e.g., Germany in Europe or Japan in Asia, will be overcome.

As shown in Figure 4, to reduce the underrun from the global leader, it is necessary to ensure the uniqueness of the used digital technologies and produced hi-tech products by domestic entrepreneurship. Government regulators ensure intellectual property protection in the economy and stimulate the digitalization of society and hi-tech entrepreneurship, which, in its turn, strives to gain the "scale effect" and high efficiency. Digital infrastructure is widely accessible and is actively used.

In emerging economies, in particular the countries of BRICS, in view of the compiled economic calendar, it is offered to start a second wave of digitalization in 2025 — to obtain advantages from the transition to a new technological mode at a double rate. Thus, it is recommended to perform digital modernization until 2025 and then start the transition to Industry 4.0 based on the formed digital economy. This will allow overcoming their underrun from advanced economies. However, the level of the USA will not be reached. For this, it is recommended to use the following model (Figure 5).

As shown in Figure 5, to reduce the underrun from the global leader, macroeconomic innovation and investment design are needed. Preference should be given to the following projects: infrastructural projects aimed at the rapid development of infrastructure, projects on the development and implementation of breakthrough technologies to create promising high-risk innovations, and projects on the development and implementation of reliable innovations — low-risk innovation with a large return from investments. This will allow supporting the sustainability and competitiveness of the economy in the long term.

For the practical implementation of the described model in the activities of advanced economies, in particular countries of G7 (Canada, France, Germany, Italy, Japan, and the UK), given their economic calendar, it is recommended to set the goal of achieving the maximum effect in 2023. This will allow overcoming their "underdevelopment whirlpools" in terms of underrun from the USA.

Based on the above, an algorithm for levelling economic time in the modern world economic system is developed: a "roadmap" for overcoming the "underdevelopment whirlpools" (Figure 6).

As is shown in Figure 6, acceleration of economic time — going through development from the "underdevelopment whirlpool" to its overcoming — envisages the consecutive implementation of all four offered differentiated models with an emphasis on uniqueness. Due to this, the economic system goes up the imaginary ladder. Contrary to this, during the implementation of the model of rapid development the

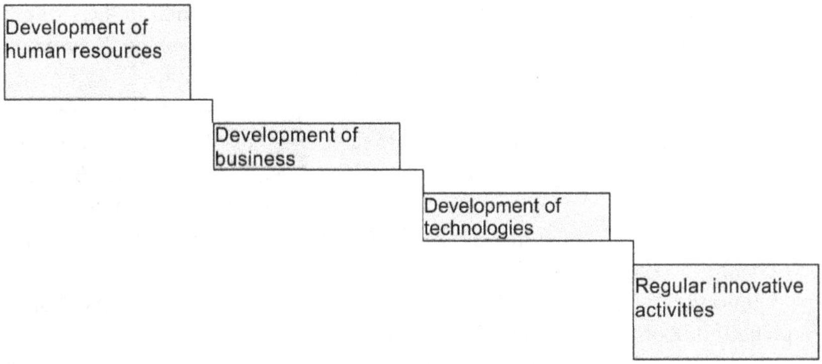

Figure 6. The algorithm of levelling economic time in the modern world economic system: "roadmap" to overcome the "underdevelopment whirlpools".

economic system finds itself under the ladder, not overcoming the "underdevelopment whirlpool".

To illustrate the differences between the existing and offered models, let us imagine an artificial ballet dancer in a box. It cannot be even remotely compared to a real, living ballet dancer. The "rapid development" model is the ballet dancer in a box, which only creates an illusion of acceleration of economic time. The offered differentiated models with an emphasis on uniqueness are the "real ballet dancer", a true way to overcome "underdevelopment whirlpools" and ensure the balance of the global economic system.

References

Bagdasaryan, N. A. (2017). Innovative development: characteristics and features of catch-up development. *Bulletin of Science and Practice*, 8(21): 208–216.

Dunford, M. (2018). Catching up or falling behind: Regional economic performance and the trajectories of regional economic development in the EU. In *Welfare State and Democracy in Crisis: Reforming the European Model.* Milton Park UK: Taylor and Francis, pp. 120–142.

Imanov, R. A. (2019). Modelling of socio-economic factors in the development of the overtaking economy. *Bulletin of the Moscow International Higher School of Business MIRBIS*, 2(18): 56–63.

Inshakov, O. V. (2011). The potential of an evolutionary approach in the strategic management of mesoeconomic systems. *Regional Development Economics: Problems, Searches, Prospects*, 12: 111–126.

Inshakov, O. V. & Shevandrin, A. V. (2007). Applied aspects of parametric assessment of types of socio-economic development of regions. *Bulletin of the Volgograd State University. Series 3: Economics. Ecology*, 11: 67–78.

Nassif, A., Feijó, C., & Araújo, E. (2015). Structural change and economic development: Is Brazil catching up or falling behind? *Cambridge Journal of Economics*, 39(5): 1307–1332.

New Economic Foundation (2019). Happy Planet Index Score. https://happyplanetindex.org/. Accessed: 07 November 2019.

Pluzhnikov, N. S. (2018). Distinctive features of the results of the study of the main models of overtaking development. *World of Economics and Management*, 18(3): 117–125.

Polterovich, V. M. (2016). Institutions of overtaking development (to the draft of a new model of economic development in Russia). *Economic and Social Changes: Facts, Trends, Forecast*, 5(47): 34–56.

Popkova, E. G. (2004a). The spatio-temporal approach in the concept of a new quality of economic growth. *Economic Sciences*, 7: 33–40.

Popkova, E. G. (2004b). Interaction of the concepts of sustainable development and the new quality of economic growth. *Finance and Credit*, 25(163): 43–47.

Popkova, E. G. (2004c). Interaction of the concepts of sustainable development and the new quality of economic growth. *Economic Analysis: Theory and Practice*, 25: 43.

Popkova, E. G. (2005). Formation of the Concept of a New Quality of Economic Growth in the Context of Globalization. Dissertation for the degree of Doctor of Economics, Penza.

Popkova, E. (2014). New prospects of economic growth in the context of underdevelopment whirlpools phenomena. *Applied Econometrics and International Development*, 14(1): 5–25.

Popkova, E. (2017a). Problem analysis of 'underdevelopment whirlpools' as an obstacle for economic growth in Asian countries. *International Journal of Business and Globalisation*, 19(2): 167–174.

Popkova, E. (2017b). Use of methodology of "underdevelopment whirlpools" with analysis of problems and perspectives of economic growth in Asian countries. *Journal of Entrepreneurship in Emerging Economies*, 9(1): DOI:10.1108/JEEE-07-2016-0027.

Popkova, E., Gornostaeva, Z., & Tregulova, N. (2018). Role of innovations in the provision of competitiveness and innovational development of economy and overcoming of "underdevelopment whirlpools" in Russia and countries of

Eastern Europe. *Journal of Entrepreneurship in Emerging Economies*, 10(3): 511–523.

Sergi, B. S. (ed.). (2018). *Exploring the Future of Russia's Economy and Markets: Towards Sustainable Economic Development.* Bingley, UK: Emerald Publishing Limited.

Sergi, B. S. (ed.). (2019). *Modelling Economic Growth in Contemporary Russia.* Bingley, UK: Emerald Publishing Limited.

Sergi, B. S. & Scanlon, C. C. (eds.) (2019). *Entrepreneurship and Development in the 21st Century.* Bingley, UK: Emerald Publishing Limited.

Shakhovskaya, L. S. & Popkova, E. G. (2004). New quality of economic growth in the context of modern globalization. *Finance and Credit*, 23(16): 71–77.

Shumakova, V. A. & Kutavina, O. V. (2018). On the South Korean model of catch-up development. *Kazan Bulletin of Young Scientists*, 2, 1(4): 70–74.

Spitsyn, V. V. (2013). Evaluation of the effectiveness of the implementation of the strategy of catching-up development of Russia. *Bulletin of the Tomsk Polytechnic University*, 323(6): 18–24.

Tsiteladze, D. D. (2018). Development of methods for assessing the innovative potential of a region in a catching-up economy. *Innovations*, 9(239): 61–73.

World Bank (2019). Indicators: GDP per capita. https://data.worldbank.org/indicator/NY.GDP.PCAP.CD?most_recent_value_desc=true&view=chart. Accessed: 07 November 2019.

Zolotareva, V. P. (2018). New sources of capital for Russia's "overtaking modernization". *Economic Sciences*, 163: 36–39.

Conclusion

Thus, our fascinating journey through the pages of the book of economic time has come to an end. We have learned from this book that time in economics, as in physics, is comprehensive but different depending on the territory. While in everyday life we feel differences in physical time with the help of the difference in time zones, the difference in time in economics is reflected in the difference in the level of countries' socio-economic development. The cyclicity of economic systems is also manifested differently.

Similarly to usual life, as we have countries with cold climates and countries with permanent heat and sun, there are also countries in the economy that are leaders by the level of economic development (this state could be compared to an eternal summer), countries that are subject to extreme cyclic fluctuations (heavy continental climate), and underdeveloped countries (eternal winter). Economic time does not coincide with physical time. For example, countries of Africa, where it is always very hot (according to the laws of physics), are in the past time from the economic point of view, i.e., they are underdeveloped by the level of socio-economic development (they are freezing, relatively speaking). Countries of Europe (e.g., Norway), Eurasia (e.g., Russia with Siberia), and North America (Canada and the USA with Alaska) are freezing from the physical point of view but warmed by the sum from the economic point of view since they demonstrate a relatively high level of socio-economic development.

Science has proven that time has certain characteristics, such as density. The density of time is a relative value that defines the flow of time in the given local sphere of space. It could be precisely and subjectively felt that there is internal time (individual for everyone) and external (obvious and same for everyone). The character of the flow of time — its acceleration or slowdown — for our consciousness depends on the volume of information that enters our brain. Compare how time quickly flies when you're surfing the internet or having an interesting conversation, and how slowly it goes when you are in hospital.

It is up to us to decide how full the unit of time is. Time becomes denser when we are far from the point "here and now". In other words, if the events of past years are set on each other in "layers", sometimes we have to make an effort to restore something in our memory.

As is shown in the book, these characteristics of time could be used in economics to study the nature and development of economic crises. An attempt is made not only to find and determine economic time but also to measure and consider it with the help of the methodology of "underdevelopment whirlpools", whose advantage is the consideration of the most important feature of economic time, which is similar to a feature of physical time — its relativity.

Now, you know that economic time has the same properties as physical time, but it has its specifics in implementing these properties. It orders the unique events in the world economy, ensuring the integrity and unity of their change during their flow from past to present and future. Economic time allows the structuring and building of logical economic phenomena and processes, forming the history of economic doctrines and economic systems. Economic time is objective and universal, but it is manifested differently in each economic system. It is irreversible and non-determinable, variable, and cyclical.

The given properties of economic time could be used for solving the current problem of economic science with the help of the offered tools of economic time management.

It is offered to solve the problem of the cyclical nature of economic development by measuring economic time at each stage of the economic cycle and increasing its density, as well as using "economic vintage".

It is offered to solve the problem of differences in the value and flow of economic time ("time machine" in the economy for provision of the balance of the world economy) with the help of setting the models of overcoming the "underdevelopment whirlpools" on the economic calendar (Figure 1).

The obtained conclusions allow developing the scientific and economic thought in the direction of precise quantitative and qualitative measuring of economic time and its management in society's interests.

Figure 1. Antifragility.

Source: Photo by scholar and photographer Elena Popkova, https://www.saatchiart.com/account/artworks/1599809.

In this book, we attempted to lift the veil of the mystery of economic time, so that everyone could realize its influence on humans, and outlined the prospects of a more precise and correct accounting of the time factor in economic research. Provisions of the theory of economic time were assembled and reconsidered, clearly formulated, and improved.

We only hope that this book will draw the attention of scholars and other readers to the phenomenon of economic time so that they would never be misguided by its difference from physical time and would learn to manage it. Though the study of economic time starts from formulating the postulates of the time theory in economics, the future will, without any doubt, bring much new information about this amazing phenomenon. Let us together look for unveiled secrets and hidden effects of economic time and solve its riddles!

Index